FROM MISTER MAGOO TO PAPA SMURF

GERARD BALDWIN

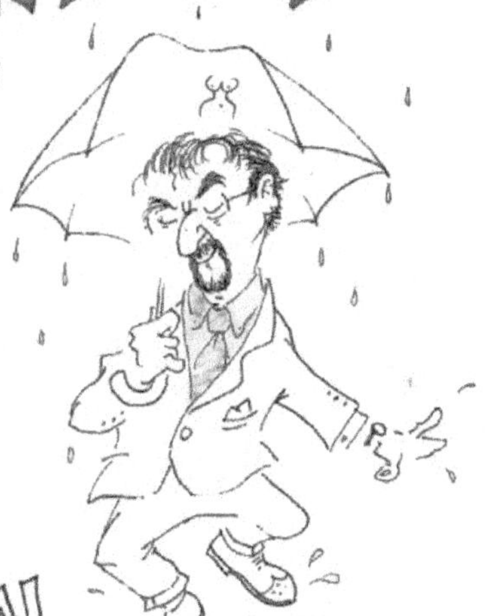

Library of Congress Control number: 2014916917

ISBN: 9780990724216

Neighborhood Publishers

3317 Manor Road

Austin, Texas 78723

www.neighborhoodpublishers.net

Cover photo by:

Frank White

Back cover painting "Papa Smurf" by Gerard Baldwin.

Mixed media on cavas board (1990)

Jacket design, and book interior by Dan Monroe.

Printed in the USA

In just about every field, there are people who go against the grain, who do things their way, who see opportunities where others see obstacles. With their iconoclastic outlook, these people often create new perceptions and reveal new possibilities and solutions. These people are often called mavericks. Gerard Baldwin is a maverick.

Gerard was schooled and apprenticed during the later years of animation's Golden Age, but when he arrived as a full-fledged animator the medium's focus had drastically shifted and the only market for his newly developed skills was in television animation. By then, budgets had been slashed to the bone and schedules were ridiculously tight. Animators were paid by the piece so making a decent wage meant working fast. Although the rules had suddenly changed, Baldwin never felt hindered by them. In fact, it appears that these limitations actually brought out the best in him, and his animation was lively, smooth but economical, and richly entertaining.

Many other animators, accustomed to the more luxurious budgets and schedules of theatrical animation, simply threw in the towel and allowed the restrictions to dictate their execution, resulting in stiff, lifeless work. Gerard, however, found inventive and unexpected ways of executing a scene and, using the budget as his ally, could execute something as simple as a walk and imbue it with personality and humor. Like an accomplished jiu-jitsu master, he turned those liabilities back on themselves and in doing so, crafted some of the most dynamic and most personal "limited" animation ever to grace the small screen.

When he directed shows for Jay Ward, he animated them as well, fashioning a number of short films that bore his unique stamp. His *Dudley Do-rights* were the funniest of the bunch and his *Aesop & Sons* ran circles around the shoddy execution of the episodes produced in Mexico. Jay Ward knew the difference and Gerard quickly became one his key men. Jay gave Gerard not just several title sequences (*Aesop & Son, Fractured Fairy Tales*) but, knowing his flair for entertainment, also gave him pilots for new productions—*Super Chicken, Hoppity Hooper* and *George of the Jungle*.

Gerard's work has the feel of spontaneity, as if the animation sprang directly from his mind onto the screen, with the feeling that the pencil and paper were almost a hindrance to the execution. Part of the reason for that was purely economic, as he has freely admitted that "the faster I worked, the more money I made." His drawings were loose but expressive while the animation was inventive, unconventionally executed and looked more full than it actually was. But due to all the years he had spent in the animation trenches, he had learned his craft to such an extent that the fundamentals were second nature to him, freeing him to push the boundaries of the medium and plumb his creativity. Gerard's work shows that it's not the tool but the artist that wields it that makes the difference.

Although he was a consummate craftsman, craftsmanship itself never stood in the way of the entertainment he put on the screen; details didn't concern him. Consequently, in a show where most characters have three fingers, Gerard's characters will usually have four. The custom in animation was to use three fingers to save money but he felt hands were key components of expression and he freely used all four fingers, posing the digits for maximum effect.

Probably the single most identifiable of all his screen moments was the darkly comedic pawn shop sequence in *Mr. Magoo's Christmas Carol* wherein Gerard (aided by an unforgettable song by Broadway's Jule Styne and Bob Merrill), takes us on a giddy tour de force of cartoon animation showcasing the plundering "Despicables'" enthusiasm for their corrupt and villainous ways. In a film filled with largely forgettable animation, Gerard's energetic execution demonstrates the possibilities of low budget animation, where the deft use of inventive execution and comedic timing can exceed even the biggest budgets and fullest animation for sheer entertainment.

Gerard had once looked down on commercial art, setting his sights on someday becoming a "true artist." Reality, however, won out and he finally capitulated, not only fully embracing commercial art but also becoming one of the most accomplished practitioners in the field of animation. His path, like many, had its share of challenges; he had several inauspicious starts, dealt with some difficult personalities and churned through his share of bill-paying jobs all the while continuing to sharpen his unconventional but inspired approach. Somewhere along the way though, between the budgets and the deadlines, Gerard Baldwin became a true artist.

For Leslie, Michael, Alison and John, and special thanks to Frances, my wife,
for her patience and help.

Responding to a question from a student:

"The newest thing in art? The newest thing in graphic art, the only really new thing in 25,000 years is the animated cartoon… drawings that move."
Don Graham -- Chouinard Art Institute, 1949.

"Only in the world of 'Fine Art' can you be a total fake and get away with it."
Gerard Baldwin - Kingwood College, 2009

Prologue

Not long ago I had the sudden and surprising realization that the father of American animation, Winsor McKay, presented his great animated film Little Nemo in 1911 and here I am, one hundred years later, having just finished a memoir about my good fortune to be involved in sixty percent of those first one hundred years.

"Where are we going today, Mr. Peabody?"

"Sherman, my boy, today we are going back in time but the past for which we search will be difficult to find."

"How come? We've never had a problem."

"The WABAC machine does not focus well on events enshrouded in dense fog or perceive landscapes lost in the mists of time."

"Who are we looking for?"

"We are searching for the origin of one Gerard Baldwin, a cartoonist, and in some way, without him and his kind, you and I would never exist."

"Really?"

"They are, to you and me and all of our acquaintances what Zeus was to the Greeks."

"Gosh, Mr. Peabody, that's profound."

"Hmm, yes. Well I guess it is."

Chapter 1

As I approach my 84th year I'm trying to figure out, like millions of other old people, what my life was, and **is** all about. Has every past event been written in the stars or is one's life a series of unpredictable accidents—some lucky—some not—a kind of mysterious crap shoot over which we have very little control?

Yes, there are choices to be made, like not running a traffic light. Or someone else can run a light and, no fault of yours, impale you on a snare of sharp steel. Surely a long and circuitous chain of events led me to be having dinner with Doctor Seuss or playing with children's blocks on the floor with Richard Feynman or, thirty years ago, driving home with the top down and the music loud and saying to myself, "I guess I really am some kind of a writer since a studio just paid me $10,000 for a short script." Moreover, I never could have predicted in a hundred years that I would be listening to Charlton Heston giving power to those words, or having a dream wherein I AM Mr. Magoo and Papa Smurf is real. Well, I try making sense of my life but there is no recollection of it ever beginning and no possibility that I can really imagine my NOT being. Sooner or later I will find out.   I'll   miss me. No. Impossible, unless you believe the heavens are infused with a googolplex of souls.

In 1928, far away in Belgium, Pierre Culliford was born. He would, someday, become the world famous creator of the Smurfs referring to himself as Peyo. Conversely, I was born in 1929 in N.Y.C., my birth coinciding with the great crash of the stock market and the world-wide depression that followed and I would refer to myself as Gerard.

My parents, I am pretty sure, had no real sense of history. Pop finished the 5th grade and Mom the 9th. They could read and write but how well I don't know. History, for them, probably began with the birth of Jesus Christ. Columbus discovered America. George Washington crossed the Delaware and was the father of our country and Tammany Hall ran New York City.

My folks accepted, with a matter-of-fact lack of amazement, the revolution they were witnessing: Automobiles replacing horses, telegraphy, telephones, radio, motion pictures, Atomic bombs and television.

I visited my mother on the day an astronaut stepped on the moon. She was not happy, felt threatened, and did not believe anyone had any business messing around up in heaven.

I am sure there were hundreds of thousands of Irish working-class families just like mine, keeping their apartments clean, going to church on Sundays, having their children attend Catholic schools. My mother saw the world divided between We and They. They ruled the world and on Sunday We put change in the collection basket.

My maternal grandfather was born in 1848 in county Sligo, Ireland. He was a farmer and a prize-fighter, and good enough to have been written about in the local press. He was also active in the rebellion against British rule and at some point the Black and Tan were after him. He fled Ireland and came to America. As was the custom, the eldest son, my grandfather, would have inherited the farm but his brother gained the land. I remember the newspaper clippings and a photo of my great uncle. He was wearing rubber boots and standing before a simple cottage with a thatched roof. He was leaning on a hoe. His son stood beside him.

According to my mother, whenever my grandfather got drunk, which was often, he would become homesick and swear he was going to return to the old sod and take back his farm. He never did.

When she was old and senile, my mom decided to clean house and tossed away everything that might have given me a trace to the past. Gone.

AMERICA, 1894 - West Pittsfield Mass.

In 1894, walking home from her little red school house in West Pittsfield, Massachusetts, my eight year old mother had to pass by the Shaker dairy farm. She told me a kind Shaker lady would always give the children cookies. When Mom was seventy she made a remarkable painting of her little red school house. It is a very wide, high angle view. Behind the school there is an out-house. Down a road a piece there is a little farmhouse and behind it a red barn. Just beyond the barn is a windmill. High up on a gentle slope is another red barn and in front of it a man and a cow. The sky is blue, the clouds are white and the American flag, in front of the school house, is in cascade. Eight boys and girls are leaving the school and walking away in different directions. One boy has a dog. I think a young child would see this panorama from a low perspective, but for some reason Mom chose to see this scene as if she was three hundred feet up in the air looking down and far away into a distant past.

Nearby there was a mine and her father, my grandfather, was a miner. When the mine ran out, the McGrath family moved to New York City to find work.

While my mother was walking home from that little red schoolhouse, my father, eleven, was probably delivering a pint of beer to some household in his neighborhood. The can was open and if you were careful and had an innate sense of the physics involved you could whirl the pint over your head on the upswing and just miss striking the pavement on the downswing - round and round and round - never spilling a drop.

My paternal grandfather had a bar and restaurant in the Colonnades, a Grand Hotel on Lafayette Street in New York City. Charles Dickens was a guest as was Mark Twain. Edgar Alan Poe hung out in the bar. From the Colonnades, President Zachary Taylor and assembled dignitaries would review the parading troops. None of this made any impression on my father, nor was he aware his father's generation was referred to as "lace curtain" Irish; part of the first wave of Irish immigrants some of whom became well established. When I visited the bar some years ago it was much as it had been in 1833. The floor was inlaid with small white tiles; only now the bar was host to a bunch of young actors and actresses from the school across the street. Once upon a time the school across the street had been the Vanderbilt Mansion. The Colonnades, a National landmark, is now a Howard Johnson's.

Harry Baldwin, my father, had two brothers and a twin sister. She died as an infant and this caused my grandmother to have, what was called in those days, a nervous breakdown. It must have been pretty severe as she was sent off to an institution never to be seen again. I only learned of this when my older sister, Dolores, after quite a few drinks, spilled the beans! Dolores, Dorothy and my brother Howard had been sworn to SECRECY! There was no insanity in our family! How would my sisters ever get a husband if this were known? That is the way it was back then. I told my brother Jack what I had learned and he was as stunned as I. My sister Dorothy was outraged by this disclosure. She was, as always, easily outraged. I imagine my poor grandmother locked away. Did anyone ever visit her? Not my siblings and perhaps not even her husband. Dolores remembered packing up Christmas boxes of food and clothing and sending them off to the Asylum. My poor grandma never saw her boys again and faded away in the nuthouse.

My grandfather became very ill and was told he was doomed to die. He turned the Colonnades restaurant over to his brother in exchange for the brother promising to raise my grandfather's three boys -- Harry, Jim and

Jack. Grandfather soon died and the good uncle turned out to be a bad uncle --like someone in a Charles Dickens novel. Pop told me that once he asked his uncle for a penny and the guy spit in his hand. Harry, Jim and Jack were soon turned out. Pop finished the fifth grade and was on the street in need of a job. My uncle Jim became a rather successful con man and my uncle Jack a bootlegger. When Harry Baldwin met Margaret McGrath, life became a whole lot better. My father, we called him "Pop", became a garment cutter . . . considered a highly skilled trade then and, thanks to his union, well paid. My mother said he made more money than a cop, a fireman, or a schoolteacher. Mom told me that when she left tiny West Pittsfield and her little red schoolhouse, she was frightened by her new surroundings. Standing up on the steps that fronted the old red brick tenement that was her new home, she heard two girls down on the sidewalk talking about her. One girl said, "She is NOT Irish. She's a nice girl."

My much older siblings told me that mom was embarrassed when the Doctor, on a house call, gathered the Baldwin family together to announce that their mother was with child. In the culture I was raised in, Irish Catholic working class families in their forties were not supposed to be having sex. They just drank beer and played bingo.

Mom was 21 when Howard was born,

23 when Dorothy was born

24 when Dolores was born

36 when Jack was born (Was Pop getting weaker?)

And there she was at 43, going to have another baby which turned out to be me. I have been told that, like a little puppy, love was lavished upon me.

Writing a memoir is a kind of affirmation of self and reaching into the long ago is a bit like reaching into a bowl of pistachios—always grab the open shells first.

When I told my family I could remember my Christening party, they laughed and assured me that it was impossible, the logic of which I must accept, so I have chalked that memory up to a creative dream that I wrote in my sleep. Yet—the memory is still there—like an out of focus image from Birth of A Nation—it is still there.

I can feel myself sitting on a little potty over a toilet and calling out to my mother who was somewhere far, far away in the kitchen—" Mommy! Wipe me." I was three.

Our gray apartment building was somewhere in New York City.

This walk- up was probably on the fifth floor since I could look way down and see the trash collectors tossing big iron garbage cans about as if they were nothing. To this little boy their CLANKITTY-CLANG-CLANG was the song of Thor.   I knew then, when I grew up, I'd be a garbage man.

We moved to Seaman Avenue when I was six and my brother Jack was thirteen. He was a Boy Scout. I knew Sherman Avenue was a good place to be. With cops on motorcycles leading the way, I clearly remember that all of Seaman Avenue crowded the curbside and cheered and waved as President Roosevelt, in an open touring car, waved us well. To mom and pop he was a second savior.

I entered the 1st grade at the Catholic School of the Good Shepherd. On the first day of school I had to take a pee so, as instructed, I raised my hand. The Nun paid no attention. I waved and waved but she paid no attention.   She wanted me to suffer.

When she went into the cloak closet I left the room and walked home. I hated school and knew school hated me.

This new apartment house was red brick. There was a small polished white stone vestibule at the entry. The door knobs and mail boxes were gleaming brass. Mom again said, Pop made more money than a policeman. I was in the vestibule playing who knows what on the white stone steps with a little girl my age that lived somewhere in the building when the stretcher came down, and they put my Pop in an ambulance and drove away. He had something called TB.

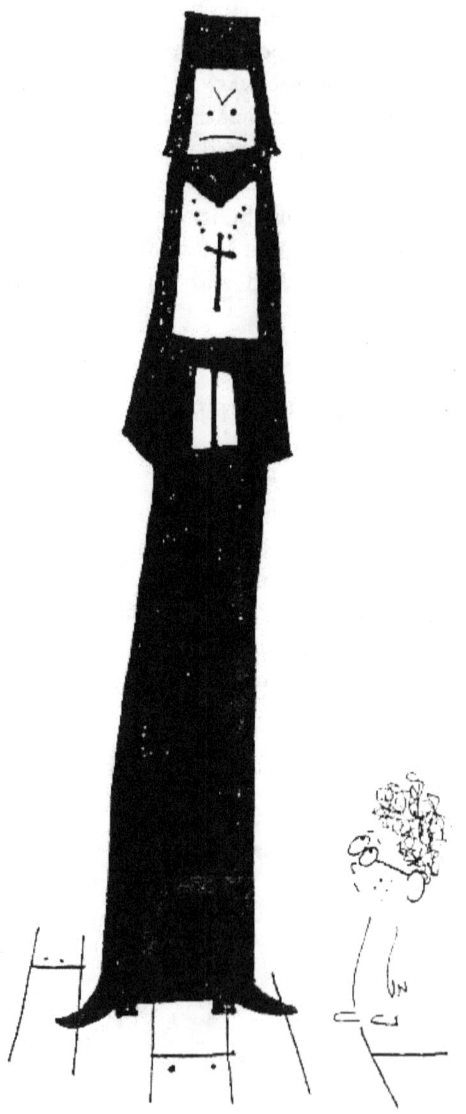
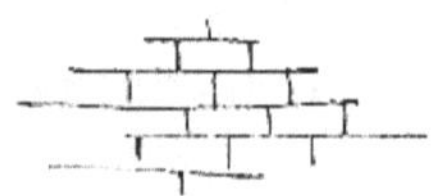

We would visit Pop at the Sanitarium on Sunday afternoons and, in the summer, we sat outside underneath a big umbrella--Mom, me and my big brother Jack--talking to Pop. The nuns were nice and one gave me a popsicle. Would Pop ever come home?

We had to move. There was no money. I had a childish impression there was no money in the entire country. Where had it gone? We were soon on relief. Mom and I would walk to some place and pick up free bags of basic food—flour-sugar-dried apples…..What little money mom did have came from I don't know where….perhaps from a State dole or from my much older siblings. Howard, Dolores and Dorothy had long ago married and moved away. Jack was attending De Witt Clinton High School and excelling in all of his classes…especially drawing. I was not excelling in anything.

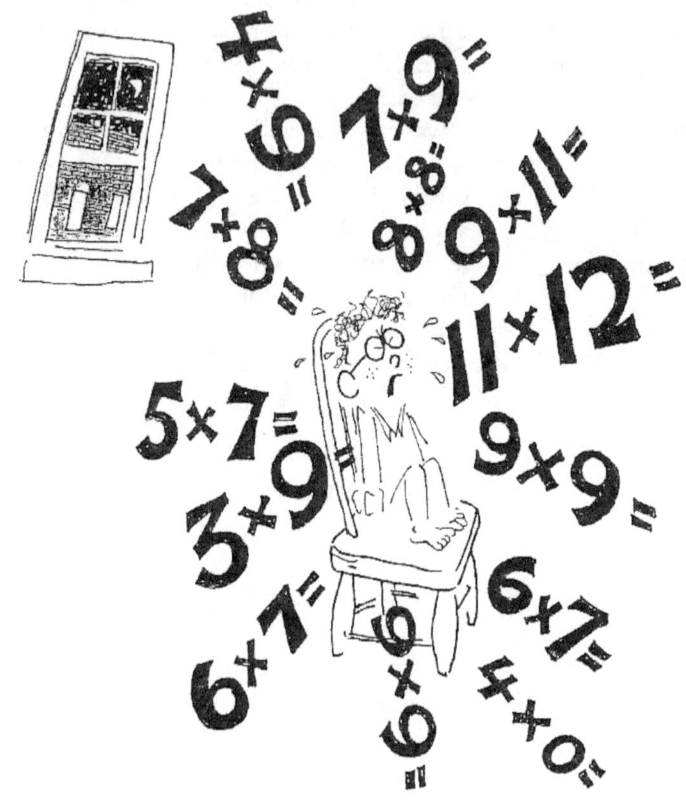

Our new apartment was in an old gray tenement on Heath Avenue somewhere in the Bronx and, when compared to Seamen Avenue, very drab —like the difference between East and West Berlin during the Cold War.

It was dark and cold when Mom sent me to the corner grocery to buy a loaf of Wonder Bread. She gave me a quarter, "Don't forget the change." Under the street lights, mountains of sparkling snow lined the curbs. On the way back I got distracted by a couple of dogs that were doing something strange I'd not seen before and I dropped a dime into the deep snow-bank. I couldn't find it. Mom was very upset by this loss and sent me back downstairs to search for the dime. I never found it.

It was about this time in my little life that my mother began to teach me about Social distinctions. We were poor. They were rich. Englishmen were bad. Irishmen were good. Public schools were bad. Catholic schools were good. Protestants were wrong. And Jews, even though they killed Christ, were good doctors. Rich kids went to college. Poor kids learned a trade.

Pop was still away in the Sanitarium when I got very sick and mom, using a neighbor's phone, called a doctor. Way back then doctors made house calls—in this case an apartment call. The Doctor was old and a bit out of breath from climbing five flights of stairs. He was wearing a suit and a tie and a vest and carrying a black bag filled with fascinating gadgets. He took my temperature—felt the swelling in my neck—listened to my heart and diagnosed me as having "the Measles!" He told mom to keep the room dark and, when I felt better, to take me to the children's clinic to have my heart checked. He didn't like the sound of it.

At the children's clinic I received a complete check- up from a very young pediatrician. Maybe the clinic took an X-ray but medicine was still more Art than Science in 1935. The doctor told my mother that I just had a little heart murmur, but not to worry. I would probably outgrow it. After he left the old hag of a nurse leaned in close to my mother and in a voice not to be heard . . .

"These young doctors! They don't know anything. If you want my advice I wouldn't even let this boy climb stairs."

Now who do you think my mother listened to? Returning to our apartment, mom hauled me piggy-back up the five flights of stairs and she did it for weeks, until Jack finally persuaded her to stop. I now saw myself as being weak and inferior and it would be many years before I judged myself differently.

One of the benefactors of the children's clinic was a Mrs. Strook, heiress to a woolen mill fortune. She also sponsored a free summer camp for sickly kids like me.

We took the subway to rendezvous with the camp's bus that would take a mob of boys from all over N.Y.C. to her camp located somewhere in the Adirondacks. Home was a lovely old summer mansion on many sloping acres. There was a softball field, a young doctor, a nurse, a couple of counselors and a family that cooked well. For breakfast there was always scrambled eggs, milk, cereal and perfect golden toast slathered with real butter. On rainy days a counselor would read to us. I wasn't good at baseball or swimming and much preferred capturing lizards down by the brook.

At night, in the semi-darkness of the upstairs dorm, I invented a running story about a heroic little Bee, just making it up as I went along, reciting it to the other kids until a counselor would tell me to please be quiet since it was time for all of us to go to sleep.

My recollection of Heath Avenue is vague . . . one boy I played with had a father who was a violinist and another kid's father was a German baker. We spent what seemed like endless hours holding toy airplanes aloft, flying around and around the block repeating Lindberg's Trans-Atlantic flight, only our ocean was cement.

The children that attended the Church Of The Good Shepherd near Seaman Avenue were only just beginning to study in preparation for receiving their First Holy Communion when we moved to Heath Avenue. I was in the third grade. I should have been in the fourth grade, but for some reason I cannot recall, I was left back. Now I was not only weak and scarred but dumb. Perhaps no one noticed I could not see the blackboard. Anyway, the children at my new Heath Avenue School had already received their First Holy Communion, a rite I knew NOTHING about. I was nine.

On the first Sunday after we moved to Heath Avenue my mother took me to Mass at our new church. It was a long walk. Adults sat at the back of the church. Their children lined up outside on the sidewalk and, directed by a stern nun, marched silently into the church. Girls sat on the left; boys on the far right. I had seen priests going through all kinds of complicated motions as they intoned in Latin. They did a lot of raising and lowering a large gold cup and moved big books about. I had no idea what it all meant or what was being said. In my pew the boys to my left and right seemed intently focused on the scene. Triggered by a gesture from a nun, one pew after another rose up and silently moved up the center aisle to the altar rail. The girls stayed on the left and the boys stayed on the right. It was all very solemn and accompanied by a droning organ. I stood behind a row of boys kneeling at the rail as a priest and an altar boy glided by. The priest would deftly reach into the shining chalice and, mumbling something, whip out a little white circle and place it on a boys protruding tongue. After a few moments the receiver, palms in serious prayer, got up, walked to the side aisle and presumably returned to his seat. Taking my cue from the others I knelt at the rail; it seemed an eternity before the priest arrived. My turn. I received it rather well . . . but what WAS it? I stood up and, imitating the others, palms in prayer, solemnly returned to my seat. What was this tasteless object in my mouth? Dare I Swallow? NO, that can't be right. By the time the priest got around to announcing Ladies Bingo night my cheeks were filled with saliva and the thing had dissolved. I dare not swallow and certainly I couldn't spit in church.

Mom, with all of the other mothers and fathers, was waiting for me on the sidewalk as I came down the church steps and hurried up to her. Then I spit the whole white slimy mess into the gutter. There was a collective gasp and mutterings of horror. Mom slapped me. Altar boys came running and doused the icky white slime with Holy Water. A nun, using a white linen cloth and whispering prayers, gently and lovingly, wiped up the body of Christ.

Chapter 2

In 1909 Winsor McCay, the brilliant comic strip artist–and graphic genius, became seriously involved in animation. I'm not alone in thinking of him as the Father of American Animation. He wrote, "Artists haven't yet taken animation seriously enough. When they do they will make some marvelous pictures."

Only 28 years later animated films had made an astonishing technical and artistic advance.

In 1937 Walt Disney made Snow White and the Seven Dwarfs.

As a kid in New York, I was aware there were real people behind Snow White, Fantasia and Porky Pig and that some of my relatives and their friends were part of a thing called animation. I was nine years old when I read an article written by my eldest brother, Howard Baldwin, in the Oct. 1938 issue of American Artist Magazine. In the interest of moving this narrative along I have cut thousands of words from Howard's essay. (Illustration by the author)

The Rocky Road to ANIMATION

By

JAMES HOWARD BALDWIN

The Animation Industry is growing by leaps and bounds with an increasing demand for skilled artists. There's money in it too. But—it's a long and rocky road that lies ahead of the would-be movie animator.

In this article the author gives young artists an idea of what to expect as beginners in the industry.

Drawn by the author

11

THE ROCKY ROAD TO ANIMATION

By James Howard Baldwin

Hundreds of well-trained artists clamor at the gates of Hollywood for a chance to demonstrate their ability and genius before the Moguls of the Animated Cartoon Industry. They are drawn to this comparatively new field for the artist by tales of fabulous salaries and sudden success. They have seen Snow White and they are convinced that the animated cartoon has grown up. The animated cartoon is definitely "going places" and thousands of hopeful artists--students and first rate professionals--are curious to know how to go about gaining a foot-hold in this fast growing business.

The animated cartoon industry is one of the few businesses today that can boast of having no unemployment problem. At the time of this writing no artist experienced in this field is without work. Of course the center of the industry is Hollywood where Walt Disney's studio is a huge showplace. Other studios of lesser importance are scattered throughout the country but the beginner's choice is generally narrowed to New York or Hollywood. Nine-tenths of the aspirants who are anxious to get into this field are doomed to disappointment.

Young Smith is an artist of exceptional ability. He has been trained in one or two leading art schools and he has enjoyed measure of success in commercial art. With the confidence naturally engendered by this Background he presents himself at one of the larger studios for an interview. One of the studio directors will carefully look over Smith's work. "There is no doubt of your ability," the director will say, "I don't think you would have very much trouble adapting yourself to the peculiar requirements of animation. Of course you'll have to start practically at the bottom and the pay won't be much but—" Smith's confidence receives a blow and his pride is hurt. "I'm quite sure I can fit into your line of work," he tells the director. "I don't really feel that I would be a beginner, exactly. After all, I CAN draw. All I want is a chance to show you what I can do. I realize it might take a few days to catch on to what it's all about but—"

"It will take you more than a few days," the director cuts in smiling. "It might take you a year to learn the mechanics of animation and after that two or three more years to get even close to the top. If and when you become a top ranking animator it will pay you handsomely but it's a long and rocky road.'

After an interview of this nature Smith will have to choose whether he is willing to plug through the long grind to the top. The only way to a large income in animation, as in most professions, is the hard way.

The game is a mixture of work and fun. There is something fascinating in animating the lovable and mischievous characters whose capers convulse millions of movie-goers [sic]. The artist must be something of an actor himself. He blows the breath of life into the hilarious animal and human characters who inhabit his delightful land of make-believe. Aside from the monetary reward there is a special creative joy in the animator's work seldom found in other fields of artistic endeavor.

If I have stripped the game of some of its glamour and blasted the myth of sudden success and wealth then I am sure that hundreds of would-be animators will approach the studios in the right spirit, prepared for the arduous and necessarily tedious first steps that lead to success and a sizable income as finished animators and background artists.

FIN

In his article Howard, more than once, refers to animators earning high incomes.
". . . fabulous salaries . . ." "pay you handsomely. . ." ". . .large income in animation. . ." ". . .monetary rewards. . . " ". . . sudden success and wealth. . ."

Well, Howard old ghost, it didn't turn out the way you thought it would. Yes, $300 a week was big money in the middle of The Great Depression, but twenty years later, in terms of purchasing power, animators were making much less than they did in 1938 and many of them were out of work.

In 1938 there were very few animators. Today there are animation studios in France, Germany, Ireland, Australia, the Philippines, Taiwan, China, Japan, India and Canada. A young artist just out of Cal Arts is not likely to be carrying a portfolio. No. She will probably be showing her animated film on a thumb-drive… whatever that is.

62 years later my eldest son, Michael, called one day to ask a question about his uncle Howard.

"Was there another Howard Baldwin in the cartoon business?"

"No."

"Well. I just saw a Bugs Bunny retrospective on TV and the credits on the first episode read—story by Howard Baldwin. Did you know about that?"

"That's news to me! I'll check it out."

Chuck Jones (Bugs Bunny, The Road Runner) and I were not

friends, but over the years we attended many a screening and shared a few drinks. I like to think we respected each other. Michael's discovery gave me reason to call Chuck just a few months before he died. Did he remember my brother, Howard Baldwin? I had to speak very loud for Chuck to hear me. DID HE REMEMBER MY BROTHER HOWARD? Yes, he did. WAS HOWARD WORKING AT WARNER BROTHERS IN 1938? Yes, he was. DID HE RECALL WHAT HOWARD WAS WORKING ON? No.

There used to be some intense controversy about the creation of Bugs Bunny and animation directors at Warner's vied for the authorship. There is absolutely no doubt that the first Bugs Bunny cartoon was made in 1938. This cartoon, Porky's Hare Hunt, was directed by "Bugs" Hardaway and the credits go on to say, story by Howard Baldwin. The line, "Don't worry chief, I'm just a little pixilated" would never have been spoken by a more mature and sophisticated rabbit, but "pixilated" was one of my brother's favorite words. Odd he never mentioned doing any writing at Warner Brothers. He never told me he worked on Felix The Cat in 1926 either - three years before I was born.

Not many animators of Howard Baldwin's generation considered the making of animated cartoons work of any consequence. They seemed to see their jobs as an extension of a high school drinking bout and none of them, with the exception of Winsor McKay, Chuck Jones and Walt Disney, foresaw that they were creating icons that would play a big part in the development of American culture or, for that matter, change the world of Graphic Art forever.

I always thought of Howard as a very successful failure. He was likable, talented and bright but for some reason a demon dwelled within. He was self destructive in the extreme and, at 60, wound up living with my Mother. I cannot imagine how she must have felt watching her first-born collapse and die of a massive heart attack on the living room floor.

Chapter 3

"Where are we going today, Mr. Peabody?"

"Today, Sherman, we are going back to the year 1938 to look in on the Baldwin family saga."

Pop, discharged from the sanitarium, announced we were no longer going to have to pay rent.

The Baldwin family, once seven, was now four--Mom, Pop, me and my brother Jack. He was 17 and I was 10. We were very poor, but you would never have known it. We lived in a large three-story house on Andrews Avenue, a lovely street near the up-town campus of New York University. This was a part of the Bronx known as University Heights, only a short walk to the Hall of Fame. The neighborhood, mostly Irish Catholic, was a mixture of apartments and private homes.

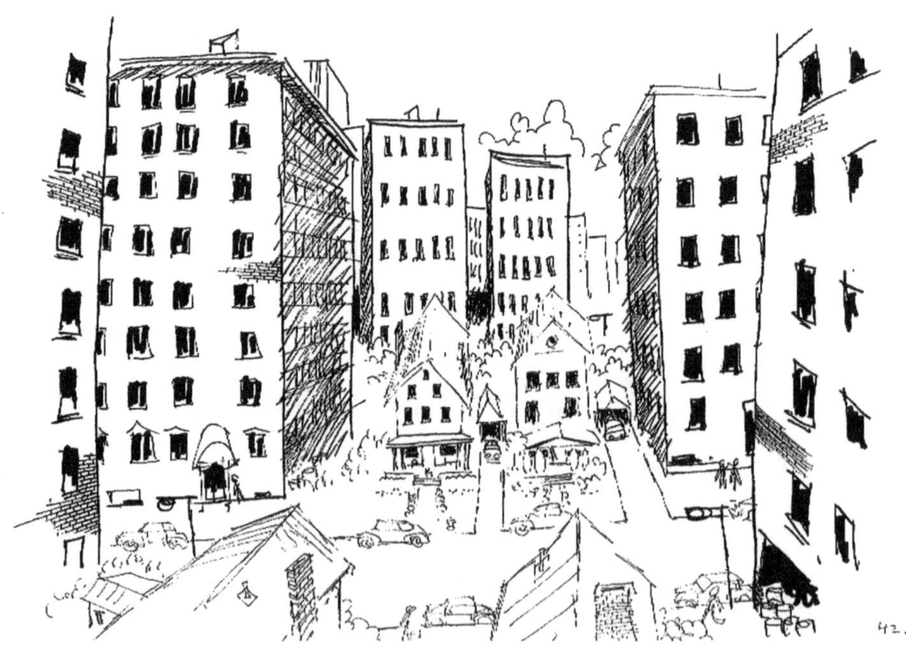

Some of these grand old places were fraternity houses occupied by energized young men fortunate enough to be in college during the great depression. They were having fun and not thinking about war.

We lived in a house belonging to my Father's cousin, John Morrisey, a widower. I remember a Sunday supper where Mr. Morrisey glorified Ireland, vilified England, praised Hitler and told us Mussolini, even though he was a Wop, made the trains run on time.

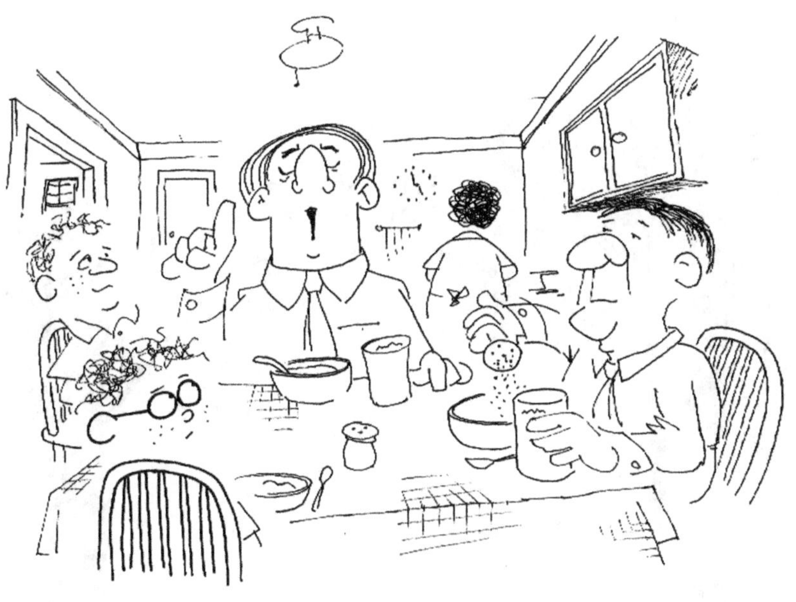

Sunday dinner was frequently an Irish version of Fricassee de Poulet à L'éstragon—a big pot of cut up boiled white-skinned chicken in a flour-based white gravy and slippery white dumplings. Dessert was canned fruit cocktail smothered in Miracle Whip. I loved it.

Mom took care of the three-story house, which sometimes exhausted her to tears. Pop, recovering from TB, did not do much of anything but putter about and drink beer. Thanks to Peggy Guggenheim, my

31

brother Jack, seven years older than I, was a full-time art student at the Pratt Institute and what he was learning about perspective, pictorial composition, color and design he was giving to me. These were concepts I would never have been exposed to in my little Catholic school. I was attending my third grammar school, St. Nicholas of Tolentine and doing poorly.

The way I looked at things it was Jack's fault that I had to wear glasses. One summer evening we were walking on the Grand Concourse on our way to see a Marx Brothers movie when Jack realized I could not read the theatre marquee just a few yards away. He told mom. She had my eyes checked. Now I could see the blackboard but it was too late--even with four eyes I would never catch up.

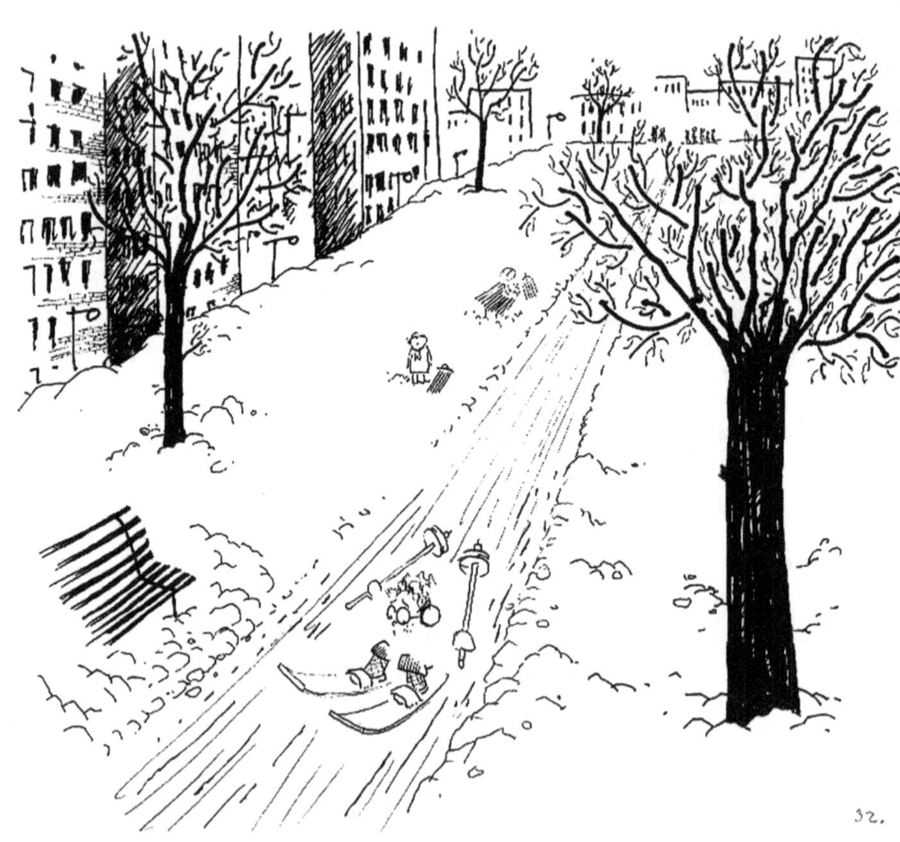

I wanted to learn how to ski, so Jack made my skis out of barrel staves. My ski poles were sawed-off broomsticks and very rigid. My slope was an ice covered road in the park and very fast.

On my third run I fell and broke both bones in my left forearm. Someone ran for help. A patrol car took me home. A taxi took me to a hospital where two very young interns aligned my bones as best they could. Many weeks later one bone had healed and one had not, so now surgery was necessary. In the 1930s surgery was a big deal and my operation required a hospital stay of many days. The Montefiore Hospital parked me in a ward with a lot of beat up men. . .burn victims. . .multiple fractures. . .ulcerous sores. I was ambulatory and soon tried to help out as best a kid could. . .fetching water. . .fetching a nurse. . .it was not as horrific as in Gone With The Wind but, to a child, this short stay made a deep impression. I can still see the white scar on my arm. . .another disfiguration.

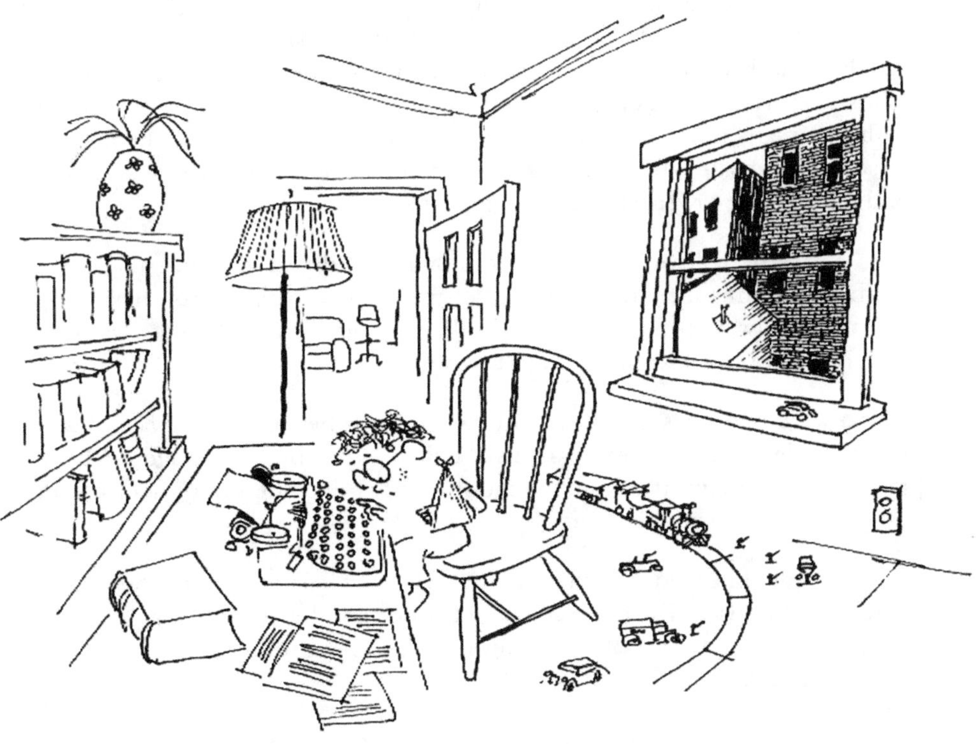

I could not play for six months so I tapped out a 50,000 word story entitled: "Felicity Island". It was a story about two boys and their uncle sailing on one of the Great Lakes and encountering an escaped prisoner and Royal Canadian Mounties.

The Major General of a nun that was dictator of my fourth grade class was not in the least impressed or interested in my book and suggested I concentrate on the multiplication tables. Fortunately, my siblings praised my book. Alas, when my mother was old and senile, she was cleaning things out and tossed my story away. The only positive thing I can remember about Saint Nicholas of Tolentine is singing Handel's Messiah at midnight mass on Christmas Eve.

The Andrews Avenue gang was composed of Irish Catholic boys – all about the same age—all went to St. Nicks. I was the troop's artist and entertained with epic drawings in chalk on the sidewalk or in the street. At full commitment the gang may have numbered thirteen.

Depending on the season we played stickball or hockey on roller skates. Only grudgingly did we allow cars to pass. After the Christmas holidays the back alleys of five story tenements would be jammed with dry Christmas trees. Working at Superman speed the gang would fan out and gather as many trees as possible—stack them in the middle of an intersection —set them ablaze—then run away and hide. Soon a fire truck would arrive and put out our towering inferno—a great sight!

In the fall we piled up huge mounds of dry dead leaves and ignited them. I do remember that once we set fire to the sleeping grass that sloped down and away from the Hall of Fame and fled with glee from the University cop who was too old to catch us.

There were two boys that were not welcome in the gang. One was a Jewish kid who lived in a new apartment building nearby. His building had a doorman and he went to public school PS 51. I liked him but, thanks to the gang, we could never be friends.

The other kid was named James Byrne. He lived just up the street in a very nice house. His father was an attorney and his mother was beautiful. The black maid wore a white uniform like in the movies. He went to a private school.

Except for Scrappy, my dog, James was the only close friend I had as a child. We built model airplanes. Down in the basement we cast soldiers out of molten lead and lost ourselves in make believe fantasy.

The gang did not like James.

One day a few of us, led by the gang's acknowledged leaders—the Cronin brothers—decided to go to the park. James tagged along but definitely as an outsider. We decided to play King of the Hill using the park's public rest room as a mountain. This square stone block structure was surrounded by deep sand. The way this building was constructed it was very easy to scale the walls and get up on the roof and whoever was on the roof was King, but not for long. It was a constant cycle of climbing up or jumping off to escape being shoved off by an attacking marauder. James was not very aggressive, so the gang began to tease him. Now their focus switched from the King up on the hill to poor James down on the ground. Up on the roof, my legs dangling over the edge, I was gazing out toward the Harlem River. I could hear the vicious taunts behind and below me—a dilemma—to defend James was to risk alienating myself from the gang. I chose the gang. Suddenly I was aware of movement behind me and turned to see James rushing toward me, his eyes projecting the hatred of one betrayed. He pushed me off.

James ran away and I joined the little mob that chased him home. We were never friends again. I avoided him. It took many years for that guilty knot to dissolve from my brain.

I did not like my name. It was bad enough having a weak heart,- wearing glasses, displaying ears the stuck out too far without having a name like Gerard. How could mom and pop have done such a thing?! In an Irish Catholic neighborhood, "Gerard" was a foreign word and I suffered with it. Boys had normal names like John, Michael, Peter, Paul or Patrick. I did not like to be called Jerry or teased with "Garage" or "Baldy" but worst of all was "Four Eyes!"

The Cronin brothers, a year apart, were very cold kids. They lived in a gloomy basement apartment under an old five-story tenement. I guess their father was the Super.

The Cronin brothers had a cousin visiting. His name was Jimmy. He was a nasty kid who used dirty words like shit and piss and damn! Sinful. The first time I met Jimmy he called me "four eyes" and, sensing that I didn't like it, he never let up. Very late in the afternoon of a summer day, I found myself walking home from a visit to the Cloisters with the Cronin brothers and their cousin, Jimmy The Mean. I must have heard "four eyes" a hundred times. Still quite a few blocks from home and very tired, we were dragging ourselves up a steep hill. It was a one-way street and automobiles, bumper to bumper, were crawling up the hill no faster than we were.

"Whatsa matta Four Eyes…can't you make it?"

"Knock it off."

With a "make me Four Eyes," he gave me a poke in the chest. I can even feel it now. In a thousandth of a second I burst into a rage and I punched him in the mouth. Before Jimmy could gather his dim wits, I was pummeling him as hard as I could ….BAM! POW! BAM BAM BAM. He was holding onto a lamppost and beginning to crumble when the Cronins entered the fight. I was backing up the hill trying to fend them off when suddenly, right beside me, the rear door of a limousine opened and a man in the back seat reached out and yanked me into the car. SLAM.

"You were doing pretty good there, kid. Where do you live?"

I stayed away from the Cronin brothers after that and avoided James whenever possible. I was no longer part of the gang and no longer had a close friend—except Scrappy—my dog. Scrappy got run over by a taxi and dragged himself home followed by the cab and a cop. I was sent upstairs and watched from a window as the policeman, aiming his pistol at Scrappy, put him out of his suffering. BANG!

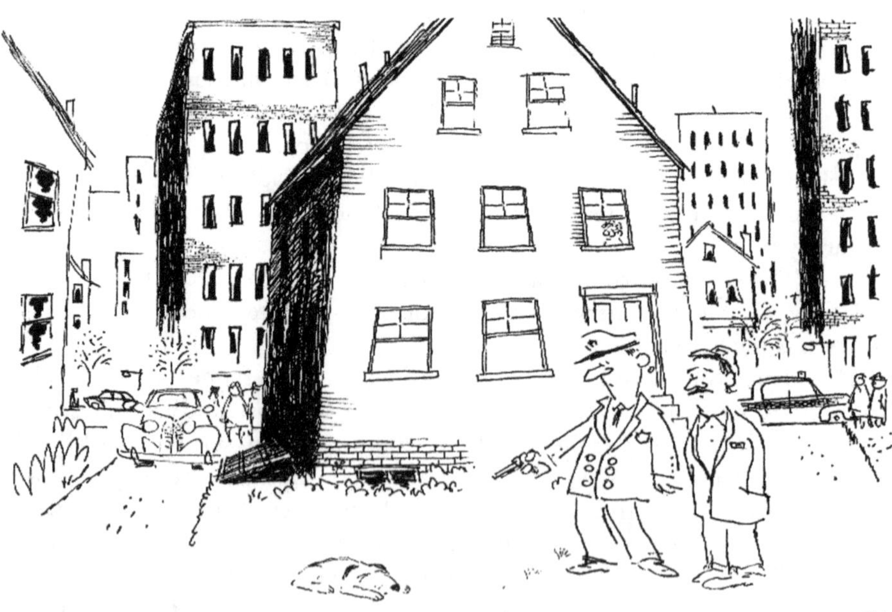

My sister Dolores, a beautiful auburn haired Irish beauty lived in a large suite in a hotel somewhere in the canyons of downtown Manhattan. The suite served as office and residence for her husband, who was a Tammany Hall politician. He grew up in the N.Y.C. that was owned by Tammany Hall. . . the Tammany that elected Jimmy Walker Mayor. . . the Tammany that nominated Al Smith for President . . .the Tammany that would decide that Jack Killgrew, my brother-in-law, would become Speaker of the House for the New York State Legislature.

My memories about my sister, state senator Jack Killgrew and their three handsome children form a kaleidoscopic montage of all too short summer vacations at a large country estate overlooking the Hudson River and on Sundays, going to Mass at a little church in Wappingers Falls.

All politicians go to church. I felt quite grand as the big black Buick Limousine pulled in front of the church steps with James, the black chauffeur, opening the car doors for us kids. After Mass there would be a stop at Napoleon's Italian grocery for pizza and spumoni. Dolores was twenty-one years older than me, so I was just three or four years older than my nieces and nephew--more like their brother than an uncle. Dolores was more than twenty years younger than her husband.

There was always something going on. Hyde Park was not far away. "Now you children stay in the play yard while Mrs. Roosevelt is here."

My nephew and I bunked upstairs in the Blue Room, which was part of the servants' wing. We would stay up late waiting for the Hudson River night-boat to pan its huge searchlight across the house. We would wave even though the ship was a mile away.

There were two dogs-- an Irish Setter, and an Irish Terrier who was very territorial. A state trooper arrived. Someone was complaining about the dogs.

"Why these dogs wouldn't scratch a flea." My little niece speaks up, "Tell him how they chased the Constable, right into his car."

One warm summer afternoon I found myself alone and I recall walking down the long, long driveway that led to the two stone pylons that flanked the gate. This gate opened out onto a narrow dirt farm road. The road separated the estate from the farm next door where idle dairy cows were chewing their cud. I climbed up and sat atop one of the pylons hoping a car would come up the hill and that the occupants, as they passed by, would think I was rich. There was no traffic.

When my brother-in-law was in the city, my sister and her three kids would visit mom and pop at the Morrisey house. She would always bring me something wonderful like the big shiny Tom Mix cap pistol I needed so badly.

Downtown, Pop was packing Jack's law books, the many volumes to be shipped to the country house. He told mom there were hundred dollar bills between the pages.

Chapter 4

I don't know what Peyo was doing on May 10th in 1940 when Germany invaded Belgium. He was twelve. I was eleven. I don't recall what I was doing either, probably collecting War Cards.

Japan did not plan well when it attacked the slumbering giant.

My brother Howard and my sister Dorothy, married to animator George Cannata, lived in Hollywood. Howard and George worked for Walt Disney. Brother Jack was still attending the Pratt Institute.

Sometimes, when my Father drank too much beer and shifted into whiskey, there would emerge a marital argument that always ended in a loud explosion of words and tears followed by my mother becoming grimly silent, which my father, a man of many words, couldn't stand. More than once he just hopped on the subway and stayed with my Uncle Jack for a day or two, returning when he, somehow, sensed mom was ready to talk again.

The last time Pop went to visit his brother and three days passed without his return, Mom began to worry. Uncle Jack did not have a telephone. On the morning of the fourth day, Mr. Morrissey dropped by my uncle's apartment. No, Pop had not been there, my mother was now distraught. On the fifth day a postcard arrived from Oklahoma. Pop was on his way to California and would send for us as soon as he had a job.

Me, Mom and Jack were soon on a Trailways Bus and heading for Hollywood. What I remember most about New York City is bricks. What I remember most about my initial encounter with Los Angeles is palm trees, open space, malted milks for 5 cents, chicken molé, tacos, avocados, Chinese food, chili with beans, and dinner with my brothers at Don The Beachcomber's, where they served exotic Polynesian food accompanied by thunder and lightning, and the sound of wind and rain falling on the roof. I saw my first stage-play and dropped my first bowling ball down one of the fifty lanes at what was then the world's largest bowling alley on Sunset Boulevard. It is long gone.

Pop got a job at his old trade as a garment cutter. Mom got a job in a laundry. Jack got a job as an apprentice in an animation studio while waiting for his orders from the Air Force. I entered a Los Angeles public school in Hollywood.

Thomas Starr King junior high was nothing like the dingy brick building that housed my Bronx prison. Thomas Starr King was a long white horizontal edifice that gave homage to Spain. It had a red tiled roof. There were classes in creative writing, art, theatre and a real gymnasium. I remember running home after the first day, "Mom! Mom! Guess what! All the kids in school talk like radio announcers!"

I spent a couple of years imitating this "radio" talk. Slowing down, pronouncing R's, enunciating every word. In New York City talk was fast.

"Hiyahowahyuhjeet?"

"Nodjew?"

In California it was, "Hi. How are you? Did you eat?

"No. Did you?"

These days, it is a rare student that spots me as a native New York kid.

One afternoon after class, I was in the Art room with my 8th grade art teacher, Ms. Frances Nugent. She was a hefty woman with a mannish hair cut. I was drawing some sketches for the Thomas Starr King newsletter. There was no one else present and soon we got to chatting about what I intended to make out of my life.

"You know, Gerard, it seems apparent that you will probably become an artist. Now Society views artists - has an attitude about artists - that they all starve in garrets, cut their ears off and, at best, are very eccentric people. We know that's not true, but since the average person holds such a view they will tolerate behavior from an "artist" that they would not accept from anyone else. Take advantage of it."

I never forgot that advice.

Somewhere within this middle-school time frame I began writing little plays based on stories my mother told me about relatives I never met or could not remember. Playing all the parts I would perform these plays, usually on Saturday gatherings of my family along with The George Cannatas, Rudy Zamoras, Cal Howards and the Frank Tashlins. They would all laugh and clap so I was greatly encouraged. Alas, these writings, too, are all lost.

My high school was named John Marshall (1755-1835), in honor of the first chief justice of the United States. I never thought about it as a student, but looking back now, it really was a snooty school.

Most high school teams are named after Tigers, Panthers, Wildcats, Mustangs and Eagles. . . names that evoke power, strength and aggression. Not at John Marshall. No. We were the Barristers!

The school was located in the Los Feliz district of East Hollywood.

The hills rising steeply above the school were home to wealthy professionals and a few movie stars.

We did not live in the hills but in a tiny bungalow which was part of a "court", a kind of horizontal apartment complex peculiar to Hollywood in the thirties when land was plentiful and cheap.

I was enjoying high-school, while brother Jack was somewhere in India on a secret project helping to build a realistic scale model of a large city. Jack told me much later it looked like a Japanese city.

Howard also joined the Air Force. He didn't have to since he was married and had two little children, but adventure called and he was, as always, irresponsible. He wound up on Okinawa after the battle.

With all of the young men off to war and all of America's factories running 24 hours a day, there was a very serious shortage of workers. Rosy the riveter would forever change the status of women in our culture.

Recently, at a dinner party, a young man asked me what my first job was: On my high school bulletin board I found out that Cedars of Lebanon hospital was in need of a Page or two. I applied and was hired. I worked after school, on weekends and all summer pedaling to and from the hospital on my bicycle.

As a Page, I wore a white jacket just like a doctor and had my own call number, which directed me to where my service was needed, anywhere in the complex. I could commandeer an elevator, wheel a pregnant movie star up to obstetrics,--turn away the unwelcome at the emergency entrance,-- deliver flowers to a sick Eddy Cantor, observe a bloody autopsy being performed, or babies being born. Down in the morgue I would open the refrigerator and check tags on the big toes of the dead to be certain the mortuary wheeled away the right body. (The still-born, also tagged, left by the main entrance in a little black bag.) I observed encephalogram examinations, gaped at the thousands of white mice sent into deadly shock in boiling water as part of a scientific study relating to the War and sometimes, on a quiet Sunday afternoon, spent time in the lab peering into a Ziess microscope as a lab tech explained to me what it was I was seeing. I had my own little microscope at home, but compared to a Ziess mine was just a toy.

When the war ended so did my job. For a while I fantasized about becoming a doctor, but that idea faded away.

Every year the John Marshall High School creative writing class published a collection of poetry, essays and short stories. Miss Mabel Herman was our teacher. She was old and frail and might be mistaken for a little bundle of twigs. One quiet afternoon, after diagramming a Haiku, Miss

Herman slipped into musing on her long career as a mentor and she touched upon how, every once in a while, a student would pass her way that displayed the gift of talent. The class saw her glance at me, but it was with an expression of admonishment. I was lazy. Perhaps three poems, written 64 years ago, give insight into the self that was me at seventeen:

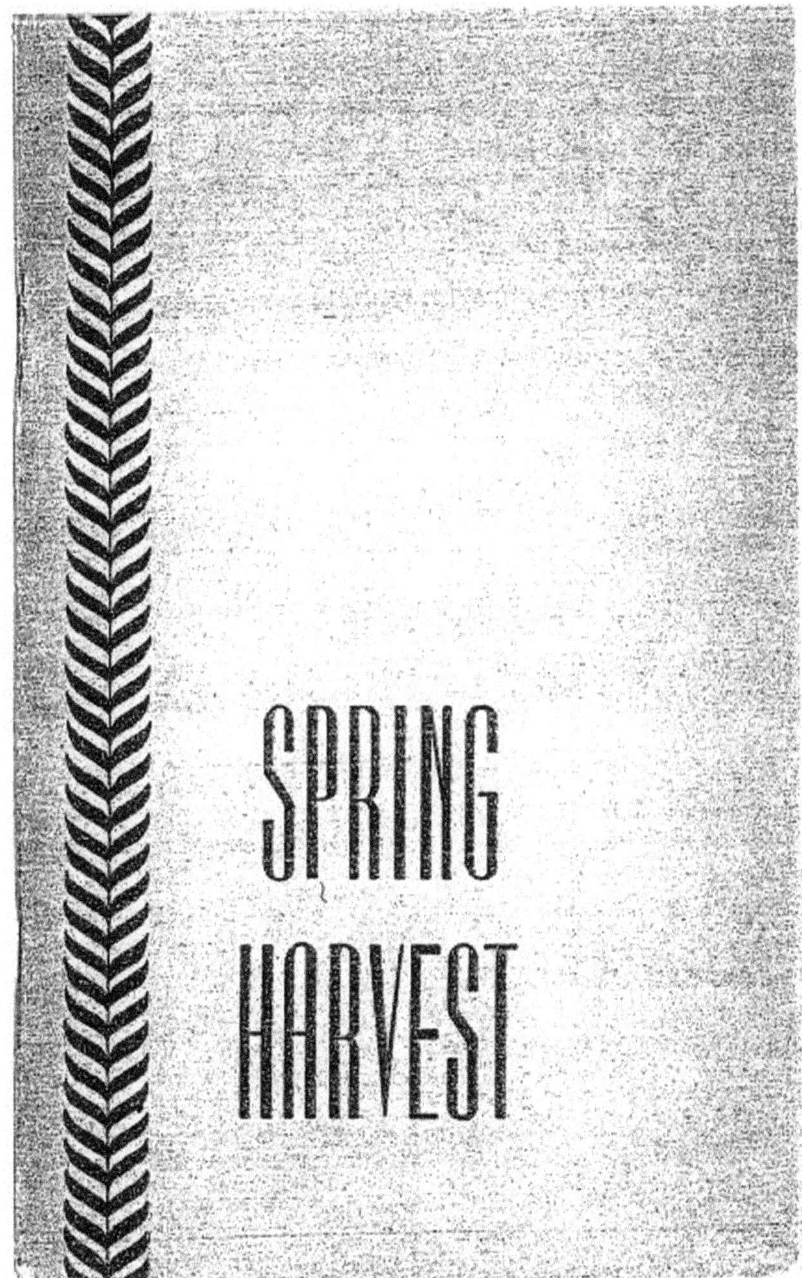

SPRING
HARVEST

WARNING

He ran alone-
    He ran till each hot breath
    Tore at his flaming throat.
    He ran wildly through the streets
    Crying out to all the world!
    Crying from the rooftops!
    Crying from the market places!
                Crying!
But the people would not listen
                And he ran alone
                And time passed.
And they marched-
    Evacuees of flaming cities,
    Skeletons of another time,
    Ghostly skeletons against the flaming sky.
    Quiet cities…..Dead cities.
                He was gone and they marched alone.

PROGRESS

A man-
    Alone in the field,
    Alone with the horse, Alone with the plow,
    Tending the crop.
                And then
A wind
    Tearing through the night!
    Beating the crop into the mud!
    Then rushing off into the darkness
                And leaving
A man
    Alone in the field,
    Alone with the horse,
    Alone with the plow.

THE MAGIC WORD

I heard the music of my soul

And it swelled within me.

And I longed to find the word,

The magic word,

That would say all that my heart felt.

Locked in contest with two high school friends, the game was to see who could read the most books in a given amount of time. Our rules required reading at least one book a week. Deep into the works of Freud, Adler, and Jung, without tutorial guidance I, somehow, got the notion that extroversion was bad and introversion was good. So, contrary to my true nature, I feigned a frown, so as to be taken seriously. The frown never went away although I dropped the introversion years ago.

World War II ended with the detonation of two atomic bombs. The world worried about what these weapons would bring to Mankind's future. As editor, I wrote the theme of our class yearbook. The bold banner across a double page spread asked,

ARE WE ENTERING INTO A WORLD OF ATOMIC ENERGY OR ATOMIC DESTRUCTION?

This Barrister is still waiting for the answer.

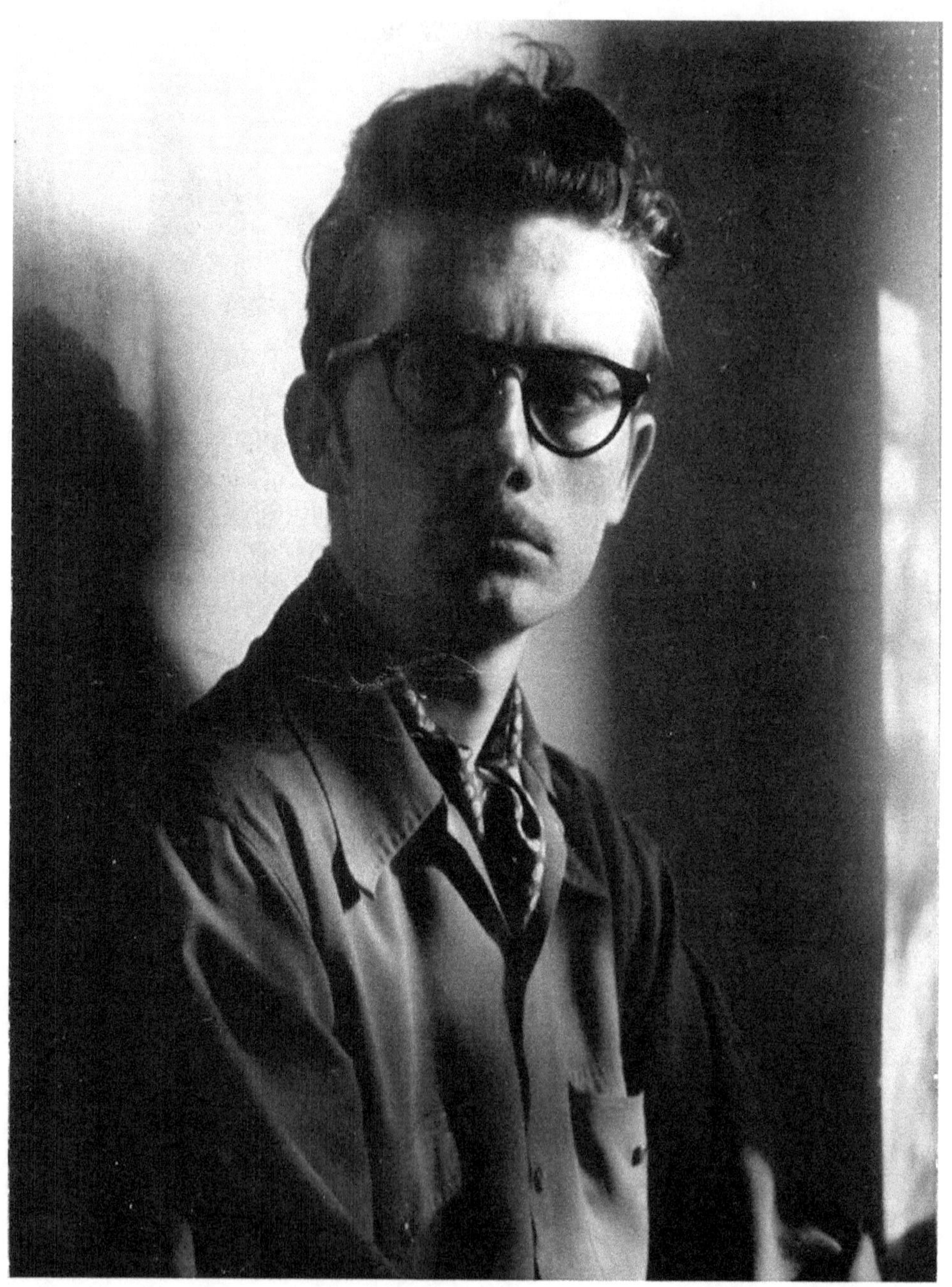

It was as a senior in high school that I, for the first time, began to wonder what would become of me. Would I be happy? Would I be rich? Would I be changing tires in a gas station or waiting tables in a crummy restaurant? I know! I'd write radio plays!

One of my brother Howard's drinking pals was actor John Dehner. Howard introduced me to Dehner, a tall and imposing man with a rich and powerful voice and much in demand as a character actor in movies. He was also the host of a CBS radio show. I cannot remember which one -- Inner Sanctum -- The Whistler -- The Squeaking Door -- The Shadow --anyway, I began writing radio plays. He graciously read my many efforts and patiently explained the proper format for a radio script. He explained the importance of sound effects and timing for keeping the listener glued to the set. I never sold a story.

Graduation was approaching. Pop thought I should apply for a job as a bag-filler at our local 1947 version of a super market and work my way up. A World War II veteran that I barely knew was attending the Chouinard Art Institute. He showed my paintings to the head of the drawing department. Madame Chouinard granted me a full scholarship. Saved!

Every year the Institute held an Open House for parents, relatives, professionals and, hopefully, future students. The school put on a good show. The industrial design department displayed models of their automobiles, refrigerators, toasters and furniture. Edith Head's fashion department, using live models, paraded elegant costumes --period and modern. Architectural renderings, illustrations and graphic designs covered the walls and, of course, there were drawings and paintings.

Entering the school a visitor had to pass a glass display window, and in that window, with a spot light on it, was a small painting of mine. Since I was a first year student I was feeling pretty good about myself. A few days after the open house I received a message from the editor of Sunset magazine: would I please call. He liked my painting very much. The magazine would like to buy it and put it on the cover. I said: No, I didn't do commercial art. How arrogant and stupid can a young man be?

Everyone in Hollywood wore dark glasses. They were either a shield against the blazing sun or some kind of a cultural affectation. I don't really know, but I do remember Howard, Jack and myself strolling down Hollywood Boulevard in our shades. On an evening stroll no one seemed to pay attention to movie stars. Even though I was only a teen-ager, my brothers never excluded me from their drunken gatherings and I soon took for granted that society was composed of writers, actors, directors, artists and animators. Most of these people, of like mind, held very strong opinions about everything. Walt Disney was a bad guy. Tex Avery was a good guy. Tex Avery, whoever he was, had their respect -- admiration -- appreciation. A long time would pass before I understood why, and 40 years would pass before I met him.

The privations of war had built up an enormous consumer demand but as I look back at the "privations" of war in America, it was really a big joke. The only ones deprived were the Mothers and Fathers whose sons were requisitioned to fight and die in battle. For the rest of the populace, insofar as a young boy could see, the war was a big party. People who hadn't had a job in twelve years were working and making money. You could buy a pint of ice cream for 10 cents. There was plenty of Jell-O and Miracle Whip. Gasoline was rationed, which meant Mae West could not drive her Duesenberg on Sunday. The propaganda machine in Washington preached sacrifice, so all resigned themselves to only buying a pound of sugar a week. The conservatives were happy when Roosevelt died and predicted Harry Truman would be a second-rate President, but he wasn't. Some day soon he would be my commander in chief.

Economically the country was booming and there was need for illustrators, art directors, fashion designers and industrial designers. Chouinard, in old downtown Los Angeles, never had so many students and a very fine school it was. In fact, it was one of the three or four best art schools in the nation -- maybe the world.

Chapter 5

In the summer of 1947, my life drawing class at Chouinard was crowded and quiet. The model was on her break and, in her white terry-cloth robe, casually talking to our Mentor, Don Graham. The demographics of the class was made up of mostly, as I regarded them, older men - fresh out of WWII, working intensely, making up for lost time. I was a kid fresh out of high school on a working scholarship. There were also quite a few pretty young girls.   Due to my sense of physical and social inferiority, I never got to know a single one. I hung out with the older guys - ex-Navy gunners, bombardiers, corpsmen and cooks. Some became life long friends. As of this writing only one is left.

On that warm summer afternoon in the life drawing class, the only sound was that of pencils on paper until someone spoke up in a loud and rather demanding voice. The school was very informal.

"Don?!"

Don Graham, a brilliant and inspiring instructor, was balding, with tufts of white curly hair framing his ears. His shirt was always open and his Levi jacket was always stained with chalk or charcoal.

"Yes, Barlow?" Barlow was the fellow that showed my paintings to Don.

"Don, what would you say is the newest thing in art - in the world of Art?"

Don Graham did not pause a moment to phrase his answer.

"The newest thing in art? The newest thing in graphic art, the only really new thing in 25,000 years is the animated cartoon... drawings that move."

Barlow kind of nodded and shrugged acceptance. The model returned to the model stand, shed her robe and resumed her pose. The class returned to their drawings.

Don walked about the room stopping here and there to give advice, make a suggestion, pass on a tip. He was the author of the greatest book on pictorial composition ever written, Composing Pictures — Still and Moving, and also a marvelous Mentor. Nothing more was said about animation - at least on that day.

I did not give Graham's assertion much thought. Animation being the only new thing in graphic art in 25000 years was not something I saw as important. I was cynical. My oldest brother was an animator and so was my brother-in-law. As a child I grew up hearing a lot of talk about Walt Disney, Winsor McKay, Bugs Bunny, Grim Natwick, Tom and Jerry, Bill Nolan and UbIwerks. None of this gossip ever gave me the impression that the "racket," as they referred to their work, was the hottest thing in Art in 25,000 years.

But I never forgot that summer afternoon. I never forgot the question or the answer. Perhaps it was prophetic, but the last thing in the world I ever considered was being a screen cartoonist. NO. I was going to cover buildings with great murals like Siqueiros or Diego Rivera only mine would be better.

In the summer '48, making use of the GI bill, my brother Jack was one of many young men studying at the Instituto Allende in San Miguel De Allende and, as his guest, he invited me to join him for a long, long summer.

The train from Laredo on its way south to Mexico City stopped only for a minute at the tiny hill-town station. Two miles away, high up on the hills, church spires punctuated an intense blue sky and mountains of brilliant white clouds. Standing on the station platform, as the train chugged away, I stood beside my long used suitcase and watched a 1936 Chevy, older than its years, trailing clouds of smoke and dust, come bumpitty-bumpitty down the hillside. This car turned out to be San Miguel's only taxi. (If you needed its service you would have to send a messenger.) Jack greeted me warmly. We were very close.

Except for a few automobiles this little city was the same as it had been two hundred years ago. Church bells tolled the time. Donkeys hauled the wood. All of the narrow streets were paved in cobblestones. The sidewalks were slate. An old man turned on the gaslights in the evening and turned them off in the morning. San Miguel must have been very prosperous at one time. Behind the brightly painted high plaster walls were many beautiful homes with lush gardens and tinkling fountains. A beautiful Cathedral lorded over the town square, at the center of which was a stately gazebo, host to a well intentioned but clunky band that played on warm summer evenings. There was a hotel or two, a couple of restaurants, a few shops and an Art Gallery. The town, because of its Art School, inexpensive accommodations and architectural beauty was becoming rather artsy-craftsy and a magnet for retired Americans. Behind their high walled villas the "rich" retired Americans paid their cooks, maids and gardeners as little as fifteen dollars a month.

Most of the art students lived in a Posada of some kind and Jack's residence was, in my inexperienced opinion, quite grand. The very large Spanish Colonial entry door opened out onto a wide tiled patio with upper and lower rooms on either side. There may have been twenty rooms. At the far end of this flowered patio was the dining room and beyond that a kitchen.

Jack's room, a tiny penthouse, had a view of the entire town. He gave his room to me and slept with Consuela, his lover and owner of the inn.

A student on the G.I. bill could throw a party, serve mounds of magnificent tamales filled with BBQ goat and hire a mariachi band for a few Pesos. Somewhere in town, there was a party every day.

During my stay the most famous person in town was world-renowned muralist and communist agitator David Alfaro Siqueiros. He had been hired by the school as a kind of artist-in-residence.

A large cavernous building made of stone blocks stood empty on the edge of town. It had once, a long time ago, been a nunnery. It was empty and cold. Siqueiros intended to revive it. He had designed a mural that would cover the ceiling, all four walls and the floor. His idea was that the viewer would not look at the mural but rather, be IN the mural. The medium was Duco, an automobile paint manufactured by Dupont. This paint was tough and toxic. Scaffolding was already up. A dozen student artists were all over the place and the Maestro, in his paint smeared work clothes, conducted his apprentices as if they were members of a symphony orchestra: I was welcomed onto the team.

A conflict arose between Siqueiros and the owner of the school. The students became involved and went on strike. Soon this was an international incident. Siqueiros loved it. Since the Escuela was certified by the Veterans Administration, the American Embassy became involved, wanting to know what was going on in sleepy San Miguel.

We drove to Mexico City in the Maestro's big black Buick. He and his driver-bodyguard were wearing black suits and black ties. Jack and I sat in the back. The drive to Mexico City was a drive of many hours.

We parked at the Embassy. I was to stay with the driver. Siqueiros reached into his inside jacket pocket and took out a pistol and put it in the glove compartment,: "Best to leave this here."

The issues were never resolved. The school lost its accreditation. The mural was never finished. Eventually a new and much better school was founded and Jack became a member of its faculty. My brother Jack lived in San Miguel for many years. He bought a piece of property and since I'd taken some courses in Architecture, he asked me to design a house. Only local material and traditional construction could be used. When finished, it was charming and I presume it is still there.

Early in my long summer stay I caught a bad cold which got worse and worse. It's hard enough to breathe at 7000 feet without having pleurisy. The town doctor gave me some medicine and advised I stay in bed for five days: a-not-very-exciting-prospect. Under Consuela's direction a few young women took care of the Posada San Miguel. These young girls did the cleaning, laundry, helped in the kitchen and served in the dining room. Consuela assigned Maria, a pretty 14-year-old Mestiza, to serve my breakfast, lunch and dinner in bed while I recuperated. Soon Maria was in my bed and I would just as soon have stayed there forever. We were not in love, but lovers. What a summer!

Finally I returned home. I had made a few paintings which I liked, but when I departed the train at Laredo I forgot them. I never saw those paintings again. I never saw Maria again, either.

Years later, on more than one trip to San Miguel, I tried to find her. The Posada was closed and the building served as a warehouse for bags of corn and grain. Consuela had long ago moved to Mexico City; no one remembered Maria except me.

Back at Chouinard the school's oil painting studio probably housed 35 paint-splattered easels and I was working at one of them. Phil Dyke, one of my painting instructors, stopped to take a look at what I was doing. He was silent for a few moments, never taking his eyes off of whatever I had put on the canvas.

"You know, Gerard, you're very gifted." I feigned modesty, "Well sort of."

"You're at a point where you have to find out what it is you have to say."

"What do you mean?"

"If you would just be consistent; paint in one style. If you can do that I know galleries will compete to have you in their stable. But your work, wonderful as it is, roams all over the place. Galleries don't like that. Their clients, the collectors, want consistency, same as you would expect in a really great restaurant."

"Don't know that I've ever been to a really great restaurant."

"Well I've not been to too many myself, but you see what I mean?"

"I see it. Don't like it. Sell out."

On a late summer afternoon, having finished my drawing class, I was in the men's room standing at a urinal when in walked Don Graham, who proceeded to wash the black charcoal off of his hands.

"Hi Don."

"You know Baldwin," he said, drying his hands with paper towels, "I've been thinking about you and your future."

"Yeah?"

"Why don't you get out of here? There's nothing more we can teach you. Get a job. Get away from home."

"What'll I do? I don't have a job."

"Try Disney. I know they're looking." Don was a consultant to Disney; a talent scout.

"But cartooning? That's a sellout."

"You too good for Walt Disney?"

"No, it's not that. I just want to stay pure to myself. Know what I mean?"

I'm sure, in his 25 years as an art teacher, Don had heard this a few times before and wondered "What is it with these pure guys?"

"I just want to paint. Besides my brother Howard says Disney is a terrible place."

"Well there are other studios. Warners, Lantz, MGM, UPA?"

"I don't even have a portfolio."

"Make one, and show a few paintings."

A couple of months later, in the winter of 1950,   reality, as it always does, won out.

I was making the rounds of the animation studios showing my drawings and paintings. There were only five places where an aspiring animator might look for a job. If there was an animation boutique out there somewhere I was unaware of it. Black and white television was killing movie attendance and there didn't seem much of a future for any of the big old-style movie studios. With the exception of Disney, all of them were contemplating closing down their animation departments.

Because of my oldest brother, Howard, being an old-timer, I didn't have a problem getting interviews, but the animation business was in a slump, so nobody was hiring anybody for anything. Disney was last on my list.

John Hubley, an Academy Award winning director at UPA Pictures, liked a painting of mine so much that he insisted the studio put me on as an "apprentice in-betweener" at the union minimum of $27 a week, which was not enough to even think about leaving home. A private in the Army made more, as I would soon find out.

Hubley borrowed my painting to hang for a New Year's party he was giving. I was not invited.

In 1950 a lot of Screen Cartoonists were unemployed. A great animator like Bill Littlejohn (Snoopy) was not the only cartoonist selling cars. The Screen Cartoonists Guild did not want to see any more animators selling cars or painting houses so, contractually, they insisted on a deal with the studio bosses that a studio would not hire any artist who was not already a member of the Guild and the Guild would not swear in any new member unless that person already had a job. CATCH 22. Bill Littlejohn was also the business agent for the union, so they bent the rule and everybody winked.

A kid right out of art school could find no more prestigious place to work than a job at UPA. Their radical changes in story, animation and graphic design were revolutionary -- Gerald McBoing Boing by Dr. Seuss, Mr. Magoo, The Telltale Heart by Edgar Alan Poe -- everything UPA did received world-wide acclaim. Never before or since has there been such a concentration of talented animation artists. Some of the aura rubbed off on even the lowest apprentice, but I still had my dream of being a great painter, so I saw this apprenticeship as temporary until, somehow, someday, I would be recognized as the great painter I really was. Meanwhile I continued punching holes in animation paper, moving desks about and learning to draw Mr. Magoo.

I barely got to know Magoo when I received a draft notice and wound up in Korea. The Doctor that gave me my physical at the induction center didn't seem to notice or care that I had a heart murmur, or that my eyesight was poor, or that I was frail.

I was not enthused about serving my country and purposely did poorly on a battery of tests in the hope they would kick me out. It didn't work.

In my Army personnel file I stated I had been employed as a Director of Animation at UPA Pictures and increased my salary by 30 or 40 times what it actually was. No one ever questioned this slight exaggeration. Someone must have opened that file because after six weeks of basic training at Fort Ord, just outside of Monterey California, I was assigned to the ASA.

ASA?

The Army Security Agency, headquartered at Fort Devans just outside of Boston, was a military extension of the top secret National Security Agency. Fort Devans was a recruiting center for the bright young kids the Agency required for its mission. In order to distinguish us from the rest of the soldiers at Fort Devans, we were issued Eisenhower jackets, the same style as worn by General Eisenhower when he was supreme commander of allied forces in World War II. Thus smartly attired I learned how to type. I was not very good at it. I also learned how to properly fill out the long questionnaires that would allow the intense probing into my background so that I could be issued a Top Secret clearance.

On a weekend pass it was not much of a train ride from Boston to N.Y.C. where I would visit my sister Dolores or my sister-in-law, Barbara. On one of these excursions I first met the world's oldest living animator.

My sister Dorothy told me that when I was a baby in New York City, the already famous animator, Grim Natwick, who gave life to Betty Boop and was later a key animator on Snow White, placed his imprimatur upon me by bouncing me on his knee and making me laugh. I would have been two and Grim 40. Twenty years would pass before I again met Grim. I was on that involuntary sabbatical from my apprenticeship at UPA Pictures. We met in New York. In 1950 Grim was not only the oldest living animator but destined to stay thus for a long, long time.   I was visiting my sister-in-law who was a tall thin black haired beauty that resembled Vampira. She and Howard were separated, he making cheap TV commercials in Mexico City; she, working for UPA Pictures in N.Y. and struggling to raise their two children. My brother was no help, ever. Barbara, myself, and Grim were to meet at some bar for drinks. It was winter. It was cold.

Natwick was tall and striking, wearing a dark navy blue officer's cape, a dashing cap and a long white scarf wrapped around his neck a couple of times, its tail flapping in the wind. He didn't have much to say. What could he say?   "My, look how you've grown!"   Five years would pass before I would again meet the world's oldest living animator. He would always be thus. Who could catch up?

On another weekend pass I visited my sister Dolores. If I write more about her husband than I do Dolores, it is because he was much more interesting. His friend, mayor Jimmy Walker, also known colloquially as Beau James, also liked to write songs and—more than once—I heard my brother-in-law at the piano, belt out in his booming baritone, "Will you love me in December as you do in May?"

On this particular visit, after Dolores and the teenagers went to bed, Jack and I stayed up until three. He introduced me to a dozen liquors, explaining what they were, where they came from and how to serve them. He also introduced me to his personal philosophy as it applied to politics and life.

"Gerard, all politicians are whores. They are all, to a man, on the take. Let me explain. You see, there are two kinds of graft, honest graft and dishonest graft. Now, dishonest graft is reaching into the till and taking the people's money. That is a crime. Honest graft is when you have the power to order 25 grand pianos for the school system or, perhaps, place an order for 25 John Deere snowplows for the Department of Highways. If a piano shows up in your living room and a small snow plow shows up on your farm well… that's just a perk."

He also offered: "Gerard, let me tell you something. You can marry more money than you can ever save." He didn't follow his own advice when he married my sister. I guess beauty conquers avarice. Jack also drafted the legislation that gave workers in the state of New York unemployment insurance.

Back in the army, the ASA sent me off to a Signal Corps school at Camp Gordon, just outside of Augusta Georgia where I learned how to send and receive Morse code. I wasn't very good at it. In order to get out of exercising in the hot sun, I volunteered to paint a mural in the company mess hall. It was probably 50 feet long and 8 feet high and was a kind of montage of Signal Corps activity. I wonder if it is still there. Unlikely.

Soon someone else was perusing my file. My impressive resume resulted in my being summoned to the base Criminal Investigation Department known as C.I.D. They were looking for someone just like me, somebody from Los Angeles. When a very close friend of mine by the name of Dion Vigne, also a draftee and attached to another Company, was arrested on drug charges, they probably grilled him and my name came up. They looked into my file and saw "Director" - perfect.

I was questioned at length by two sergeants. I sat across from them at a long table and had fun playing with their dumb questions. I even took the fifth a couple of times just for the hell of it. Up to this point in my life the only drug I used was alcohol, but these two guys assumed otherwise. At the far end of the room sat a Major. He only listened. When this futile interrogation was finished, the Major took me aside and made an offer. The base had a drug trafficking problem. Since I was from Hollywood and knew all about such things, perhaps I would like to work for the C.I.D. There would be no trouble getting me a transfer. The plan was to set me up in the Augusta hotel as a civilian, giving me a nice car of my choosing. I suggested a Desoto convertible with wings. I would need money of course. No problem. The traffickers would find me or I would find them, which would ultimately lead to a sting of some kind.

WOW! This was exciting!

When I returned to my barracks our company commander, a young lieutenant, wanted to know what was going on. I told him about my good luck. He was not happy. He was aghast. He informed me that the last young man playing the role they wanted me to play was found dead along the highway. Murdered. He hinted that the C.I.D. was in on the money.

I turned this opportunity down.

When I finished Morse code school I received my orders. Still assigned to ASA, I was to report to Vent Hill Farm somewhere in Virginia. I never heard of such a place and neither had my company commander.

When the Greyhound bus dropped me off at Vent Hill Farm, it also sped away with my duffle bag. Two old men, smoking pipes, were sitting on the front porch that fronted a general store. This could easily be a scene in a movie. Did they know how to get to Vent Hill Farm?

"Why sure, son." One of the two old gents walked into the store while I expressed my anxiety about losing my duffel bag. I was wearing a flashy nylon shirt, grey flannel slacks and loafers. At least I still had my orders. The old guy comes out of the store, "Cab will be here in a minute."

"Thanks."

The taxi and its driver, innocuous in the extreme, took me a few hundred yards down a well-manicured dirt road and stopped at a little striped guardhouse - another movie scene. The spiffy guard was wearing a .45 on his hip and the police dog was straining at its chain. A barbed wire fence flanked both sides of the guardhouse and disappeared into the deep pine forest. The guard studied my orders carefully and bade me enter. I strolled onto Vent Hill Farm as the taxi turned about and left. The dog snarled.

It was a long walk until I came upon the barracks. They were one story as were all of the ancillary buildings and well tucked under the trees. A big red barn and a couple of old fashioned silos dominated the scene. Only later would I learn that the barn and silos were packed with listening devices of extremely advanced design.

Vent Hill Farm, it turned out, was a place where the Agency, using a battery of tests, sorted out its new recruits and began the investigations that would determine if these young soldiers could be exposed to Top Secret information or what kind of further schooling they were to have. The food was excellent. The farm was peaceful and as close as the military can come to creating a resort.

I'm sure I did well on most of the tests, but I definitely failed the aptitude test for learning a foreign language. About three days later ten of us draftees boarded a small bus and headed for Arlington just outside of Washington D.C. and the headquarters of the National Security Agency where we would be going to school. The NSA was housed in a large office building surrounded by barbed wire and heavily policed.

This was the place that monitored and recorded every message transmitted by every ship, airplane, cable, radio and short-wave transmitter in the entire world, and probably even native drums. NSA receivers were listening 24-hours a day and all of this great mass of information was fed into computers that searched for THE secret message that might be harmful to the United States.

There were as many civilians as there were Army, Navy, Marine and Air Force officers and there were peons like us. Some people were hurrying about. Some were quite still and sipping coffee. Some were far away and deep in thought.

A master sergeant ushered we ten into what looked like an old-fashioned schoolroom. There was a blackboard at the front and desks with arms for writing. We drank coffee and smoked while waiting for Godot. We had no idea why we were there. When the 1st Lieutenant entered we stood up at attention. He motioned us be seated and said this formality was no longer necessary as long as we were in this building. Then he picked up a stick of chalk and wrote a long sentence on the blackboard in Chinese Characters.

"Anybody know what this says?"

"Nope."

"It says you're all going to Korea but first you're going to learn to speak a little Chinese."

Many weeks later our class of ten, still privates, boarded an Army chartered DC-6. Our MS number said we should have been Master Sergeants but the army had a freeze on pay. Our fellow passengers were a mix of officers representing the United Nations. At 300 miles an hour it was a long slow trip, stopping only for fuel: DC to San Francisco to Honolulu to

Wake Island to Tokyo to Seoul.

About five miles south of the fighting was our final destination. In April of 1952 the ASA encampment was still under construction when my class of ten arrived on a truck from Seoul. Five miles north of our little encampment, people were being blown to pieces. You could hear it. The choppers flew over, back and forth, just like in MASH. Our group numbered about one hundred fifty including Officers, cooks, guards, cryptographers and Morse-Code operators. But I wasn't there to send messages, only to listen. There was also a cadre of Chinese officers from Taiwan. These former Chinese Generals, as civilians, were in the employ of the ASA and very well paid, as well they should be, as the Chinese army would view them as spies to be executed. Rumor had it that if the Chinese broke through, our guards had orders to shoot us. We had our own plan.

Before we could do the job for which we were schooled, a huge amount of hard work was waiting.

Located on the rising slope of a small alluvial fan that had once been terraced rice paddies, we were surrounded on three sides by high escarpments and atop these were three 50- caliber machine guns. First things first. Eventually these guns would be manned day and night by full-time guards. All of the equipment needed for this company to function was still in boxes, crates and trailers while we all toiled at digging latrines, fox holes and troughs to divert water. The distinction between officers and enlisted men still remained, but there were so many officers that formality had to be dispensed with. We put up two Quonset huts, one a kind of "office" and the other a mess-hall with a fully stocked bar open 24-hours a day.

The snow had melted. The streams were full and it was warm. The earth was damp and green.

When not working we hadn't much to do. We'd watch movies every night and sit in the "bar" and drink. I tried drawing but my sketches, for some reason, were not good. I wrote a lot of letters, mostly to Jack, who was still living in San Miguel, adding the final touches to the house I had designed for him. He saved my letters.

With one exception they were all scrawled in long hand at lightning speed and barely legible. Even less clear are the rush of words from a young mind flooded with so many mental meanderings that, like a bumper car ride, these thoughts crash into each other—BAM BAM BAM—it's hard to make sense of any of them. So, I have edited these letters, leaving only that which contributes to my story. Reading the ME of 60 years ago was a shock. I was so mixed up and naïve! Most of the writing is a twisted and garbled mess

filled with arrogant affectations of interest only, perhaps, to a psychiatrist...
or my children.

April 30 I952
Dear Jack and Bunny
          For many reasons I can't pin-point to you my location--one
of them being I don't quite know where I am--in the arms of rolling
foothills ultimately rising into rugged peaks and with a sweeping
view of the valley—that is where we are and where I hope to stay
for awhile.   It looks very much like a miniature San Fernando
Valley. There is much traffic, ALL of it military. There are no
civilians up this way—the rice paddies are dry and uncultivated—
there are no houses—all the villages have been demolished. Every
hill is a honey comb of fox holes and trenches—every mountain is
dotted with emplacements to make it a fortress. A few of us took a
late afternoon hike up to one of the loftier peaks and, bottom to
top, it was littered with empty shells of every caliber, old
grenades, burp guns, clothing, boxes and crates riddled with slugs,
bones, skulls, feet hanging on the limbs of shattered trees. But
then, one tends to over dramatize one's situation.
          We live in ten-man tents and have a gasoline stove and it is
as comfortable and cozy as a good sleeping bag, a cot, and a dirt
floor can be. A house boy does the laundry; sweeps; lugs water,
etc.
          Due to the few of us here at this time it is necessary to
pull guard duty every night (practically), and tonight at I2 it
becomes the month of May and the communists attach importance to
this so that the guard is doubled and holes are being dug to fall
back on but in the event of a push we have all intentions of
getting out fast—the artillery has been pounding day and night.
BOOM BOOM BOOM since I arrived.
          What few meager sketches I have made are not satisfactory to
date but I have a few months yet.
          I look forward to my 7-day "rest" leave in Tokyo—a fine
hotel—a beautiful girl—ah me. Time to eat lunch. Please write
soon. Love, Gerard   PS send photo of house when completed.

MAY IO I952
Dear Jack and Bunny,
        Hoping still, for a truce.
        Another hard day—standing about and trying to put together a
Quonset hut.
        A latrine pit is being dug—myself and two others hacked away
for a morning and hit rock—the Capt. Moved the site and work was
begun again, with a new crew—after four and a half feet down
another rock bed was hit so the Capt. had the position moved again—
again rock was hit.   So the Capt. decided to build the latrine pit
up…..with sand bags and steps and thereby making the latrine the
highest structure in the area and topped by the American and UN
flag. Dismiss this letter. I find no content at all. Gerard.

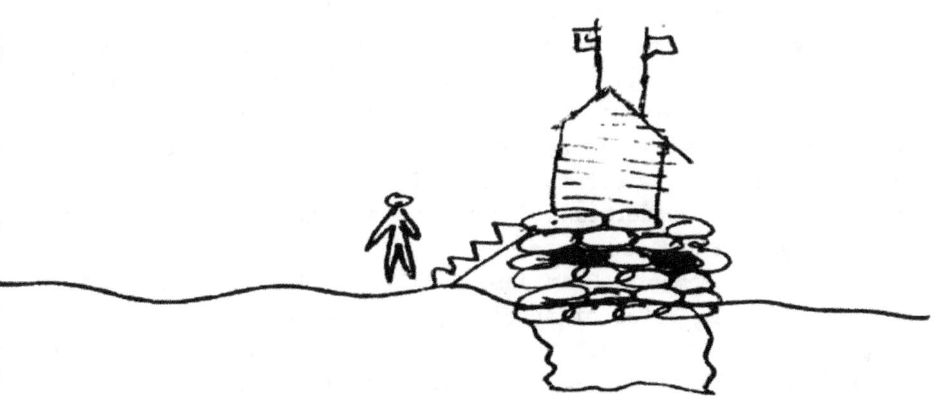

        By mid May the Company was in business—no more construction
work—no more guard duty—we were isolated and alone and other than the
front line, five miles to the north, there was no other military establishment
of any kind within miles. It was as if this little enclave was totally detached
from the rest of the Army and it was.
        I wrote many long and tedious letters. What follows are dated
excerpts.

May I8 I952 I2:30 AM
Dear Jack and Bunny
	Working the night shift -- I2 to 8 AM and swallowing pints of black coffee—listening with one ear to music - jazzy - symphony - and other kinds of strange and fascinating music.

	It is amazing the wonderful music that travels the airways across the Pacific—Japan—Australia—Canada—USA—Ireland—Asia and so on

	You know, I have seen but two motion pictures since leaving USA—One in Seoul and the other, earlier this evening—"Painting The Clouds With Sunshine" and the greatest piece of rot imaginable.

	On my desk, before me, and I think that best describes it - though not accurately—on my desk is my pipe, the Sherlock Homes job with a fine luster—the result of polishing it frequently with my cap. Also there is a bright red tin of Prince Albert, particularly striking against the olive color of my desk's surface and the generally subdued color scheme of my enclosure. There is a package of Phillip Morris cigarettes, a clip with thirty rounds of carbine ammo, a tin coffee cup, a peanut can ashtray, matches, crumpled candy wrappers and the assorted forms and papers necessary for my work. Things are rather dull on Night shift (every seven days we change shift) so understand I jot down all this trivia as a means of passing time and for amusement.

	At the moment, I am inside of a small windowless trailer, listening to the Voice of America. I manage to get all points of propaganda—and in English. It is the season for Anopheles mosquitoes and quite a few flit about me. I don't feel aggressive enough tonight to swat one. Today I managed to down a quinine pill, the most distasteful poison. It clung to my palate like an acid-salt and imagination is enough to recall its horror! Thinking I still have 8 hours to write this letter, I wonder what stuff it will be composed of by 6 AM, if I'm awake. Probably I'll lose interest in writing by then and just sit back in my chair puffing my pipe and letting the music carry me hither. . .
The Star Spangled Banner is playing in one ear. . . interesting.

	It is a pleasant bunch of young guys I work with. Some I have known over a year and a half and others about one year and some only a few weeks. I've convinced two of the guys that Ulysses is a worthwhile undertaking and they are taking turns delving into the labyrinth of its complexity.

I have changed from script to Quink and from black to blue.

Bob Topping, one of the guys I've known for some time is a good Joe, as the expression has it, but small in concept and given to carelessness, especially with fire arms. His unloaded rifle blew out a bulb and ripped through the roof of the tent. Today a mouse ran across our tent floor and Bob whipped out a 25-caliber pistol and, taking careful aim, bounced a bullet off the floor, through a duffle bag full of clothes (putting 5 holes in folded garments), and out through the side of the tent wall. The mouse hurried off unscathed. Bob has been warned.

Out of the rusted boilers, tanks, pipes and the junk of ruins has come an (unreadable) …a huge structure that bellows smoke all day as it consumes gallons and gallons of aircraft fuel. Nothing but the best for ASA. Pumps hoist water from stream to boiler, etc. We now have a shower and it's quite hot.

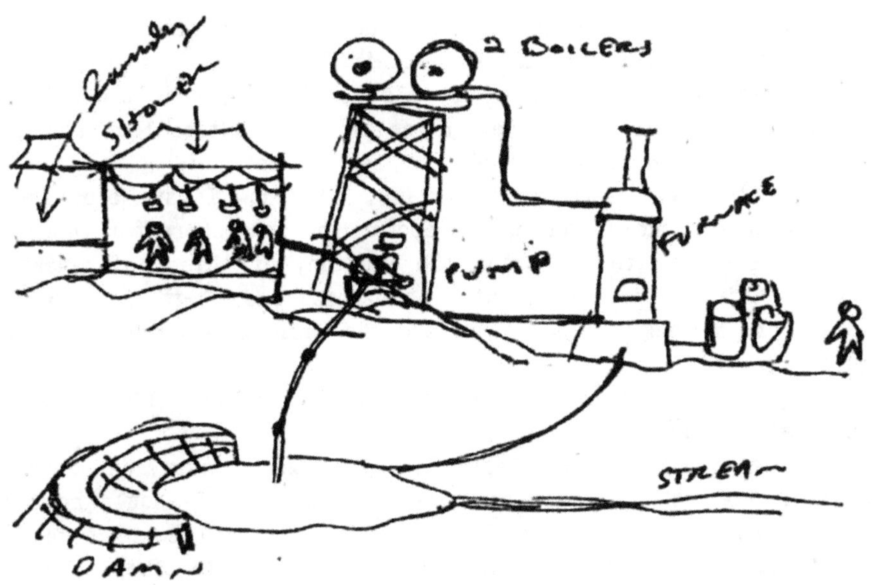

This is drawn to scale—the lumber is massive 8 x 8s.   The boilers etc. are brown with rust.   Little streams have been damned to provide the pool.   It is an amazing gadget.

Of all the flights of fancy the most recurrent, other than sex, the most insistent, are the dreams of being a civilian again. As I see it now (World War III not considered) I shall have to work for awhile and I have reasonable assurances of my job at UPA. Sending mom some money every month.   I still expect to leave the army with enough money to ease my purchase of a good car.   Hoping to keep myself highly organized, I believe I can work—draw—paint— and experiment, on a small scale, with film.

The GI bill seems certain and I will take advantage of it when working becomes unbearable - zip to Mexico and relax a few years—writing—painting—considering future possibilities, this is so much Alice In Wonderland!   Full war will probably break out 2 days before my discharge.

I haven't heard from Howard (or received a letter from you for that matter).   Please ask him to write and include his address. He is a strange man who seems to detach himself so easily from close relationships that one wonders whether he ever gives of himself at all.

I am now listening to a symphony—and I imagine that young, talented and ambitious minds with their friends or lovers, at this moment, in the Soviet Union, are also listening, near their books and perhaps, as I do, curse the negative of Nationalism and the general stupidity of (unreadable)   …few indeed.

Methinks I shall fill my pipe.   And now I have blue smoke and the odor of moist tobacco to add to the atmosphere—for there is time to pass—and to withstand the monotony of this confinement I see drama in the insignificant.   A corporal and a Sgt. have joined me and are discussing logarithms and the basic workings of a slide- rule.

Pardon while I change the station…sounds like English (Australian jazz).

Later 3:30 AM they left.   I try to sketch every day—even by candlelight—working nights this week.   Next week I should be able to draw by daylight… it is discouraging   It will be nice to sit about tomorrow and do nothing… perhaps get a little sleep.   Ah!   A

French station. No, it's Belgian. No, it's Vietnamese.

5 AM: So here I sit wide awake; picked up a good jazz station and tapping—drum like—on the table top. When starting these ramblings I was wondering what I'd be up to at 4—here it is 5 and I am going strong---it is daylight and it rained a bit awhile ago while I was reading a detective story.   No doubt when you've read this far in this letter you will wonder at the pointlessness of it all…well so do I but what the hell. They are playing Latin American rhythms and I think of Mexico the life fantastic

San Miguel… Fly time! FLY...! Please write

Buenos Noches Amigo   Gerard

May 23 Chip-ori, Korea (typed on a MILL ALL CAPS)
Dear Jack and Bunny

The cooler hours of late afternoon and early evening are not only more comfortable for hiking but seem to throw the rugged hills into sharper and more attractive focus and recent downpours have intensified the greenness of the stubby growth and washed the dust from the scrub pines. As a party of four we began climbing the sandy slopes that zig their way upwards eventually locking into the almost vertical mountains that characterize Korea. Every foot of this area was assaulted…. defended….. assaulted. The bunkers, 25 yards apart, line the crest of rise, hill, and mountain and the black threads of field wire, more common on the modern battlefield than barbed wire, give evidence the American army was here. The lack of many ration tins indicates they didn't stay long. The pounding must have been terrific. . .wherever a shell hit large trees are broken, snapped outward, away from the center of the concussion and imagination projects oneself into the fear.

Two of the guys decided to continue the climb aiming at a towering crag -- myself and Nelson choosing to descend on a narrow path into a deep canyon devoid of sunlight. It was quiet, except for the birds and we moved slowly, almost cautiously though there was little chance of trouble. We had become hunters and our alertness was for game. It amazed me that two reasonably civilized and specialized men should suddenly tap into the knowledge of their ancestors. We found the animal trails and the prints of the rabbit, fox, deer and a large cat. From the looks of the terrain and available food this cat would be similar to our western lion.

We reached the end of the canyon without seeing anything but a lizard and a few birds which we examined with binoculars. The canyon floor, with a small stream at its center sloped downwards and grew ever wider. Nelson walked on one side of the stream and I on the other...carbines at port. . . In hopes of flushing something from the brush. The brush ended abruptly and we stood at the edge of a plowed though neglected clearing...typical of the Koreans peasants farming methods and desperate need for tillable land. The country is so mountainous it is necessary they extend the workings as far up into the hills as possible, as in this case, where the area was scarcely thirty yards wide and dotted with rocks. Then I heard the HONK. I had heard it before, near our camp, and someone had said "that is a pheasant." HONK! Startled, I whirled about and gaped as a large pheasant rose up and away, disappearing into some trees about fifty yards below us.   Nelson offered, "We'll have to come back in the morning and wait." It was getting dark and we started back up the canyon. Somewhere, above on the ridge we heard the others whistle and answered. As we trudged up hill we talked little and I kept thinking of the bird and its great beauty and whether there wasn't enough killing and murder in this land. Certainly it could be justified….army food was no delight and we were all sick of pork…. wondered how I'd feel if I had shot it. I recalled the time, when as a kid, I had shot a jack rabbit, wounding him….and his leaps and writhing…..hot desert sand soaking up the blood….its lower jaw shot away…I decided I would not hunt anymore…..so pointless.

Then it occurred to me we had not decided to hunt at all. It had just happened there in the quiet of the canyon...something or some series of things had tripped the trigger to a deep rooted past. I heard the thunder of distant artillery and wondered how far behind us was the screaming babe and the stalking hunter.

We joined our friends where we had left them and they had no souvenirs. The first stars were out and MARS...we talked, standing high on the mountain, of when the first of us would land there…we rambled to the limits of our comprehension and believed it and the belief was faith and future.

-Gerard

July 30
Dear Jack and Bunny
     It has been raining steady for two days and the little
droplets, swept by a fair wind relentlessly gut the ground—and the
ground, now soft and mushy, gives in. . .swirling brown water
cutting little canyons that twist and turn down every slope and
come up to, then rush around every rock following the path of least
resistance. At night, walking by flashlight, I imagine the
"canyons" to be great ones and the rivulets part of the Colorado.
We have some very deep foxholes outside our tent...they have
straight sides and the small frogs that find themselves in these
pits can't get out. I don't know why they would act so stupid as to
deliberately jump into, what to them, must be a bottomless pit. My
theory is they sit motionless in the wet darkness waiting patiently
for prey and when it passes within range, some fluttering moth or
droning fly, they strike. Now I imagine some frogs, by chance, land
near the edge of one of our chasms and when they hear the buzzing
and there senses tell them the time is right…they spring…and go
hurtling into the pit. What a shock it must be! Nah. Can't happen
like that.
     Every morning that I think about it, I check the pit to see
if any of them have mistakenly gone to hell during the night, in
which case I set them free with a lecture.
     Tonight Bob Heller saw a mouse or small rat in the pit and
fetched his pistol and aimed and fired and it doubled up in an
instant…They rummage through the food and carry fever.
     This sort of weather is very bad…the air is warm and the
wind is refreshing and I personally don't mind the rain BUT it
softens the roads, bogs down the tanks and limits the use of our
aircraft…generally putting the enemy on an equal footing . . . the
sort of situation where an old-fashioned infantry marching
offensive would be feasible. We all think about it.
     The billions of tiny droplets carried in the air have a

peculiar effect, apparently, on sound waves. Noises we don't
normally notice, like distant artillery, sound like their origin is
only a few hundred yards away when actually it is miles. My guess
is that each droplet bounces a sound wave onto the droplet next
door with little energy lost in the transfer, and this accounts for
the magnification of our hearing. . .
 CLOD-A-BOOM   CLOD-ABOOM   CLOD-A BOOM and machine guns that
THUD A DUD DUD DUD   THUD A DUD DUD DUD   THUD A DUD DUD DUD I
awoke this morning thinking they were storming up the canyon but
it was just the droplets . . .
      Well, I'll stop and chat with the guys awhile working
tonight from IO to 8 am   write soon Gerard   hope you can read
this scrawl   it's not worth revision

Sept I4 I952
Dear Jack and B
      The day your letter arrived was a particularly provocative
one—Four long letters and each containing enough material to keep a
writer busy for a week.   One letter from animator Bill Littlejohn,
one from Dion, one from Bill Hurtz (director at UPA) and yours—
which I answer first.
      Your argument on film vs painting etc. is reasonable and you
made your point clearly enough—In the main I agree with you. I
reiterate, the Pollacks and their backers are symbols of the
painters' refusal to accept a less prominent role in the world of
graphics—so they do the spectacular to gain attention etc. I
certainly intend to continue painting and will try and exhibit.
      Mike and myself have no intention of putting anything ARTSY
or intellectual on film—if we did there would be no problem.   We
could just go ahead and spill a lot of Pollack bile on strips of
film and we'll be in the avant-garde film business.

      —Gerard

Korean houseboys cleaned our carbines, shined our shoes and made up our cots. To make people use their brains they must be treated well. We worked around the clock spying on Chinese army communications—8 hours on and 16 off. It was summer and there were lots of mosquitoes but I rarely took my quinine pills.

It was 3 o'clock in the morning and, in a cramped trailer, I was hunched before my giant radio receiver and listening to a Chinese opera. General Chow, seated beside me, was explaining the story and helping me to appreciate 5000 years of Chinese literature. I could easily tune in on much of the world but the focus is on North Korea where Chinese armies are massed and always pressing. At this point in history only superior United Nations firepower is keeping them away.

I imposed an intermission on the opera and, spinning the tuner, listen for what is now a very familiar noise: A Chinese radio operator sending his Morse Code message in spoken Chinese. The Chinese, short on equipment, spoke their numbers, which I jotted down. These operators were not very disciplined. Sender and receiver frequently broke into conversation and this is when General Chow would determine what province they were from and, therefore, what army division we were hearing and finally, bringing all of ASA resources to bear, just exactly where, on a map, this transmission was coming from.

The next time we heard this guy, his delivery was cut off mid word. He's been hit. Dead. And that is one of the many ways we interrupted Chinese military communications.

Six months later, just before the first heavy snow, my two years of service were up; I was on my way home, thinking about using the GI bill. Maybe I should study at the Pasadena Playhouse and become an actor?

As a young man my politics were way left of center. I read Marx and Lenin, admired the Soviet Union and thought that working at a commune would be a nifty and honorable life-style. The army showed me otherwise. It is the perfect commune. Just follow the rules and you need not worry about a thing. Two years in the army taught me that the individual is more important than the state.

Wanting a yellow convertible that had a nose like a P-38 and desperately needing a girlfriend, I returned to United Productions of America where Mr. Magoo was waiting, as were Mom and Pop.

Chapter 6

In 1952 not only was animator Bill Littlejohn the business agent for the Screen Cartoonist's Guild, but he was also a car salesman for Otto Zipper Motors, an importer of spiffy European automobiles that were soon to be the rage.

It was hard to spend money in a war zone, so I managed to save a few hundred bucks toward my future vehicle and wrote Bill a letter from Korea telling him how much I could put down on a used convertible. He had it waiting: A 1947 yellow Studebaker Regal Deluxe convertible, designed by industrial designer Raymond Loewy who also created the Coca-Cola bottle.

One problem. My down payment was sufficient but I had no credit nor did my folks, or anyone in my family. Bill wanted to make that sale. We went across the street to Zippers' bank and Bill co-signed my loan, which, for a young man he barely knew, was a very generous and trusting gesture.

Years later Bill would reveal the less generous side of his character.

On my first day back on the job as an apprentice inbetweener, Steve Bosustow, President of UPA, called me into his office and, welcoming the returning hero, enquired what aspect of the craft I might want to follow. I told him what I really wanted was HIS job. He received my arrogance with amusement and offered it might take awhile. I returned to my animation desk and continued my struggle to draw a decent in-between of Mr. Magoo. It was not easy.

There were no schools teaching animation. USC and UCLA offered classes, but there was no real immersion. The screen cartoonists really were a guild in the medieval sense of the word. Artists tend to be a highly individual lot, but animation demands extreme discipline and conformity. Every gargoyle must look the same.

One pleasant California afternoon, animator Art Babbit asked me to fetch him the inbetween machine. Ask Paul Julian if he can part with it. Paul said "no," he didn't have it. Probably in Tee Hee's bailiwick. Tee didn't have it. Check with Bill Melendez. Nope. Betcha it's with Grim Natwick. No. Try Tony Rivera? I finally caught on. I was the in-between machine! It was all innocent and wonderful. What, for me, was a daily tedium was relieved by AM and PM coffee breaks. Ping Pong was popular and Grim Natwick was an All Star horseshoe pitcher.

Just about every Wednesday, during lunch, in its small well appointed screening room, the studio ran animated films from all over the world and an occasional cartoon animated in America although not many, other than their own. The UPA staff deemed few American cartoons worthy of a serious look.   They saw American cartoons as too violent, too sweet and too stupid and there was some merit in their view. Animated films from European studios, particularly from the Eastern bloc, were greatly admired, although more for their content than their form. I thought they were boring but wisely never said so.

It was at one of these lunchtime screenings that Chuck Jones arrived to show us his latest Warner's cartoon, the second Road Runner, or was it the first, I can't remember. Animation was still a very small industry if, indeed, it could be called an industry at all. Everybody knew everybody or so it seemed to me.

The projection room went dark--roll it. The Road Runner was wonderfully violent and very funny but no one laughed. I could have easily cracked up but was too intimidated by my mentors. When the lights came up there was no applause. Someone mumbled, "Thanks Chuck, very nice." As the audience shuffled out, the projectionist handed Jones his 35mm film can. I caught up with Mr. Jones as he was pulling out of the parking lot in his open convertible. He was obviously wounded and in a hurry to get out of there. I breathlessly offered something like "My name is Gerard Baldwin… you probably know my brother Howard… I just want you to know I think the picture is really funny! These guys are so filled with themselves and their mission to end violence not only in cartoons but in the whole world they just can't see how great your film is."

"Thanks, Gerard."

I went back to punching holes in animation paper and learning how to draw Mr. Magoo. You rarely see a UPA cartoon anymore but The Road Runner is still out there.

The short time I worked at UPA before being drafted along with the months since my return to the studio added up to about a year and, as required by the union contract, I was offered a one-week paid vacation – my first and only.

I met Michael Murphy in art school and we had become very close friends. He had become a cinematographer and a very good one. His father, Dudley Murphy, had been a movie director and made pictures featuring Bess Smith, Duke Ellington, Joel McCrea and Paul Robeson. David Alfredo Siqueiros painted a mural on Dudley's Pacific Palisades home.

The mural is now in the Santa Barbara Museum of Art. When I met Michael's dad he was the owner-operator of an upscale hotel and restaurant in Malibu. Holiday House was perched atop a cliff that fell into the sea.

Dudley gave his son some acreage way up in the hills above the Malibu Colony and at the end of a narrow dusty and dangerous road Michael designed and built himself a wonderful house. The nearest residence was a small ranch probably a mile away and far below. On a clear day you could see the sun glint on the Pacific. Michael was going off to Arabia or some such place to shoot a documentary film for Lowell Thomas and offered me his house while he would be away. Great! This is where I would spend my vacation. I packed my yellow Studebaker convertible, the one with a nose like a P-38, with food and art supplies and snaked up into the hills. I filled a watermelon with wine. I could forget about Magoo and just paint-paint-paint.

That first moonless night was black and still except for the howling of the coyotes. I did not sleep well. Awake with the sun I was ready to paint. I cannot remember what it was I was going to paint, but I'm certain it was ambitious. No sooner had I waved a brush when I suddenly felt weird....a bit like that feeling when your leg falls asleep and then tingles as it comes back to life. I buzzed inside and all over. I tried to work but I was too weak. By noon I had a high fever. By mid-afternoon I was freezing. This cycle of tingling and boiling and freezing continued thru the day and into the night. In the morning I was driving myself home. Mom put me to bed and alternated bathing me with ice water or covering me with blankets as I trembled from cold. A local doctor came by and looked me over. He said he'd never seen anything like it and suggested I better go to a hospital.

When I walked into the Veterans' Administration hospital and up to a guy behind a reception desk he gave me a raised eyebrow once over and called out to someone nearby: "MALARIA." They put me to bed in a ward with some quiet old gents. A young doctor gave me a shot, some pills and told me my Malaria would not return. They kept me a week. Some vacation. Always take your Quinine pills.

The Chouinard Art Institute was located in old downtown Los Angeles in a neighborhood that, in 1890, was an upscale suburb just a street car ride from the city hall which was completed in 1928 and, at thirteen floors, the tallest building in the city. In 1953 it still was.

Los Angeles was growing West and leaving behind the three story wooden houses, once grand, that were now run down and somewhat dilapidated. Most had been converted into apartments and many of these were rented by art students who, pooling their money, lived sometimes five to a floor although usually segregated by sex, if only for appearances.

The students were a mixture of war veterans on the G.I.Bill and upper-middle-class young people whose folks could afford to send them off to Art School.

What better place to look for a date. My niece and nephew, the George Cannata kids, both on scholarships and just three or four years younger than me, were part of the Chouinard "scene," so I had entrée to parties I otherwise would not have known about. It was at one of these Saturday night parties that I saw this striking girl leaning against an arched doorway a step above the dark smoke-filled room that was crowded with dancers and pulsing with music. Some of the smoke was clearly not from cigarettes. It would be a few years before I gave pot a try.

Patricia Durst looked every bit like a Sacramento California Country Club girl and, as it turned out, she was.

As I approached I took off my glasses so as to hide at least one of my self-perceived negatives. We chatted. She was intelligent. I couldn't dance very well and neither could she, but we pretended . . . just to be close.

Patricia Durst wanted to be an artist of some sort and had studied for two years with WayneTheibaud at a college in Sacramento. The way I read her story, Chouinard was seen by her parents as a kind of finishing school.   She dumped her date and I walked her home to one of those old buildings where she shared a third floor with four other girls.   At the front door I did not kiss her goodnight. Yes, a movie tomorrow would be great. Thus began a romance that would end in marriage.

I always thought marriage was like what it had been for Mom and Pop. No matter what, you stuck it out. I had some anxiety about getting married. Marriage seemed such a huge commitment! I was on the phone talking about my hesitation to a young woman I'd gone to high school with and had dated a few times. Her father was the drama critic for a Los Angeles newspaper and she lived in a hill-top house designed by Shindler. She was very sophisticated. After listening to my fears she offered,

"Stop worrying. You can always get a divorce."

That shocked me.

Chapter 7

Five personalities played major roles in my development as an animation artist. The aforementioned John Hubley was the first. He assigned me, as an apprentice inbetweener, to UPA director Pete Burness, who won his Oscar for Mr. Magoo. Pete Burness was big influence number two. Over the years Pete and I became pretty good friends. He was a Hollywood version of an English squire. He wore tweed jackets with patches on the sleeves and a hat tweaked with a little feather. He was given to grumbling and screaming at other motorists. I noticed he never bought a new car, which I thought was odd since we lived in a city where car was King. Pete always had a good job but he never went on a vacation. The furniture in his home was old and sturdy just like his jackets.

One day we were having a very long lunch and quite a few drinks and I felt comfortable to ask him, how come? Why so frugal? Pete told me that when he was a young married, his wife's parents didn't think much of their daughter marrying a poor cartoonist. So Pete made a decision that when he died he would leave more money than his in-laws!

I did a lot of animation for Pete and later with Pete -- and finally we worked side by side as directors on the Bullwinkle Show.

The last time I saw him he was home and dying of cancer. He was heavily doped up. As we chatted about nothing in particular, he offered that as soon as he was well and back at work he thought he would buy a new car. He never did.

Ray Patin Productions, a small boutique that cranked out TV commercials, called me to see if I would be interested in joining them. They would move me up a notch, from in-betweener to break-down artist. This came with a little more money. I learned a lot and soon was doing some work as an assistant animator.

So, what does an inbetweener do? The animators drawing of an open door is drawing #1. The animators drawing of the door closed might be #9. There are seven drawings between #1 & #9. The assistant animator will make drawing #5. The breakdown artist will make drawings #3 & #7. The lowly inbetweener will make drawings #2,4,6 and 8.

Meanwhile, back at UPA, Steve Bosustow had hired Disney-Bambi animator Ken Hultgren and put him under contract. Ken was a fantastic draftsmen and a master academician, but his drawing was not at all compatible with UPA's graphic style. Big mistake. What to do? UPA called me to see if I would be interested in returning to the studio as a full fledged assistant animator. My job was to take Hultgren's anatomically correct, beautiful drawings and smash the shit out of them, flatten them out and force them into the UPA "look". This was a task a bit like taking a beautiful drawing by Michelangelo and shaping it into Gerald McBoing Boing. The studio placed the two of us in a little bungalow behind the main building. Ken would happily make his drawings and I, just as happily, would destroy them. He did not seem to mind. During a dinner conversation at his home in Pasadena, Ken told me he was a Swedenborgian, which is a weird religious sect based on the 1744 revelations of Emanuel Swedenborg. Perhaps Ken's faith in Swedenborg was why he was so tolerant of my destroying his work.

Steve Busustow, president of UPA Pictures would frequently walk up the street to a terrific deli that was just across from Warner Brothers' main gate. Half the customers were always in make up and costume. One day it was obvious we were both headed for the same deli and Steve suggested we have lunch together, Dutch treat. Can't hurt to have lunch with the boss. He ordered something as did I-

"Gerard, is that all you're going to have?"

"Steve, on what you're paying me that's all I CAN have."

He laughed.

I liked Steve and I think he liked me, but that didn't get me a raise.

I got a call from John Hubley, founder of Storyboard Productions, and he asked me to join his staff. More money and a feature film, an animated version of Finian's Rainbow, was about to go into production. I left UPA and Ken Hultgren to his revelations. On my departure, the UPA production manager told me if I kept jumping around like this I would get a bad rep and not get very far.

My mother-in-law did not understand any of this job switching. She thought I should settle down and grow with a firm. Nah, I thought. The concept of job security is self-delusory.

AND THEN A WONDERFUL THING HAPPENED!

Television discovered animation. Madison Avenue found animation to be the perfect medium for advertising cigarettes and selling cereal. ABC, CBS, and NBC discovered the animated cartoon, the Education Industry discovered the animated cartoon and corporate America discovered the animated cartoon. The cottage industry was now in great demand, so for the first time in years the talented and ambitious had opportunity.

The quickest path to becoming a journeyman was either as a layout artist or a background painter. I was impatient and tempted. Animator Mike Lah (Tom & Jerry dancing with Gene Kelly) gave me some good advice. Become an animator. It will take much longer but it is the only path to being a director and that is where you want to be.

It was 1949 when J. Ward debuted Crusader Rabbit, the first cartoon series for children's television on NBC. Not long after, Joe Barbera and Bill Hanna were trying to figure out how to produce a television series for $2700 an episode.

McCarthyism was still infecting Holllywood and Hubley, blacklisted, was unable to proceed with Finians' Rainbow, so I wound up working exclusively on television commercials designed by John Hubley and great commercials they were. I jumped about, assisting one animator after another and great animators THEY were. It was not boring, but I was dying to be a Journeyman. I borrowed an animation disc from the studio and was practicing animating at home. Knowing almost nothing except how to draw well, my efforts were overly ambitious and not very good. There is a huge difference between being an assistant animator and the real thing. It was a gap to close.

In 1954 one of Storyboard's four animation directors was a balding gentleman with a long string of credits in animation and live action. His name was Arnold Gillespe. I think he held more than one Academy Award. Arnold was also a great billiards player but he lost to Minnesota Flats. He was my Mentor # 3.

"Gerard, how would you like to animate this ten second spot? It's not much, just a spinning top."

"Really? Will you help me?"

"Gerard, there are only 23 things you need to know to master animation. Spinning this top is one of them."

He then proceeded to show me how to spin a top with five drawings. The magic number 23, which was just something he plucked out of the air, had nothing to do with acting or imagination or creativity. It is all too common to mistake great craftsmanship for creativity, but there is a wide divide.

There are more bells in the belfry of one mind than in all the churches of Mexico. To most people their ringing is noise. To the more sensitive their tolling is music and to genius, their sound is the Dance of the Sugar Plum Fairies.   The problem with orchestrating all that noise in an orderly, coherent structure and translating it on to paper, or stone or blueprints is a very difficult and demanding thing to do.

There are many reasons why, at the beginning of the 15th century, there was a sudden explosion of Art and Science as Europe emerged from the quiet meditation of the Middle Ages. The almost sudden stability of city-states allowed for greatly expanded trade resulting in the accumulation of surplus wealth, which, in turn, encouraged and paid for an increase in human creativity. During the 15th century the geniuses of the renaissance (Leonardo and Michelangelo being only two of many) saw no distinction between art and science:

"Design, by which another name is called a drawing, is the fount and body of painting and sculpture and architecture and of every other kind of painting and is the root of all science." - Michelangelo

"Principles for the development of a good mind: Study the science of art. Study the art of science. Develop your senses, especially learning how to see. Realize that everything connects to everything else." - Leonardo Da Vince

An artist was a scientist. A scientist was an artist. The separation between art and science came later. In a span of sixty years I have worked closely with hundreds of Artists. They were all, to greater or lesser degree, very talented, but not one, in the Einstein sense of the word, was very creative, including myself. There is quite a difference between being talented and being creative. Horowitz was extremely talented. Beethoven was creative.

During that exciting time when NASA was preparing to send a man to the moon the Jet Propulsion Laboratory housed so many scientists they were tripping over each other and, brilliant as they all were, and many of them were extremely brilliant, one creative genius was working next door, lecturing at Caltech. I was a lucky man to toast with Nobel Prize Winner Richard Feynman. He was a kind of silly, simple man, like Mozart as portrayed in the movie Amadeus. He was to numbers what Mozart was to music.

Intelligence is one thing and creativity another. A person can be intelligent and not be at all creative. One can be creative and not be particularly intelligent, but an average person is never creative and a creative person is never average.

A pass receiver making an impossible catch is one thing. Doing it repeatedly borders on High Art. But it is not Art. When the game is over the game is over. Same with chess. Not so with Art. A painting of a little angel by Raphael is outrageously cute and clearly a work of Art. One aspect of a work of Art is that it be potentially repeatable. Raphael painted dozens of cute little angels and all of them are works of Art. Jackson Pollack could never make the same painting twice which tells us something about his "genius."

As a young boy I was already a voracious reader. I remember, as a kid in N.Y.C., going to the library by myself and taking home as many books as I could carry or the library would allow. In my late teens I was consuming book after book so as to have an education beyond what the Chouinard Art institute would provide. Art Through the Ages was the only required reading at the school. Twenty-three years my senior, brother Howard made it clear that if you didn't read James Joyce you had no chance of ever participating in the culture of the intellectually elite.

I began with Portrait of The Artist As A Young Man. I enjoyed it very much and connected. I followed with Dubliners. Reading Ulysses was an excruciating experience. Was there something wrong with me? "Everybody" said it was a great work of Art so I figured I would never be part of the intellectual class. Why couldn't I see what they saw?

I could hear the THUD, THUD, THUD of artillery when, somewhere in Korea, I again read Ulysses and followed with Finnegan's Wake. Nope. I still don't get Joyce. Probably never will.

Only 63 years separate Huckleberry Finn and Ulysses. Twain's book is a creative masterpiece while, in my opinion, Ulysses, at its best, is the product of a very talented man who lost his way.

So who am I to judge? Do you need a Master's degree in English Literature to enjoy Finn? No. Do you need a Master's degree in English Literature to enjoy Ulysses? It would help … but not much.

Newspapers and magazines frequently run articles proclaiming that everyone has creative potential. These stories assert that creativity is a "thing" sitting on a shelf and safely stored in a vault within your brain. All you need is the combination to the lock that will allow that massive door to swing open revealing your creativity. Nonsense.

Whether you "get" Joyce or not, an artist or a scientist is being "creative" when he shows us a new connection between things that were not previously perceived to be connected.

Being creative is not the process of making order out of chaos but something more. It is the ordering or perceiving of chaos in a new way.

In 1955 the second piece of animation I did, also for Storyboard Productions, was much more than ten seconds in length. Under the tutelage of Arnold Gillespie I was assigned to be the animator on the main title of a movie, The Seven Year Itch starring Marilyn Monroe.

Great graphic designer Saul Bass did the basic layout, which was a simple wide screen checkerboard. These multi-colored squares, like little doors, were to spring open revealing someone's screen credit…then the door would close and, somewhere else on the field, another door would spring open revealing another credit. All of these openings and closings were synchronized to music.

I did my best, which, looking at it again many years later on TV, was not very good, but I guess it was good enough.

I well remember the screening which took place in a large and dark theatre located somewhere on the 20th Century Fox lot on Pico Boulevard in Los Angeles. There were not many seats for such a big screen, no smell of popcorn; it was gloomy. I sat next to the designer, Saul Bass. Two elderly Hollywood Producer types arrived and sat down in front of us. The introductions were perfunctory. These two gentlemen were beautifully yet casually attired; confident; maybe a bit bored. One raised his hand slightly as if to signal. The theatre is suddenly very dark, almost black when POW! The screen is ablaze with a checkerboard of color. The music is near deafening. All that hard work and in a minute or two it's over-gone-screen dark-silence-lights up.
Producer #1 leans over toward producer #2 as if to keep his words almost to himself.

"Well?"

"Do you think Daryl will like it?"
There is almost contempt in the reply.

"I'm too old and too rich to worry about what Daryl Zanuck thinks."

I was impressed. Boy, this really IS Hollywood.

The following paragraph is from my website:

One morning while shaving, Baldwin had the sudden realization that he was not Pablo Picasso. It was not too painful. Perhaps the realization was a blessing. It is hard playing a genius when you are not one. Baldwin settled, to use his words, "for being occasionally brilliant." And plunged into an intense and continuous effort to be the best animator he could be.

I managed to put together a short reel of the few television commercials I had done and began to shop myself around looking for work as an animator. While some animators, like Arnold Gillespe, were extremely helpful in passing on their knowledge of animation and took pleasure in teaching, many others were protective of their skills fearing, I suppose, of being replaced by the possibly more talented. They continued to encourage the myth that it took years and years and years to master their craft.

Bill Littlejohn (Peanuts), the animator who had so generously co-signed my first car loan was an extraordinarily talented artist, who should have felt quite secure, but he responded to a question of mine with: ". . .you know, I've spent years polishing all this shit, so why should I pass it on to you? Figure it out for yourself."

Whew—I guess he was beginning to sense competition and didn't like it.

Another famous animator, Art Babbit (Fantasia), responded to my little animation reel by suggesting I go to Disney's and get a job as an assistant and spend a few years learning the craft. It hurt.

I remember well that in the mid nineteen fifties Southern California was stricken with a plague. Most researchers think this ambulatory malady was carried to California via the Panama Canal although some investigators feel it more likely the disease was carried from the East coast to the West coast in infected trucks. However the virus arrived, it found the perfect environment where-in to multiply: Los Angeles.

Medical professionals, themselves not immune, soon categorized this extremely infectious curse as a social disease of near pandemic proportions, its transmission impelled by the psychological needs of a certain segment of the population which, even today, is not well understood.

No accurate records having been kept, there can only be an estimate as to the number of cases, but most experts agreed that two hundred thousand was about right.

It infected mostly males. The poor victims experienced a strange euphoria and, given to hallucinations, often saw themselves as Mickey Rooney astride a thoroughbred thundering down the track at Hollywood Park.

In a few years most of the patients recovered and the vast majority gained permanent immunity although later studies indicated a slight rise in Melanoma was possibly related.

In Hollywood, if you didn't drive a Sports Car you were socially quarantined. A Sports Car is defined by THIS driver as a two-passenger convertible. The most elegant of these machines had wire wheels, no air conditioning, displayed leather seats and were extremely sensitive to road feel. Road feel was good. The snap-on side curtains, made of plastic, must be easily scratched and, with only modest age, show off some genteel cracks, like the patch on the elbow of an old tweed jacket.

When Patricia Durst and I got married, I bought my first really new car so that we could motor to Lake Tahoe in style. My MG TF was positively, undeniably cute and beautiful. I was a young animation apprentice and its $2700 price tag meant I had to finance a loan, my first venture into serious debt.

The large log cabin at Lake Tahoe built by Pat's grandfather sat on the only natural sandy beach on the North Shore and offered, through a large picture window, a spectacular view of the lake and snow-capped Desolation Valley twenty miles away.

No one paid any attention to us honeymooners, but they sure gave a lot of attention to my 1955 shining black MG TF. One night as we left a casino, the MG gathered a small, curious, and admiring crowd. Amidst the Cadillac's my little car was a Lacewing.

That night, in bed, Pat told me that her mother had advised her that too much sex was not a good thing. Now I knew why my father-in-law was always nervously squeezing his thumb. I knew then, this marriage was not made in Heaven but in a Hell of old ideas.

Most of these sports cars were bolted together in England. Why in heaven a cold, damp, wet and foggy nation would manufacture so many open-to-the-weather automobiles is still puzzling to me.

There were sports car clubs. One club might be exclusive to Jaguars. Another might be exclusive to Morgans. I think there was an Austin Healy club, and how's this for a moniker: "The Austin-Healy Riverside County Sports Car Club". They had a flag.

We sports car drivers distinguished ourselves from the common man with special paraphernalia, driving gloves, car coats with clips instead of buttons, caps that would not blow off and emblazoned with insignia. The very rich wore goggles with corrective lenses.

On a Sunday morning thousands of sports cars could be found puttering about Southern California looking for old comrades at some way-out-of-the-way restaurant, to have brunch and champagne, and talk knowingly about the virtues of rack and pinion steering or the importance of cylinder displacement. Not one in a hundred of these guys had ever touched grease.

I had a few friends who did not own a sports car, but they were, in the final analyses, just ordinary people, not like "us." Despite the exclusivity the sports car drivers were very democratic. Jaguar drivers would wave at MG drivers and Morgans would wave at Healys and Healys would wave at the occasional Alpha Romeo. Aston Martins only nodded. This mania only lasted a few short years. I knew it was all over when one Sunny afternoon, my wife beside me, I was driving down the Pacific Coast Highway and gave a little wave at an oncoming Triumph.

He gave me the finger.

Returning from our honeymoon we moved into a little house we had rented from animation director Ted Parmalee, whose much larger house was right next door. Ted was mentor #4 and while at UPA had received an Oscar nomination for The Telltale Heart by Edgar Allen Poe and starring James Mason. Ted gave me my first fulltime job as a journeyman animator at Graphic Films Corporation. Animating was much more difficult than I ever thought it would be. Sometimes I felt I was drowning. I struggled. Will I ever get it? I remember how patient Ted was. Also, I remember how exciting it was to sail on his two-masted trading bark to Catalina Island and back in the same day. I was not on board when, anchored off of Avalon and diving for abalone, my mentor died of a heart attack.

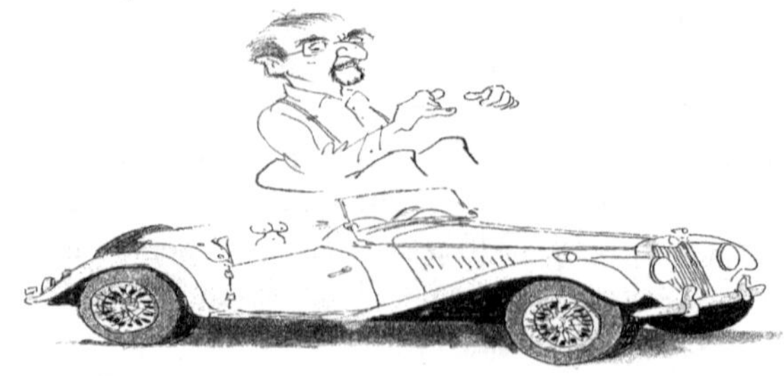

Chapter 8

How in the world my father, an Irishman, ever became a garment cutter in an industry totally dominated by Jewish immigrants and their descendants I don't know. In the 1920s The Ladies Garment Workers Union, its members numbering many thousands, was a powerful force in the political and economic reality of New York City. Pop participated in a long and bloody strike. Cops and thugs hit on the strikers and the strikers hit on the scabs. Anarchists and Communists struggled for control of the union. Both were defeated by David Dubinski, a man my father much admired. After many months the union finally won its strike and the front page of the New York Times heralded the EIGHT HOUR DAY!

My pop was very proud of this achievement. He advised his three sons, "Learn a trade--join a union--and you'll be okay." His three sons became artists, but that did not make them anti-union.

The Screen Cartoonists Guild (SCG) was probably the smallest independent union in the world. To my knowledge no copies have been kept of its colorful newsletter, **The Pegboard**. It was filled with some wonderful editorials and clever cartoons, all lost to History's dumpster. I guess the membership, at one time, including New York, might have numbered somewhere between one and two thousand, but closer to one than two.

The Guild first asserted its power by calling a strike against the Disney studio in 1941. The union won and for the first time, minimum standards for wages, benefits and working conditions were established for screen cartoonists. I was twelve.

Politically the union was way left of center and there was some truth in Walt Disney's accusation that Communist party members were involved. Many years later, brilliant artist David Hilberman was working for me on the Smurf show. I felt free to ask him if he was a member of the Communist Party at the time of the Disney strike. His answer, "yes." All of this political stuff concerning McCarthyism, black lists and outright bribery is well covered in Charles Solomon's wonderful book, The History of Animation-Enchanted Drawings.

Because of television the production of animated films was increasing rapidly. New studios were opening in New York and Los Angeles. There was, suddenly, a shortage of talent. The Guild needed a new President and opened up the post for nominations. At a union meeting someone at the back of the hall nominated me and I accepted. Also running for this honorary unrenumerative office was a very talented designer, Bill Perez. Bill had a very annoying smile. It snapped on like a dog bearing its teeth. There was anger in there somewhere and it was displayed every time he smiled. He lost; I won.

Mom and Pop were proud of me, especially my father. Twenty-three years later the ghost of Harry Baldwin would shrink with shame as his youngest boy drove through a picket line.

So there I was at 27, the youngest president of a labor union in the world and, as such, probably a candidate for the Guinness Book of World Records. I was freelancing nights and weekends and surely did not need another job at the helm of a labor union that was soon to call a strike. I felt, at that time, kind of indestructible.

The animation producers decided they would form an Association. The purpose of this Association was to prevent them from cutting each-others' throats and, collectively, to better defend themselves against Union demands.

The Screen Cartoonists Guild executive board became paranoid in its fear of a strong Producers Association, whose sole purpose, in our view, was to weaken us. The Union must act before their association could be established!

One fine California day I called for a lunch-hour meeting of the entire membership at the union hall; its purpose was to inform the cartoonists about the gravity of their situation. So many members showed up we held the meeting outside. I had no prepared words but spoke passionately and sincerely about the executive board's opposition to the producers' objective. Lastly, I suggested, as a demonstration of our resolve, everyone enjoy a very long lunch and not return to work that day. To my amazement they didn't go back to their studios. In my role as President, I learned a lot about human behavior. I learned that man is a herd animal and willing to accept leadership from anyone who asserts it. I learned how you can be a hero one day and vilified the next. The board decided not to call for the strike until after Christmas, so, on my own volition, I sent each producer a telegram wishing them all a very Merry Christmas. When the executive board heard about my telegrams it exploded like a string of firecrackers and called a special night-time meeting. I got out of bed to attend. I survived their wrath but a few days later, while driving to work on the Hollywood Freeway, a sudden pain shot down my arm. A very old and wise doctor advised me that

I was killing myself with overwork. I resigned the Presidency, and Bill Perez, he of the growling smile, assumed the role. The Union, picking the studios off one by one, saw to it there would NEVER be an animation producers association. Eventually the Screen Cartoonist Guild was swallowed up by The International Alliance of Theatrical Stage Employees and became local 839.

Looking back now, with the perspective of 53 years, the Guild was shortsighted and made a huge mistake. If the producers had been allowed to amalgamate, the union would have had a strong organization with which to bargain for residual payments as enjoyed by actors, directors and writers. Too bad.

My marriage had its ups and downs. We never quarreled about money. There always seemed to be enough. We quarreled about sex of which, for me, there was never enough.

Lunch "hour" for upper echelon cartoonists, was always much longer than an hour, sometimes two or even three.

In The San Fernando Valley we hung out and ate lunch in the bar of the Far East Terrace across the street from MCA's Black Tower. In Hollywood we gathered at Steve Boardners' bar and grill across the street from a seedy parking lot and, in West Hollywood, we met at Frascottis Belgian restaurant on Sunset Blvd., across the street from the Jay Ward Studio.

At one such lunch, I believe it was at Steve Boardners, the group included animator Ben Washam, designer Tony Rivera, directors Ted Parmelee, Pete Burness, Arnold Gillespe and the Muppet Man Jim Henson. The subject of divorce came up. I remember clearly and forcefully stating that, as for myself, if Pat and I ever separated and divorced, it would be an indicator that Society had collapsed. Seventeen years later I was divorced and "Society" never noticed.

Buying a house in 1957 was not easy. The Savings & Loan required one third down. Patricia and I bought our first house for $ 21,000 and borrowed the $7000 down payment from my father-in-law, good Doctor Durst. I know he was surprised and pleased to be paid back in one year.

The house was new and the most beautiful house I ever lived in. It gripped the side of a steep canyon and was cantilevered out into space like a diving board. In the simplicity of its design it looked almost Japanese but was much heavier in its construction. It was a big wooden box 30 ft. wide and 80 ft. long. Very heavy beams supported the flat roof. Exotic and gleaming mahogany floors were from the Philippines, one and a half inches thick, maybe two. Most of the interior walls were tongue and grooved, the wood of equally exotic origin. The outside was sheathed with redwood. Our home, on a dead end, opened out onto The Verdugo Hills to the south and on the north, the San Gabriel Mountains touched the sky. This house was filled with light.

Some of this wonderful light came from our two children. Leslie was born in 1960 and Michael was born in 1963. The children pretty much grew up in the Haines Canyon house except for a three year sojourn to a nearby community known as Shadow Hills where, for a while, we played cowboy. Then, for reasons I will touch on elsewhere in this memoir, we moved back to the house of light.

Occasionally, usually on a Saturday evening, Grim Natwick , the world's oldest living animator, would drop by my sister's apartment in Hollywood, for dinner and boxing on TV. Grim and my brother-in-law, George Cannata Sr. had worked together in the nineteen twenties in N.Y.C. and they did a lot of reminiscing, which I, as possibly the world's youngest living animator, enjoyed very much.

I never worked with Grim. I only knew him socially and we were never really friends. Perhaps my arrogance got in the way, or the great difference in our ages. I recall an event where the Screen Cartoonists Guild was awarding fifty-year pins and Grim was one of the recipients. Now I have one. During the milling about and drinking that preceded the sit-down dinner, Grim introduced me to someone I don't recall. But I do remember the introduction, "…..and this is Gerard Baldwin. I really don't know quite what he does… a jack of all trades…" He didn't finish, but I got the slight.

Once the tiny animation business went beyond the novelty stage, animated cartoons began to make money. In the beginning, because there were so few, animators like Grim Natwick were making very high salaries — $300 a week was a lot of money in the depression 30s.

In 1935, in order to complete Snow White and the Seven Dwarfs, Disney instituted a training program and created a very LARGE pool of animation talent. Now animation workers were no longer in short supply. In fact there was a surplus and it would be 15 years before the little animation "industry" would expand enough to absorb them all. The country was still in the great depression. Jobs were scarce, so very few were in a position to make wage demands including all of those newly created animation workers. They believed, although there was no proof, that the producers, Warners,

MGM, Fleischer, Lantz and Disney had a secret agreement to keep an anchor on wages. The Animators felt they were being exploited—and they were.

As a group the animators were not too fond of anyone that could be seen as a boss. That included Directors, who by the nature of their role of having to judge talent and make decisions as to who works and who doesn't —a money spigot—could not help but be aligned more with management than with their fellow artists.

Some outstanding and talented animators decline directorial opportunities because they do not want the responsibility or have a fear of failing. It is a position filled with constant anxiety. Grim Natwick never chose to direct or—possibly—no one ever asked him to. He animated and animated and animated for 70 years and with each passing year his persona was more and more romanticized. The workers needed a hero and they chose Grim. He was there at the beginning of the first new art form in 25000 years. He was one of them. Someone wrote, "Some seek fame and never find it. Others have it thrust upon them."

I can still see him 57 years ago in New York, the dark blue cape and the long white scarf flapping in the wind. In the legend of Grim Natwick, the Screen Cartoonists found their hero, their own Lawrence of Arabia.

This memoir is not meant to be only an autobiography, but an account of what it was like to be an animation artist from 1950 to 2000, a period during in which the industry rapidly expanded and rose to new levels of Artistry. Not being famous or celebratory, I don't think my personal life is of much interest or concern to any beyond my immediate family and, even there, we all die with secrets.

What and where I animated from 1956 through much of the 1970s is a chronological jungle. It is a tangle that probably could be sorted out, but this is not a history book and, as John Adams said about the American revolution, "Does anybody care?"

Animator, director & producer Shamus Culhane (Snow White), had a New York studio specializing in TV commercials. In Hollywood he opened another office that would venture beyond TV ads. Bill Hurtz was his West Coast producer and director and, pretty much, ran the place. I animated on two of Frank Capras' Bell Telephone science series.

Hemo The Magnificent-1956
Our Mister Sun-1957

The head animator and strict teacher was Ben Washam.

I do recall animating at John Sutherland Productions on a film for AT&T that purported to teach telephone operators good manners in dealing with difficult callers. I was working alongside my brother-in-law George Cannata Sr. He was a wonderful mentor.

On the occasion of my second wedding anniversary, Pat gave me a beautiful stop watch calibrated in 35mm and 16mm feet per second. I showed it to our director, George Gordon, who, holding the watch aloft, shouted out to the crew, "He's got the watch! He's got the watch! There's no stopping him now!"

It still works. It feels like part of me. This old Minerva is well travelled and covered with scratches and dents. What little sheen remains comes from my caressing it in the palm of my hand for 60 years. I wonder about its worth.

There is, on the internet, an extensive filmography listing many, but not all, of the animated films I have worked on spanning a period of over sixty years. I don't know why it was compiled or who did it but in my mind much of it is forgettable. What floods my mind as memorable? Mr. Magoo, Rhapsody Of Steel, Bullwinkle, Energy-The National Issue, The Caterpillar And The Wild Animals, George of The Jungle, Dr. Seuss, Fred Flintstone and The Smurfs. All of the television commercials I have animated, no matter how beautifully executed add up to nothing. In 1963 the first Captain Crunch commercial was mine to do. I animated and directed for a short while on the Linus The Lion-Hearted show. My nephew, George Cannata Jr., designed the wonderful characters, one of which was Sugar Bear. I did a few brief stints at Sutherland Productions, working on what used to be called Industrial films and did a lot of long forgotten television commercials that emanated from New York studios.

1958 Rhapsody of Steel

John and Ross Sutherland somehow convinced U.S. Steel that they should sponsor an animated film about the history and future of mankind's use of metal. This one half hour movie would be for theatrical release and would be, up to that time, the most expensive "industrial film" ever made. It was 1958 and the film was called, "Rhapsody Of Steel." Dimitri Tiomkin would compose the music and the Pittsburgh Symphony would play it. As a young animator I would be working with some of the most talented designers and animators in the business.

Eyvind Earle was one of them. He had designed Disney's Sleeping

Beauty and later would become an extraordinary and successful purveyor of fine prints. Eyvind, it seemed to me, saw nature as a crystal palace. His world was made of colored ice. His Art is beautiful but cold and never troubled by human beings. He was very stingy. Just before Christmas he slipped me one of his stunning Christmas cards and told me not to show it to anyone as he didn't want to give anymore away.

There is a sequence in Rhapsody Of Steel where a huge meteorite strikes the earth and Carl Urbano, the director, assigned it to me. In a flash of inspiration I received this great idea about how to animate the meteors' descent and impact. Nothing like this had ever been done before and it was hard to explain. Yet I could see it clearly in my mind, an inner vision. The sequence could not be animated in the conventional way. There would be no pencil test, not even my assistant could help me. OK. Go ahead.

For weeks I piled up hundreds of drawings . . . hundreds of cels that I painted myself. At last it was finished – camera – shoot – develop -- Let's see it!

What we saw was the most incomprehensible, meaningless mess of something happening on screen that had ever been seen by man. What was it? My great inner vision wasn't there. Nothing usable was there. Nobody said much of anything. Carl gave the meteorite sequence to great animator Irv Spence and he did, without any inspiration, a fine piece of work.

At the studio Christmas party I found myself talking to John Sutherland. We had both been drinking. I apologized for my failed sequence, the waste of time and money. John was kind -- "Gerard, my young genius friend, just think of what you learned."

I did many other sequences in that movie and what I really learned from my work on Rhapsody of Steel was that I finally was a master of my craft, and from that picture forward whatever I animated would turn out well.

American Airlines wanted to direct its advertising toward upscale ticket buyers. Their agency came up with a concept that focused on an obviously upper middle class man and wife having a conversation about their next trip. This was to be the first of a series of commercials. The voice delivery was low key with no hard sell. The well-known New Yorker cartoonist Chuck Saxon would be the art director. His sophisticated and unique drawing style was perfect for portraying the well off. Who else reads the New Yorker? Saxon was not an animator, so the problem was to find an animator that could so perfectly mimic that Saxon "look" you would swear he had done the animation himself.

There were some try-outs. As they say in show biz, I got the part. The ad agency arranged my trip to New York and of course I flew American. They knew. The pilot came back to my seat to chat.

There would be no animation director involved, just Saxon and myself choreographing the characters. He had ideas. I had ideas and together we planned every move. Day after day we acted out every gesture, expression, and nuance. He would draw a key pose and then I would emulate it. I used the same pencils, the same paper and soon I couldn't tell his drawings from mine.

HE COULD.

Saxon would painstakingly go over every one of my animation drawings and show me how I had missed some subtlety in his work.

I went back to L.A.; returned with more drawings. No. You still haven't got it. I returned to L.A., this time taking many of his drawings with me.

On my next trek to New York I made sure to slip some of his drawings in with my own. I never said a word as I watched Saxon correct his own drawings and explain to me in excruciating detail how I had just missed some little "touch." Time ran out. The commercial got done. It was great and we did others. Chuck Saxons drawings never looked so good.

On one of these Saxon trips I made plans to visit my now widowed sister, Dolores, who lived somewhere in New Jersey not too far from the Big Apple. I hired a limo and, on the way, decided on a detour. I thought it would be interesting to check out the old neighborhood, St. Nicholas of Tolentine Catholic School, Andrews avenue, the Morrissey house, and, of course, the Hall of Fame where I played as a child.

The driver was firm.

" NO! Not to the Bronx. Not to the war zone and certainly not in THIS car!" I took his advice. As we cruised northward I just got a glimpse of a long row of tenements high on a bluff. All of the windows were punched out. It was a funereal image, little black rectangles decorating slabs of gray.

Chapter 9

By 1959 Peyo was creating successful European comic books. These are not like the American cheapies but hard cover and well printed. Gerard was soon to become an animation director. The animation business was expanding rapidly and us new guys gauged our importance by how few of us there were in the entire world. At one lunch time fantasy, we created a situation wherein all the "old" directors would board a plane to attend some film festival, the plane would crash and us new guys would replace them. Time passes quickly; it didn't seem very long before another batch of new guys were waiting for my plane to crash.

Mentor #5 was Director Bill Hurtz. He did not win an Academy award in 1953 for his brilliant UPA short, "The Unicorn In The Garden," but he should have. Written by James Thurber and narrated by Edward Everett Horton, it is a small masterpiece. I got damn excited when Bill called to see if I would be interested in being a director on a new J. Ward show, "Rocky And His Friends," a series to air on ABC. I remembered all of those talented directors I worked with and how I had always envied their creative jobs. WOW!
A director! I loved the sound of it and still do. Bullwinkle, here I come.

I was very fortunate to have five extremely talented, knowledgeable and giving mentors. Does the mentor choose the student or is there something reciprocal that just kind of happens? I dunno.

On the strength of a 3 month contract, Pat and I left our nice new house and flew to Mexico City. There was not enough money to produce the animation in Hollywood, so most of the work would be produced by Val-Mar productions. This company was hurriedly put together for the sole purpose of putting the Rocky show on film. There weren't even five artists in all of Mexico with any animation experience, so there would be a lot of teaching.

My salary of $350 a week would prove more than adequate. At 12 pesos to the dollar we had an awful lot of pesos, 4200 to be exact, and since, at that time, one peso could buy almost what one-dollar bought in the U.S.; we felt quite wealthy. We rented a furnished apartment in a nice part of town just off of Chapultepec Park and sent money home to cover the mortgage and utilities and dined in Mexico City's finest restaurants every day.

Mexico City was not yet totally immersed in poison gas when Hurtz, Hiltz and Baldwin arrived to oversee the studio that was going to produce "Rocky And His Friends." Jim Hiltz was another young and aspiring director. He got this job based on his animation for the main title of The Pink Panther.

A couple of other guys representing the New York interest in this series arrived at about the same time: Bob Schleh and Harvey Siegel. Harvey told me, 40 years later, that he was also on the FBI payroll to make sure there were no communists lurking about. He also told me they were not worried about me. I was okay what with my Top Secret clearance and all. Harvey also told me that he liked to hunt bears.

With delivery dates for the first episodes fast approaching no work was being done. No artists were drawing. No cameramen were shooting. What was going on? Something strange.

Enter Gordon Johnson, SR V.P. for Dancer, Fitzgerald and Sample. He was the account executive for General Mills, the sponsor. Big Gordon Johnson did not want to look foolish. Limousine-ing in from the airport he established himself high up in the Hotel el Presidente. It was Posh. Really posh . . . at least back then.

It was a warm summer evening when Hurtz, Hiltz and Baldwin met with Johnson in his luxurious suite. Outside, above the city lights, the sky was roiling. A storm was forming; two actually. Gordon Johnson had his own. Room service wheeled in an entire bar, as he demanded to know why we were not in production. Phone calls were made and one after another the Mexican management came and went. Jesus Martinez, Ernie Terrazas and Carlos Rodriguez all had a different and somewhat vague explanation as to why there was no work being done. Where were the artists they had promised? What the hell was going on? The sky was ripped with lightning. Now Gordon was furious. "Damn it! I'll cancel the whole thing!" Thunder was slamming through the walls. Hurtz was pleading to save the show.

"But what about those cameras? You'll never get them out of the country."

"I don't give a damn about the cameras. They can stay here and rust!"

My heart sank. I really SO much wanted to be a director. The next day Gustavo Valdez, owner of the studio, but never involved, finally explained that the reason nobody was coming to work was because the Union boss had not received his cut. The next day he was paid his mordida and, as if by magic, artists showed up and work began.

Mexico, as everyone knows, is a dangerously corrupt country. Just before returning to California I thought I would try, one more time, to get my work permit. In the Capital the man behind the counter shook his head sadly side to side, "No, no, no Señor, your work papers are still not ready." As I was leaving and walking down a rather dark and dismal hallway, a man approached and quite openly said that for x number of pesos I could have that permit right now. No thanks.

Gustavo Valdez, that never-involved owner of the studio told me never, ever, get involved with the police even if you hit someone with your car, "Just run, scram fast and come see me. I'll fix it."

Pat and I returned to Los Angeles to find our lovely isolated hillside house surrounded by a huge housing project. New black roads snaked all over the hills and the houses, packed side by side, created the image of a centipede with black rectangular legs.

I continued directing on Rocky with much to learn.   What can I say about Bullwinkle, George of the Jungle, Dudley Do-right, Fractured Fairy Tales, Aesops' Fables, Hoppity Hooper, Peabody and Sherman, and Tom Slick, that has not already been masterfully and kindly covered by Keith Scott in his well-documented book "The Moose That Roared." In this book J.Ward comes across as a complex, cuddly eccentric. I liked Jay and I think he liked me although I can't be sure. I think it was Bill Hurtz who said I was 'barely lovable'.

Jay Ward was very paternalistic. It was the only studio in Hollywood with its own, always open, ice cream parlor. There was always some kind of a contest going on with prizes for the winner. I thought it was childish and did not join in the fun involved in seeing who can grow the biggest mustache by some given date. Jay had a stable of race horses known as the Bullwinkle stable. One contest offered two free tickets to Paris for the employee who came closest to predicting the date and hour of the arrival of a foal. I did not participate. At the big award luncheon at Frascotti's restaurant I recall Ben Washam receiving the prize. There was a second award: "…and for Gerard Baldwin, a one way bus ticket to Bakersfield." It was funny and everyone laughed, but beneath Jay's laughter there was CHASTISEMENT.

Ward gently coerced all of his employees to each contribute $500 toward the making of the Hoppity Hooper pilot, in return for which we were each to receive an interest of one-quarter of one percent of any money the series made. Hurtz directed the pilot. Ben Washam and myself animated it. It was funny. It sold. After the sale Jay gave everyone their $500 back sans any interest in the show or any interest for the use of our money. Complex and cuddly, indeed!

There was a period of well over a year when animation production in Hollywood just collapsed. I don't remember why. More than half of the cartoonists were out of work. If you were lucky enough to have a job, better hang onto it. That's when Jay's business administration schooling came in. Knowing the staff was trapped, he cut our salaries by one-third. REPREHENSIBLE.

From 1959 to 1967 I functioned as a director at Jay Ward's studio, doing some animation as needed. I animated the title for Fractured Fairy Tales, the pilot for George of the Jungle, the pilot for Hoppity Hooper, the title for Aesop's Fables. I animated something-or-other for the Smothers Brothers show and the first Captain Crunch cereal commercial. Twenty-four years later I'd animate the second - in Spanish.

Over the years I was in and out of the Ward studio numerous times. The reason for one of these departures was my new role as Vice President in charge of animation for John Sutherland Productions, a company that specialized in Corporate and Educational films of very high quality. The company produced a lot of films for the department of Health, Education and Welfare. Since Sutherland contributed lots of money to both political parties, it didn't matter much to him who won a presidential election. He had access to Government grants.

I was impressed with my gold embossed business cards, wore suits to work and I felt secure. After all, I had my contract. The studio produced a half hour documentary film which was nominated for an Oscar, a film I had nothing to do with.

On the big Oscar night my wife and I, decked out in our finery, mine a rented Tux, were walking down the long red carpet past the bleachers when we heard someone ask: "Who's that? "
"That's nobody."   CORRECT.

After a few months, when it turned out the studio had no new projects coming up, John Sutherland told me to lay myself off. WHAT? Lay myself off? I called my attorney. "He can't do that. I have a contract." My attorney told me, yes, my contract was enforceable but Sutherland could also have me sweep the floor, which the contract had not ruled out.

"How badly do you need this job? " Could I get another?
"Probably."
"Then just chalk this up to a bad experience."
So I left. I called Jay Ward. Did he have any work? Jay laughed,

sure, come in Monday.

When I showed up at the studio there was a box of gold embossed business cards on every desk, which properly identified each employee, and their position at the studio and all of them, of course, were Vice Presidents.

At some point I realized I did not really know everything there was to know about making animated films. In a sense, I felt vulnerable, so I decided that I would produce my own animated film. Not only that, but it would win an Academy Award. If my mentors could do it, then, damn it, so could I.

First I needed a story and chose a Masai folk tale from a book published by the Bollingen Foundation, "African Folklore and Sculpture." The story was titled The Caterpillar And The Wild Animals, a short tale about a caterpillar who withdraws from the world and retreats into a hole belonging to a rabbit. It was a perfect story for a short film. I obtained the rights and would produce this movie with my own savings. That's a no-no in movie-land. Since I was also directing all that Jay Ward stuff, it took about two years. The narrator was Greg Morris and the music was composed and recorded by Fred Steiner. Wall Batterton painted the backgrounds. When it was completed I knew every step in the process of making a film from idea to fruition.

The Motion Picture Academy required that to submit a film for nomination, it had to play in a pay-to-enter movie house in Los Angeles for one week. The Laemmle theatre on Vermont Avenue in Hollywood obliged. During that week I attended every screening to gauge audience reaction and the reaction was very positive.

On the evening of the Academy screening for short film nominations I, now a member, was very excited to be competing. The Academy theatre was packed with my short subject peers. I just knew my film would be nominated and surely win an Oscar. After all, my story, an African folk tale, was politically correct! The narrator was an African American TV star! The music was superb and I had designed and animated a gem.

The lights dimmed. OH NO! The first film to screen was a beautifully made African folk tale by some very talented fellow from New York. I was dead. The pro-African vote split 50-50 and so, that year, another film took the Oscar. My little 7-minute short cost ten thousand dollars and though it never made the money back, it was as close to being a work of art as anything I would ever do. Most of the technical craft I mastered then is now obsolete. An Oxberry animation camera belongs in a museum alongside the white bones of a dinosaur.

In 1970 the Caterpillar and The Wild Animals presented me with a surprise I never could have anticipated in a hundred years. My wife and I were invited to participate in the fifth international festival of films for children sponsored by her Imperial Majesty Farah Pahlavi, Empress of Iran . . . all expenses paid. Once again I rented a tux and Pat bought a couple of very formal evening gowns, the expected attire at palace banquets. Our two young children would be watched over by Grandma and Grandpa Durst. I took a two-week leave from my third stint at Sutherland Productions and off we flew to London-Paris-Rome-Tel Aviv and finally, Tehran.

In Rome our tiny taxi stopped at the end of a very narrow street that opened out onto St. Peters' square. Even though I had been raised a Catholic, and even though I no longer was one, I was unprepared for the sight and felt a rush of emotion. Here, before me, was Catholicism's Mecca!

Between the outer wall and the inner wall of the Basilica is a very narrow winding staircase that spirals up, up, up, step, step, step, and finally, after a very long ascent, opens out onto the roof where we were greeted by a Coca Cola stand. I wondered if the Pope had the concession.

The next stop was Tel Aviv. There were soldiers everywhere and we were not allowed to leave the plane. Through the little window I looked down and watched workers stealing cases of Scotch.

The Tehran airport was a fortress surrounded by tanks and machine gun emplacements, waiting for something to happen. The Tehran Hilton was surrounded by a fleet of Mercedes and their drivers were waiting for us 24-hours a day. Our assigned guide was a very modern young woman in a well-tailored uniform who, a few years hence, would be forced back into the dark ages.

Her Imperial Majesty's guests, about thirty in all, were taken to view Iran's royal treasury. Under armed guard and looking through bulletproof glass, we gazed upon mountains and mountains of emeralds, but the real treasure was underground and it was black.

Leaving Tehran behind, seven black Mercedes began the long and gradual descent across the barren plateau that is Iran. Unlike a caravan of old these camels are well apart so as not to choke in the clouds of dry fine sand that billow out behind each car. We were on our way to Isfahan, 200 miles to the south. There was little traffic in either direction, mostly dusty trucks. We passed a few nomads on their slowly plodding camels. I picked up a bad cold, which got worse.

We found Isfahan a beautiful city fast asleep, dreaming of its golden age 500 years ago. Today, as I write this, the city is wide awake, alert to the nuclear facility that is its neighbor and praying the great mosque can, in some way, shield the Uranium stockpile from attack by Israel or the United States.

I recognized the symptoms of Pleurisy as our caravan continued south for another 200 miles headed for the ruins of Persepolis. Persepolis was once the capital of Persia. It was destroyed by Alexander the Great, 300 years before Christ was born. Nothing remains but a few very tall and stately stone columns. At the turn of the last century, Stanley, of Stanley & Livingston fame, added a little destruction of his own by scratching deep into one of the columns "Stanley was here." I thought this was almost sacrilegiously arrogant.   Leaving the rest of the tourists below, coughing and heaving with illness, I felt impelled to scramble up The Mount of Mercy and, gasping for breath, paid homage to the tomb of Artaxerxe III. I don't know why I did that -- didn't even know who he was.

The film festival went smoothly and ended in a formal banquet at the Palace. It was almost dark when our car arrived. We found it ominous that the Palace was surrounded by army tanks with their engines running.

As a representative of the United States, Iran's most important ally, I would be presented to the Empress. She was tall, gracious and beautiful. As Pat and I approached Her Royal Highness protocol demanded my wife be half a step behind me and a bit to my right; her left foot behind my right foot. The Empress said something formal and welcoming, and I stammered something like, "…uh…well… gee…I've never met a Queen before." No one noticed Pat's little kick to my Achilles heel that clearly said, "You jerk!"

So the Caterpillar took me on a great adventure, an adventure I would probably never have experienced if I hadn't animated those wild animals.

We left Iran with some concern for the bright young woman who had been our guide. The further you got away from the elite, you could not help but notice the intense hostility. Expressions of glaring hatred were everywhere. To most of the population we, and our kind, represented something evil. We were symbols of Satan.

Chapter 10

The railroad ties are rushing toward me as, pumping my own hand-car, I propel myself down a long straight track toward an ever receding horizon and a vanishing point I will never reach, well, not for a while, perhaps in a second? In a year? I can't get off. My feet are nailed to the deck.

Clickety-click-click-click Clickety –click-click-click

There is only time for a momentary look at the space between each tie as it widens before me then slips beneath the car and vanishes. If I glance back the experience is reversed as the ties rush away toward another ever-receding vanishing point.

Clickety -click-click-click Clickety –click-click-click

Searching into my mind is much like looking into a file cabinet that has not been properly organized. The file folders are not in alphabetical order. The time line has gaps, the work of a sloppy file clerk. Each folder contains a sheaf and each page, when turned, reveals another. Some of the pages are blank.

Clickity-click-click-click Clicity-click-click-click

So, this memoir has a Yin and a Yang.

In 1963, I had a dream. This dream was so powerful and filled with insight that, for a while, it changed my life and can only be described as an epiphany of a high order. Immediately on awakening and in a state of near trembling elation, I wrote it all down as best I could. . .on scraps of paper. . .in a scrawl barely discernible. I vowed, at the time, never to read those words again. I felt such an intrusion would spoil the magic of the gift given to me from somewhere in the deep recesses of my subconscious. I dropped the few scrawls into the bottom of a file cabinet where they stayed, and decayed, in the dark, for fifty years.

Why I recently decided that now is the time to unfold these fragile scraps of paper and insert them into this memoir I do not know. Perhaps I sense the Reaper. Even now, some voice within me says don't do this.

At the time of the great dream I was married and had two children, a lovely home and had just leased my first Mustang convertible. I was very busy practicing my craft as an animator. I worked as a freelancer and life was, and still is, very intense.

My dream, like a movie from the 1930's, was in black and white. Once written down the motion stopped and the scenes, now stills, were encased in a tall black and white stained glass window. This window was just one of many that lined, and still line, the Cathedral that is my mind. Only the final climactic scene, a small circle at the window's apex, was in Technicolor. The images, until this resurrection, have existed as a frozen kaleidoscopic montage without continuity or movement.

My Cathedral, over many years, has been struck by multiple storms and one of these, a hurricane, knocked the window out of its frame. It crashed onto the floor of myself and shattered into a thousand shards. Later, the cleaning lady swept it all up and deposited the fragments of my dream in some dark alcove where they have waited all these fifty years. I don't know why I wanted to do this. No matter how expertly I fit all the bits back together, they will never come alive and be charged with the energy this experience once held, but I can try. I never forgot the aftermath and how the effect of my dream impacted me in a most profound way.

MY DREAM

I was there, somewhere, with hundreds of other young men standing in a long line as we waited to be inducted into a strange new Army. As in most dreams, I am an observer and a player at the same time. I think I am on the Moon although this place might also be an asteroid. I'm unsure.

Why I don't know, but I DO know I'm definitely not on earth. This place is a dark and gray world...a world with out shadows. We are a crowd of nothings, shuffling along in a very slow line and following orders shouted from a sergeant major, a crude coward of a man who is never happier than when herding people. Our line is imprisoned by a tall gun-metal gray chain link fence which leads to a building that is fifty yards into the future. The ground on which I stand is warm and composed of a powdery gray sand. My loafers are already covered and it is working its way into my socks.

This building I am being bullied to approach looks like a long trailer except that it is made of wood. It is attached to another of its kind and that to a third and so on. The connections are imperfect and the whole string reminds me of a line of freight cars that have jumped their tracks. They zigzag away, disappearing into a black void.

Letting others pass, I keep falling back but finally succumb to the screaming sergeant and the magnetic pull of the open door over which a simple sign reads:

INDUCTION
WELCOME

How much of what I am putting down here is true to the original and how much is a re-creation by my mind, of its own volition, just filling in gaps so as to satisfy its need to create order out of chaos. . .I do not know. I do know that in those first waking moments, in the very act of trying to put it all down, some threads were broken and the fabric therefore is imperfect. You cannot return to the loom and weave again.

Inside the barracks the light is very dim. There is a row of 13 desks at which sit 13 corporals. I begin at desk #1 and by the time I have reached the back of the room and responded to 13 barking dogs and filled out the 13 forms that will create my army profile, Pinocchio comes to mind and I can see my fellow conscripts turning into braying donkeys.

Suddenly I stand in a long line of naked young men. Our advance is stop and go. . .stop and go. . .stop and go. A bored doctor jams a needle into my buttocks. I wince. A guy faints. Another doctor wants to know if I had slept with my mother or got excited showering in the high school gym. As I fill out the 100 questions that purport to be an IQ test, I am engulfed in a Gregorian chant. The monks intone only two words: YES SIR, YES SIR, YES SIR. The chant drones on and on, fading in and out depending where I am in what is now a maze of ever darkening rooms.

A couple of privates first class are taking my measurements. They definitely do not approve of loafers, of gray flannel slacks, or of violet nylon shirts. One measures and calls out the size numbers. His buddy fills out the forms that will allow supply to issue my uniforms, I think of the Emperor's new clothes.

Suddenly, I am alone and it is creepy quite. The monks are still. It is always darker. Moving, almost floating, down a long hallway that ends in my out-of-self reading a sign on a wooden door. . .but to my left, in a narrow alcove, is another sign, on another door.

DO NOT ENTER
OFFICERS ONLY

I glance back down the long hallway that now looks more like a tunnel in a coal mine. I must get out of here.

DO NOT ENTER
OFFICERS ONLY

I open the DO NOT door and close it behind me. Click. It is too black to see but slowly, like a fade-in in a motion picture, I see I am in a small room. It is a bedroom and against one wall is a king-sized bed. Covered up to their necks under a white sheet are four beautiful Raven-haired women. Not only are they quadruplets but they are my sister-in law. Two crowd the left side and two crowd the right and between them is one serene baby. I have seen this image before in The NEW YORKER. I am startled by a loud and angry masculine voice:

"WHAT THE HELL ARE YOU DOIN' HERE!?"

Suddenly I'm standing out on the gray and featureless surface of the moon. I am freezing and trembling in my sand filled loafers. The sky is black and so is the huge stallion that stands over me. Astride this armored animal is an army colonel in full plate armor. The armor is black and has the sheen not of metal but of plastic. I don't know why I know this or why I know that the man within the helmet is a Colonel but I do. His admonishment is intense and grave.

"Now that you know what the others do not know you are not fit for fodder. LEAVE. GO HOME!"

The Colonel and this horse vanish and I turn away, focusing on the moon's horizon. Rising above that horizon is my Earth, that famous shot we all know as seen from outer space. It is in full color and I am warmed as the camera that I am begins zooming in on Earth as I wake up.

For a few days I felt as if I were barely grounded and for a few weeks I was sharply aware and sensitive to everything and everyone around me. Not making much constructive use of my blessing, it slowly faded away leaving me with the memory that, once upon a time, I experienced the arrogance of feeling very, very special.

In 2007 I received a phone call from Darrell Van Citters, an animation producer and director in Los Angeles.

Darrell said, "I'm doing research for a book on the making of Mr. Magoo's Christmas Carol."

"You're kidding!"

"I'm not."

"You're writing a book about THAT?"

"Yeah."

"WOW, God works in strange ways."

The book arrived in 2009 and on page 79 it says: "…Gerard Baldwin was issued the Despicable Song, apparently the last song to be written (by Julie Styne and Bob Merrill). Abe Levitow gave him carte blanche to do as he saw fit with the sequence, and after Baldwin got the director's approval for his thumbnail storyboards, Dick Ung began laying out the sequence. Baldwin had only two weeks to animate the entire sequence, but those two weeks were well spent, since it is probably the most memorable and most entertainingly animated sequence in the entire film. Baldwin was performing his duties free-lance and as he put it, "the faster I worked the more money I made." Despite his mercenary approach, it is a brilliant example of what cartoon animation does best, heightening the humor in any given situation, and beautifully underscores the characters personalities and their delight in being evil.

At a gathering of designers and sequence directors for the premiere, Baldwin somewhat immodestly declared that it was the best thing in the whole special. He can be forgiven his boast; it was indeed a show-stopper."

By 1964 UPA had degenerated into a schlock house and I found myself as a freelance storyboard director working on a TV series, "The Famous Adventures of Mr. Magoo". The only good part of this show was my ability to pick up a script, drive to my wife's family cabin on the beach at Lake Tahoe, work on the board, play with the kids, then drive back to L.A. and pick up another script. It was a lousy show but not bad duty. Only now, when I look back, do I see how privileged I was to have so much freedom.

Far away and certainly far out of my mind, Peyo was turning out more than one successful comic strip. In Peyo's mind the Smurfs were secondary characters in a strip entitled "Johan et Pirlouit." Eventually The Smurfs pushed Johan aside, just like Bullwinkle pushed Rocky aside and, on their own, took Belgium and Holland by storm. Much of the world soon followed and merchandise licenses were in the thousands. At the time, America was unaware of these little blue creatures.

In 1965 The creator of Batman, Bob Kane, came up with the idea for a TV series, "Cool McCool" to be produced by King Features and animated in London. Cool McCool was supposed to be a parody of James Bond and the structure of this series was a rip off of a live television show "Get Smart", just like The Flintstones was a rip off of Jackie Gleason's "The Honeymooners". King Features wanted to send an American to London as a supervising director. After a chat with Kane I was offered the job and accepted with the proviso that if I didn't like the situation I wasn't bound. That was okay with Kane.

Just before my flying off to London, our neighbors, John and Sonia

Winfield, who lived across the canyon, held a little going away party. They were English, as was their house guest Edward Mulhare, at that time, star of the TV series "The Ghost and Mrs. Muir".

Pat took our two young children to Mass every Sunday, a ritual I rarely attended, but this must have been some special Sunday, maybe Mothers' Day or Easter or something . . . Anyway, on this special Sunday, Mulhare, who was Catholic, asked if he might join us.

Holding my five-year-old Leslie by the hand, Edward Mulhare gave one of his finest performances as he marched up the center aisle and the parishioners of Our Lady Of Lourdes Catholic Church, in Tujunga California, were properly impressed.

At the parting party Sonia told me to be sure and contact her sister who was married to big time English movie director Basil Dearden. He had just finished Khartoum starring Lawrence Olivier and Charlton Heston. Sonia gave me her sisters' phone number. She would alert them.

I had some romantic notion of tooling around England and Scotland with my little family all tucked into a little English motor car. Friends who had worked on animation in London assured me that my salary was more then adequate. What I didn't realize was that these encouraging endorsements were all from single young men who had slept in furnished rooms and ate in pubs.

I would go first. If all worked out, Pat and the children would follow.

It was early June and I would arrive on the eve of a 3 day holiday. The studio business manager would meet me at the airport and take me to my hotel. I would recognize him because he would be wearing a red carnation. I cannot remember his name but he was pleasant enough, though quite formal, and my first impression was that he felt he was my superior. First we would just drop by and meet George Dunning at his flat. The chat was brief and perfunctory. Dunning, it seemed to me, was in the grip of a terrible hangover. He was also more concerned with the upcoming Yellow Submarine, which he was directing, and showed little interest in Cool McCool. Understandable. I never saw him again.

The red carnation dropped me off at my hotel and drove off, left me there, alone, for the long weekend. No American would ever do that to a foreign visitor, never, ever, ever. The hotel was nice enough. The food was boring.

Saturday morning I went for a walk. My California blazer was not up to the penetrating cold. This was summer? I bought a newspaper and checked out rentals. Anything adequate was three or four times what it would cost in Los Angeles and none of the apartments had a place to house my little fantasy automobile. Not enjoying this long and lonely weekend, I called Sonia's sister. Why of course they would love to meet me. Was I free for dinner tomorrow? Great. We'll send a car.

Lord and Lady somebody had also been invited. We sat on deck chairs out on the lawn shooting champagne corks into the swimming pool while the cook prepared an American Thanksgiving dinner with all the trimmings.

The following morning I showed up prepared to go to work on the first episode of Cool McCool. I had model sheets, a storyboard, exposure sheets and a sound track. I needed a small tape recorder on which to hear the track. There wasn't one available. Couldn't I use a moviola? No. Need tape recorder. The management would order one. Can't you just go down to a store and buy one? No. I was in an odd social situation. The management treated me as if I was just another coal-miner. The animation artists treated me as if I was a coalmine Operator. Out of the entire crew only one cartoonist befriended me. His name was Gerald Potterton. He migrated to Canada and became a producer. Years later I would write for him. One of the studio's directors questioned the authenticity of my animation reel because it was so eclectic. I explained that a really talented animator could play any part, just like Alec Guinness. By the end of the first week I still had no tape machine, so I gave a weeks notice and called Pat who, leaving the kids at home with Grandma and Grandpa, soon joined me. When she arrived in London we did all the tourist things then flew to Dublin, rented that little car and toured Ireland, the land of my ancestors. It was great. Ireland really is GREEN.

In 1966 I did not much enjoy animating on two films produced and directed by my first mentor, John Hubley. John, a brilliantly creative man, had never been an animator and I found his directorial input vague. He would hand me a sheaf of blank exposure sheets and a piece of music with the instructions…" make these skyscrapers dance" or "this taxi is racing around like crazy!"

Urbanissimo was interesting but no great work of art. Tijuana Taxi starring Herb Alpert and his band won an Academy Award, but I don't think my contribution had much to do with its success. I can only think of one or two directors who were not animators before assuming the mantle and these directors usually wind up working with a very small coterie of animators who can read their minds.

The Hollywood chapter of the International Animated Film Society known as ASIFA, held a festival at the 1967 Canadian World's Fair in Montreal.

After dinner, barrel-chested Dimitri and skinny Nikoli, the official Russian delegates to this event, invited Larry Kilty and myself up to their room for drinks. Larry was the Business Agent for the Screen Cartoonists Guild and since I had once been the President, the Russian delegation probably assumed we "labor" types would have much in common with comrades from the Soviet Union.

This exclusive little celebration numbered six--Dimitri, Nicoli, my wife Pat, myself, Larry Kilty and a rustic woman from Poland who had something official to do with animation behind the Iron Curtain.

The Russians opened up two very large cans of Beluga caviar, which they generously slathered onto slices of Wonderbread. I figured soft white bread was pretty classy in Moscow. No peasant bread for these guys. One suitcase was packed with a dozen bottles of Russian vodka.

The room held twin beds, a couple of chairs, a tiny table, a telephone and a collection of small glasses, the kind you find in every hotel bathroom. We sat where we could. It was awkward to eat globs of caviar on limp white bread that wanted to bend. Hotel Kleenex served as napkins. With much flourish Nikoli proceeded to fill our glasses up about one third. Dimitri inflated himself and raised his glass high to offer a toast. We all stood up: "To animation. The greatest art form in the world!" We all raised our glasses high, clinked all round and spoke as one…
"…Nazdoee-Nazdrowee-cheers"
Following Dimitri's lead we quaffed our vodka down in one slow swallow. It burned. A mouthful of caviar soothed the throat as Nikoli refilled our glasses up one third and Larry Kilty proposed, "To the happiness and well being of working men and women everywhere!"
Six clinks. "Nazdoee-Nazdrowee-cheers"

And thus began a kind of rondo.
Nikoli "To world peace!" six clinks "Nazdoee-Nazdrowee-cheers." My wife, laughing, offered "To understanding. I can't drink anymore and I'm going to bed." Six clinks. "Nazdowee-Nazdrowee - cheers." With gracious nods she was excused and left with a hint of insecurity in her step. We had drunk a bottle of wine at dinner.

The Polish lady stood up, "To all your good health. I too cannot drink anymore and I'm going to bed. Good night." Poland was graciously waved off. Now we are four in a Russian instigated contest as I raised my refill, "To Nikita Khrushchev!" Four clinks " Nazdoee-cheers."

Dimitris turn, "To President Johnson," four clinks "Nazdoee-cheers." The phone rang and Nicoli picked up the receiver. He listened for a moment then handed the receiver to Dimiti, who began an animated conversation in Russian. Larry Kilty did not look so good. He was sweating and had a sickly green pallor. He whispered to me, "Gerard I gotta go to my room... I'm going to be sick." As poor Larry lurched out the door Dimitri, still on the phone, and Nikoli, with just a hint of victory in their smiles waved Larry goodnight. Nikoli refilled the glasses another one third as Dimitri said goodbye in Russian and hung up. "That was Moscow. We keep in touch."

Here I was all alone defending my country's honor against two Russian tanks. After a couple more toasts, an unspoken decision was made that we stop or face mutual annihilation, and so we did.

During those years, Pat and I were blessed to enjoy, as neighbors and friends, Dr. Walter Higa and his family. Their house was just across the canyon. Walter was the leader for Maser Technology Development at the Jet Propulsion Laboratory. We didn't talk much about his work. Some of it was secret and all of it way beyond my ability to crunch big-time numbers. So, we talked about other things -- cabbages and Kings and the delicacy of Japanese food.

George Hobby and his family lived a couple of houses down the canyon. It was not unusual to be walking in the Verdugo Hills, under the hot sun, with my friend, George. He was an excobiologist who also worked for the Jet Propulsion Laboratory. Nor was it unusual that we were kicking around ideas how to design a machine that could collect and analyze soil from the surface of the moon, assuming, of course, that the device ever got there. There were some problems, conceptual and technical, with what the scientific journals refer to as "The Carbon Assimilator Experiment" -- looking for signs of life in outer space.

"Jesus George, I'm not an engineer."

"...yeah but that might be good...a different perspective." I was no help.

The Viking Lander touched down on the Moon in 1976.

George was a big guy and built like a circus strong man. He had some serious problems. One very late night after some very heavy drinking at a nearby bar, I dropped George off in front of his house and within a very few seconds pulled up into my own driveway. Got out. Looked down.

There was George laying in the middle of the street and weeping. I hurried down to help him.

"George, you gotta get up." Suddenly, a snarling beast rose from the ground and was attacking me. He was pounding me and knocked me down. I was backing up the hill – bam -- bam -- bam -- it hurt. Finally George stopped and became passive. I guided him to his house and knocked on the door. It opened and Palma, his big fat sleepy wife said, "oh shit…" as I shoved him into her arms.

The next morning I realized my shirt was ripped, my trousers were torn and my ribs were hurting. After seeing a doctor and finding out I had a couple of cracked ribs, I called George. He was genuinely contrite and began to see a Psychiatrist. We remain good friends to this day. I just got off the phone with him. He's 95.

It was through George that I met and became friends with Al Hibbs, a second in command at the Jet Propulsion Laboratory and his Mentor, Nobel prize-winner Richard Feynman, who, at the time, was lecturing at Cal Tech.

I don't know if Al Hibbs was a genius or not but he sure was brilliant. Time magazine reported that Al and a friend or two figured out how to beat the wheel at Las Vegas. They made a lot of money. Las Vegas changed the rules. He seemed able to master, in minutes, just about everything he found interesting. Hear a Japanese musical instrument? He buys one and is soon playing it. Get a pilot's license? SNAP. Fly a glider? I went up with him. GREAT. What did we talk about? We talked about black holes and the incomprehensible vastness of space. I had problems with the black hole idea. "Hey Gerard, so long as it works, helps, for now. When it doesn't work we'll drop it." He was an avowed Atheist and I was well on my way although I still felt God was just as good an explanation for existence as a Big Bang.

Al had two children, also brilliant. At a party his first wife confided in me it was extremely trying and depressing living with three geniuses. Some-time later, she committed suicide.

Al threw a lot of big parties and it was at one such party that I met Richard Feynman. He was off to one side of a very large room surrounded by almost adoring students. On the other side of the room enclosed by another cluster of adoring students was Murray Gell-Mann, Nobel prize-winner and inventor of Strangeness. I sensed there was competition for attention and realized such folk are just like everybody else.

Mix one part Nobel Prize recipient with a generous amount of Cal Tech types, add a couple dozen people who are going to put a man on the moon, and one artist and you have a recipe for an interesting cocktail.

Hibbs and Feynman were both receptive to the Arts but they found graphic art difficult to master. Their efforts at drawing were stiff and plodding…lacking any spontaneity. I couldn't crunch numbers, but I sure could draw and that was the basis for our friendship. Both were puzzled and mildly pissed that they could not do what I did, which was to make a sketch in seconds where idea and execution were seemingly as one.

One evening after dinner for eight, while the wives were off somewhere chatting, Al produced and dumped on the floor a very big pile of children's building blocks. They were unpainted and presented a variety of configurations. Four children -- Al, Feynman, a JPL public relations man whose name I cannot remember, and I sat on the floor and began to play. The game was to take turns building towers which would then be analyzed as to what the structure meant, along with what it revealed about the architects personality. Fortified with Cognac we played this game until two in the morning.

After Pat and I divorced, my social life changed dramatically and I didn't see either of them again. These two scientists taught me a lot: Don't ask stupid questions and in so far as it works, 2+2=4, but the probability is that 2+2=3.99999999 or 2+2= 4.9999999999999.

Chapter 11

My brother Jack was an Art Professor at the University of Ohio at Athens. He was also a successful sculptor and his hundreds of statues in fiberglass, welded steel and cast bronze dot America. No doubt he would be classified as a "fine" artist.

On one of my many visits to Jack, I brought along my portable animation board so that I could continue working on a Dudley Do-Right episode that had a deadline. Jack, not unfamiliar with animation, gave a glance at my drawings. "How can you stand doing that shit?" I was a bit hurt but let it go.

Contemporary sculptures and paintings are certainly major art forms, but they have very little social impact. Animation, on the other hand, may be, as of this writing, a minor art form to many critics, but it has an enormous social impact. In the 21st revised edition of Art Through the Ages the word, animation, does not appear in the index, nor does it appear in my many books on drawing. These books are never written by Artists but almost exclusively by college professors who cannot do the thing they teach -- at least not very well.

On another visit to Ohio I attended an exhibit at the University's large and beautiful art gallery. The entire Art Department was in attendance. The male professors all wore their tweed or corduroy jackets with patches on the elbows and the females, wives and teachers, were also academically attired. The purpose of this exhibit was to display the artwork by a young woman about to receive her Master's degree in ART. This show, in effect, was her thesis. On one wall of the gallery was a manifesto that explained the rationale behind the display. This manifesto was written in typical Art Speak, the kind of convoluted and incomprehensible jargon you read in Art News. The Art consisted of several pails of sand, all tastefully placed around the room. Today such an "event" would be called an installation. A deeply involved couple was staring into one of the pails as if it was The Holy Grail. My brother, by briefly placing his finger over his lips, cautioned me not to laugh. This young woman, officially sanctioned, will now go out into the world and get a job teaching the innocent.

You cannot fake your way into a ballet company. You must know how to dance. Nor can you play in an orchestra if you cannot play your instrument, or write for Atlantic Magazine if you can't write. Only in the world of "Fine Art" can you be a total fake and get away with it.

Bullwinkle has had much more influence on America than Andy Warhol's Marilyns and The Smurfs have influenced, and will continue to influence many more people, world-wide than Rauschenberg's leftovers.

In 1997 author and art critic for Time, Robert Hughes, published American Visions : The Epic History of Art in America, a work I greatly admire, but in six hundred and twenty pages you will not find McKay, Disney, comics, graphics or animation. There is some mention of the movies but only as the motion pictures were influenced by painters. This is a weak assertion. More likely the reverse is true.

Consider what Hughes writes on the last page,

> "...with the millennium at hand, in a society founded on messianic optimism, more imps and goblins will appear than ever before; the sleep of reason will produce its monsters. But there is little reason to suspect that it will also bring forth a Goya to record them."

> Mr. Hughes, in his search for a Goya had only to look at Snow White and the Seven Dwarfs or Fantasia to see that graphic art in America had not died but was very much alive and kicking.

> Hughs continues, "For the smaller field of the visual arts is equally fatigued, and its model of progress—the vanguard myth—seems played out, hardly even a shell or a parody of its former self. This however, only seems unnatural or disappointing to those whose expectations have been formed by vanguardism. Cultures do decay; and the visual culture of American modernism, once so strong, buoyant, and inventive, and now so harassed by its own sense of defeated expectations, may be no exception to that fact. One thinks, with regret, of W.B. Yeats's lines: "The best lack all conviction, while the worst are full of passionate intensity." But on the other hand, in the equally durable words of Scarlett O'Hara, "Tomorrow is another day."

In The Moose That Roared by Keith Scott, I was quoted as saying, in 1959, ". . .having brainwashed myself into believing that the animated cartoon is a potential high art form I have had little success in proving this thesis - to date."

That was true then. I am still an animator, and a very good one, but computer technology has made many of the crafts I mastered obsolete and I must salute a new generation of animation artists that have, at last, raised animation to the level of a high Art form. From the 1950s through the 1990s animation was supported by the television industry. Now animation is supported by feature length films, many of the best produced by Pixar Animation Studios. I will never forget that Sunday afternoon when my teen-aged children and their friends were gathered in the den in front of the old TV. We were all, for the first time, about to see - "experience" would be a better word – the movie "UP" directed by Pete Docter and Bobo Peterson. This audience, myself included was extremely attentive and when our eyes welled up with tears, it was clear to me that the art of animation had reached the level of high cinema and that this film, in particular, would take its proper place in the long history of fine art.

In 1969, Sesame Street, supplying a list of words, numbers, phrases and concepts sent out a nationwide call for storyboard submissions. Those who best solved the communication/teaching problem would get the work.

Sesame Street budgets were so low the big studios didn't even bother. Working with Fred Calvert Productions, I set off to N.Y.C. to pitch our ideas and the Street said okay to buying fifteen or so. We had such a small amount of money to work with I could only allow a laughable fifteen minutes for direction on each spot. They all turned out rather well which somehow proved that big budgets do not necessarily guarantee good pictures. They aired for years and years.

I was 38 and working for Jay Ward again. I animated the pilot for George of the Jungle and animated a Tom Slick or two and some Super Chickens. John Sutherland Productions called again. They had a really BIG animation project and would like me to direct. John will toss in a car.

The San Antonio Texas school district received a grant from the United States Department of Health and Welfare. The grant was to fund a hundred or so films aimed at young Mexican-American school children. Dan Weisbird, a very talented writer, would be the producer. So I quit Ward again and started to direct Tony & Tina, a worthy and wonderful project. Thus began the most chaotic period of my entire life.

Leslie was ten. And what would you like, Leslie? I would like a horse. Okaaay. Michael was seven. And what would you like, Michael? I would like acting lessons and an agent...and maybe a horse. Okaaay. And what would you like, Daddy? I would like a love affair....and perhaps a horse. Okaaay. And Mommy, what would you like? I would like a love affair of my own, but it's all so awful and messy I will need therapy. Okaaay. Boarding horses is very expensive. Let's buy a little ranchette in Shadow Hills: a lovely old house on an acre and a half atop a hill with a grand view of the entire San Fernando Valley which will sparkle at night.

We kept the Haines Canyon house and rented it to a beautiful couple. She was Penny Singleton's daughter (Blondie). They drove a Bentley but were frequently late with the rent.

One of Walt Disney's many dreams came to fruition with the creation of The California Institute Of The Arts, now known as Cal Arts. His idea was to merge The Los Angeles Conservatory Of Music (est. 1863) and the Chouinard Art Institute (est. 1921) and build from there. He had long supported Chouinard. Bill Hurtz, my old mentor, had long been teaching a class in animation at Chouinard and, in conversation with me, pretty much assumed he would head up the animation department when Cal Arts opened.

English movie director Alexander Macendricks was appointed Dean of the new film school. He was famous for directing a string of English comedies, one of them being The Man In The White Suit starring Alec Guinness, a classic of its time.

Bill Hurtz was somewhat stunned when the dean hired Jules Engle to be the director of the new animation department. Jules was a good enough background-painter but he really excelled in social manipulation. He was always involved in Beverly Hills fund raising events in support of the Arts. He asked me, one time, to contribute a painting to an auction that would raise money for some worthy Art project, which I did. It was a small painting in the style of Giorgio de Chirico and somebody bought it. I wonder where it is? I digress. I was surprised when Jules asked me to teach animation at Cal Arts two days a week with all of the benefits of a full time professor. John Sutherland was fine with it. So now I had two roles and two jobs. As a Mentor I would have to write and deliver a lecture every two weeks.

Not long ago I was having lunch with my good friend Max Addison and for some reason Cal Arts popped up in the conversation. I told Max about my dozen or so lectures on animation now tucked away somewhere in a dark closet. Max made me realize that as the first person to lecture on animation at the now prestigious and world famous California Institute of the Arts, surely, the school library would like to have them and maybe that is where they will rest. But in the meantime, I offer one here.

Circa 1971, these morning lectures were delivered from notes scribbled in pencil on a yellow legal pad. The pages were covered with little drawings that, as I spoke, were transferred to an old blackboard. The class, not all animation majors, might number fifteen.

The CalArts lectures: Dean, Alexander McKendrick -   Dept. Head, Jules Engel - Mentor, Gerard Baldwin.

ANIMAL LOCOMOTION – WALKING

When preparing this talk on animal locomotion – or more specifically – walking, I went first to the Encyclopedia Britannica – which had some lovely things to say about the Art of walking. Let me quote...

"Walking in the nobler sense is a measured progress inspired by the woods and hills—by rivers—and the flowers of the field – a serene partaking of the enduring sources of joy."

"Walking and meditation are bound together in the very name peripatetic—as they walked they pondered—as they pondered they walked."

To say that walking is a means of animal progression accomplished by methodically setting one foot in front of the other is not enough. Certainly Aristotle would not like it. I feel somehow responsible for making such a mechanical process more exciting than that. I suppose I am trying to make walking seem romantic and wonderful – which it really is when you think about it -- and I hope that by touching on various kinds of animal locomotion -- the ability to move from place to place -- that struggling with an animation exercise involving the basic principles of walking will not seem such a tedious, mechanical and boring task.

There is a science of human locomotion and it is called Kinesiology - the science is an attempt to understand the function of the various limbs, ligaments and muscles etc., that are involved in the mechanics of our ability to move in some coordinated way. I do not recommend investigating this highly specialized branch of science -- it has about as much to do with animation as the study of anatomy has to do with drawing - which is very little.

Yet, on opening a textbook entitled Animal Mechanics by McNeill Alexander I found on the first page of chapter one Newton's three laws of motion, and a quick glance through the contents reads like a book NOT on animal locomotion but on animation.

Force and energy, center of gravity, motion with constant acceleration, moments of inertia, circular motion, joints and mechanisms, elasticity, viscosity, friction, stress-pressure, buoyancy, drag, gliding, vibration and on and on and on.

In thinking about walking it is interesting to note that nature never evolved an organism based on the wheel, nor is there any organism whose method of locomotion resembles a wheel. The reason for this may be that a lever system - walking - is more efficient and more adaptable to the Earth's terrain, and this is why we have feet on the end of our legs instead of wheels.

And so we walk or run or trot – gallop – leap – or creep.

The Amoeba

Amoebic movement is probably the most primitive mode of animal locomotion – much studied but little understood. It seems to move along about 3 quarters of an inch in an hour by gripping the substratum with a delicate external plasma-like membrane, which is continually giving way anteriorly and being reinstated posteriorly.

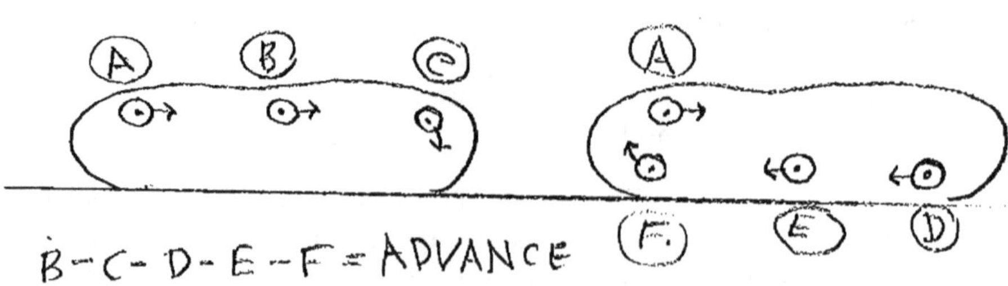

What impels it – food-light-warmth – is, to say the least, considerably shrouded. Apparently it doesn't really glide along or flow along – as it seems to do under a microscope – looked at from the top…

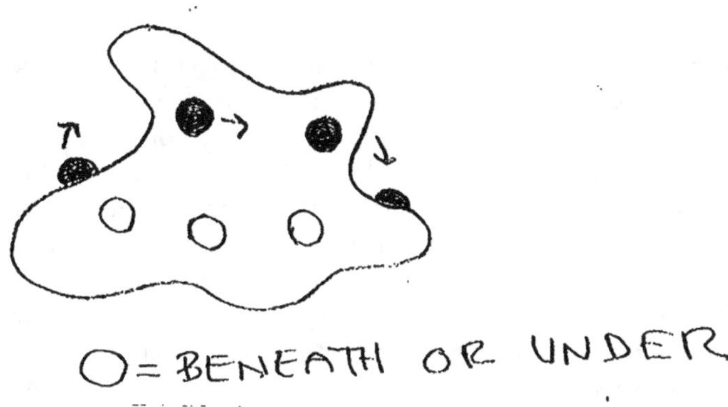

A recognizable particle may be seen moving along the "upper" level – gets to the "front" which in this case means the direction in which the Amoeba happens to be moving – the particle disappears over the top – only to reappear some time later at the back – a kind of mad internal – outside in – caterpillar tractor

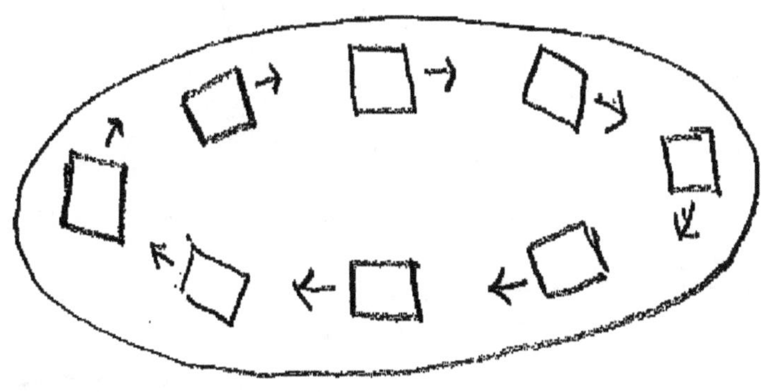

So this, perhaps, is how we all, in some dim past, began walking and, for all I know, we may be impelled NOW to move about by some urge we have in common with the Amoeba. I have dragged the Amoeba into this because I feel strongly that motivation is a factor you must take into account when animating a walk.

I have tried to imagine some long ago simple life awash in the sea or lying in the sand—never having moved of its own volition—yet somehow—propelled by some inner force – or attracted by some external one – or a combination of both – suddenly filled with a desire to be 1 thirty second of an inch more to the left of where it is and not having the faintest idea (much less self - awareness) of how to get there – it must be something like having your arms tied to your sides – your feet set in cement – and wanting to go across the street for a drink of water – imagine the frustration. How unconsciously we accept our locomotion – how unappreciative of the eons that went into its development — how little aware are we of the amazing biomechanical process that is walking.

For whatever reasons we animals need to propel ourselves—be it food-females-or flight—there are four chief methods of animal locomotion – though, no doubt, there are exceptions – these four basic methods may best be illustrated by picturing a man in a boat.

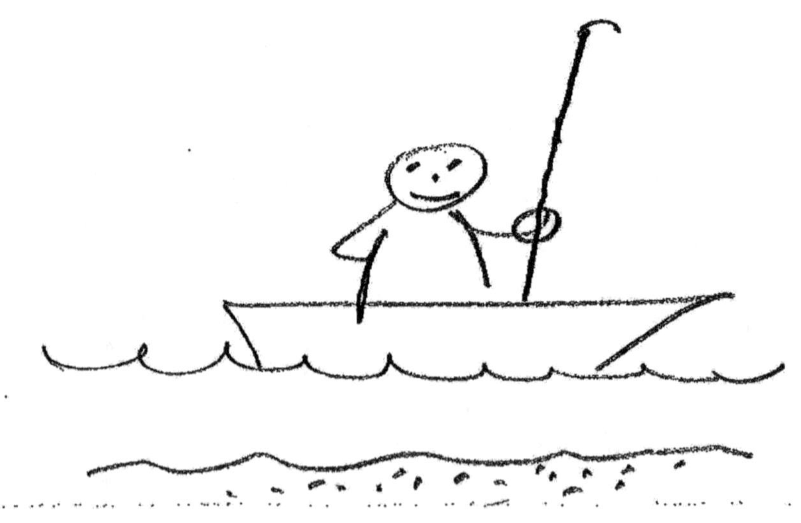

The four methods are pulling-punting-culling and rowing.

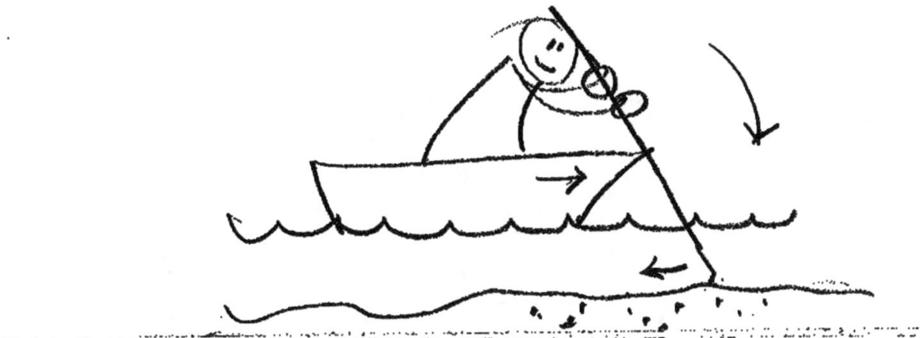

PULLING

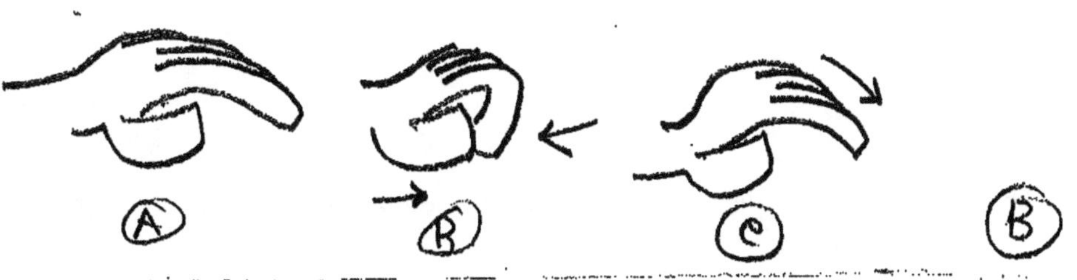

You reach forward with a boat hook and pull the boat forward. Leeches and starfish are animals that move in this fashion and… under extreme circumstances… so might a human.

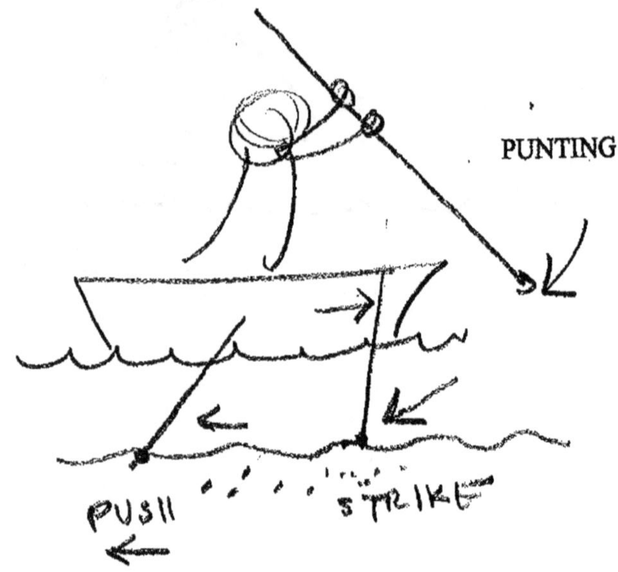

PUNTING

The man uses the pole as a lever—pressing it against the floor of the stream
—this is how we walk…and beetles and camels

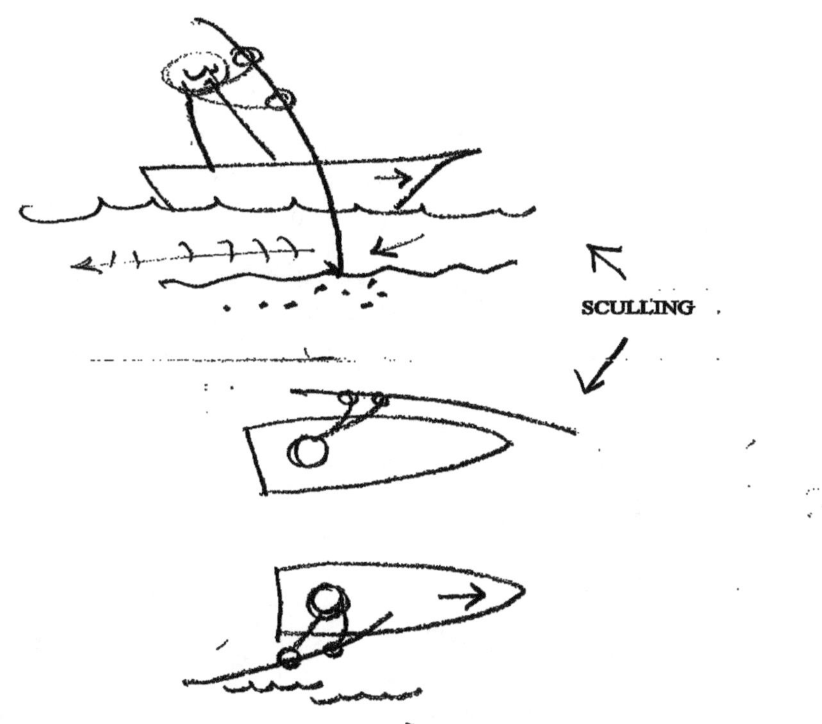

SCULLING

The man in the boat stands in the stern--displacing masses of water alternately on one side and then the other--thus propelling the boat forward – this is basically the locomotion of fishes or whales.

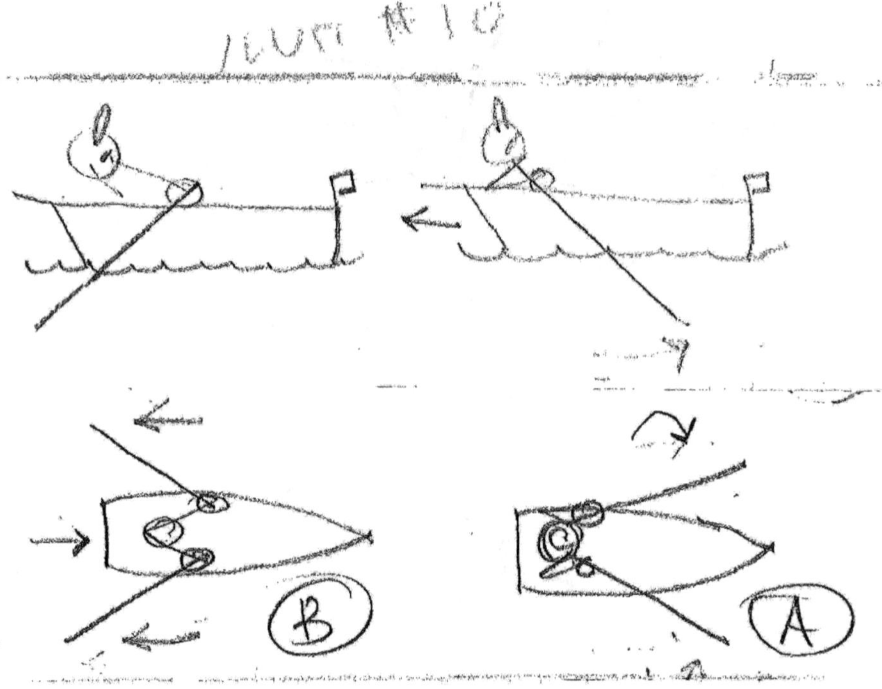

ROWING

And finally the man in the boat may row – exerting pressure on both sides with two poles. This is excitingly illustrated by a bird – it may be said to row in the air.

WALKING

The mechanisms which are involved in throwing a baseball, or lifting a trunk, or walking are no less awe-inspiring than the mechanisms involved in metabolism or photo synthesis or sending a man to the moon.

The muscular-skeleton system is provided with many of the mechanical principles basic to machines: the lever – the wheel – the axle – the pulley

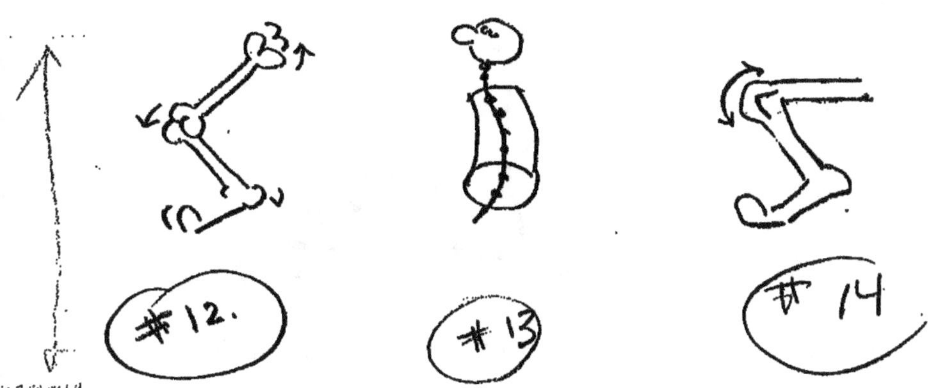

The lever may be illustrated by the leg – rigid bars turning at a fulcrum point.

The wheel may be illustrated by the rotation of the upper trunk and the axle is the spine around which rotation occurs as in the movement of the head.

The pulley may be illustrated by tendons moving over knee joints and across knuckles.

Locomotion in man is the progressive movement of the entire body from one position to another by means of self-propulsion … perhaps also there must be an "attraction" to justify the self- propulsion … and understanding the "attraction" may be as important – in animation – as understanding the mechanics of the process.

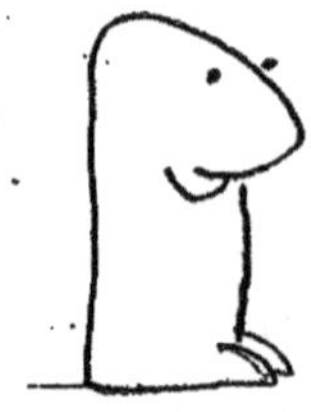 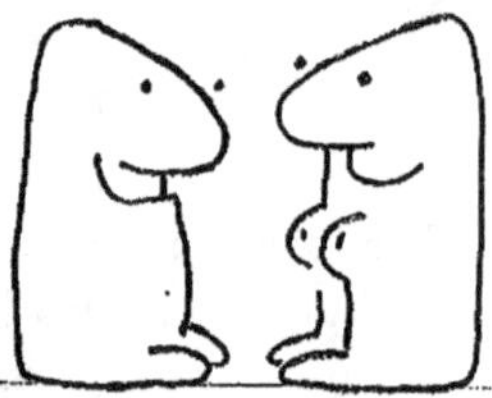

There are three basic kinds of animal stance that effect walking

Flat footed – like a bear

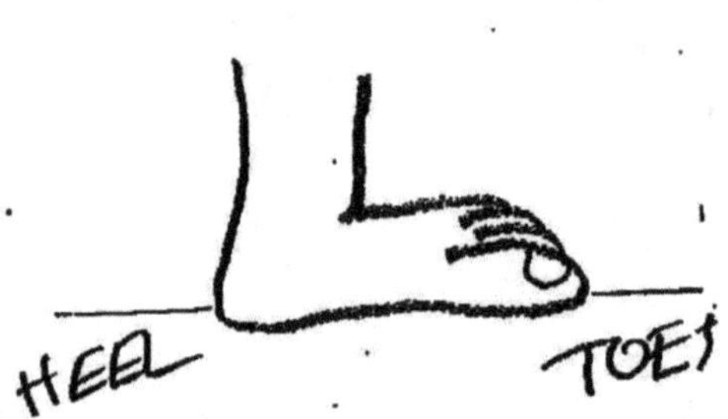

This kind of walk on the sole of the foot is called Plantigrade

The faster dog or cat are Digitigrades ... they stand and walk on their fingers with the heel permanently raised.

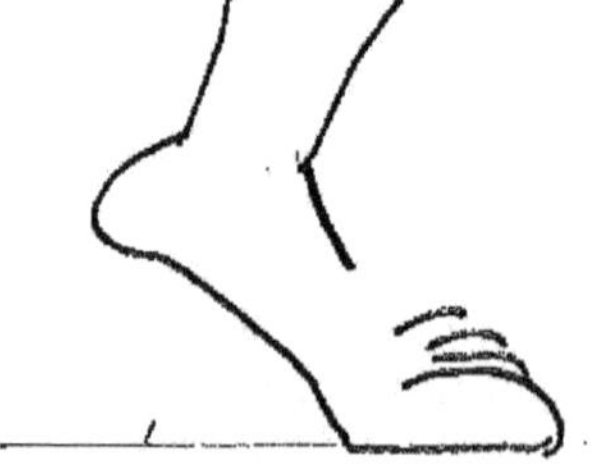 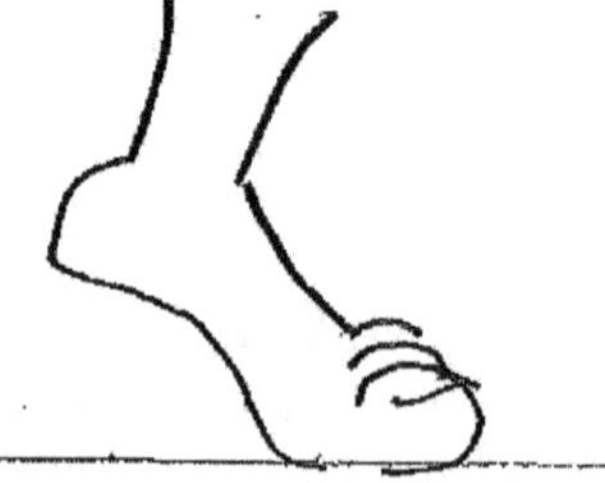

A third category of mammals, including horses, is Unguligrade – progressing on the tips of the "fingernails" which we call hoofs.

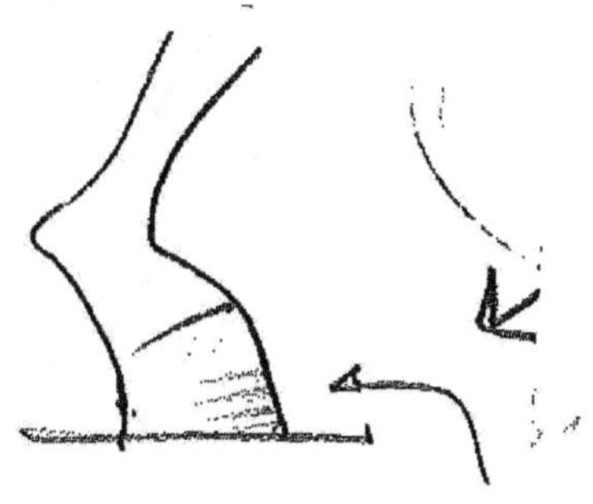

Man is a Plantigrade – flat footed like the bear – but as a stance, we have perfected it. Walking has been described as an alternating loss and recovery of balance. In walking the inertia of the body has to be overcome at each step because it is necessary, which each step, to overcome the opposing forces of gravity and air resistance. As unaware of it as we are, except in a high wind, the forward moving trunk meets with air resistance and the restraining push of the forward foot, as it strikes the ground has to be overcome at each step.

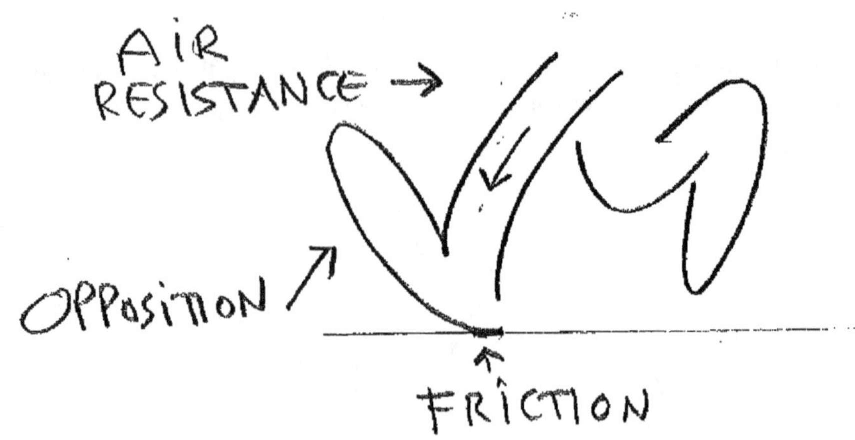

It seems obvious, though we never really think about it, that without applying energy or force at each step you would come to a rather abrupt halt. Because the amount of work involved is so great – conservation of energy becomes a factor – a factor in how the audience will interpret your animation of a walk.

In an animated walk exaggerated up and down movements indicate that extra energy is being used unnecessarily. How many animators have their characters bouncing up and down – just to put some "animation" in – not realizing that this "body language" says something about the character they are portraying – conveys meaning to the audience at an unconscious or semi-conscious level. The animators may be displaying some knowledge of movement but very little about acting.

I like to think of walking as falling over and catching yourself – sort of throwing yourself toward the target – and then not knocking your brains out with some very tricky leg work. Walking and similar forms of locomotion involve a complicated balance of forces.

The inertia of the stationary body is overcome by the horizontal thrust (self-generated). This cycle or periodic movement is characterized by an alternating increase and decrease in speed. This change in speed is usually so subtle as to go unnoticed and usually need not be accounted for in an animation problem ... still, inertia must be overcome at every step.

As the upper mass moves forward it passes beyond the support base and a temporary loss of balance results – at this point the downward pull of gravity threatens a complete loss of equilibrium.

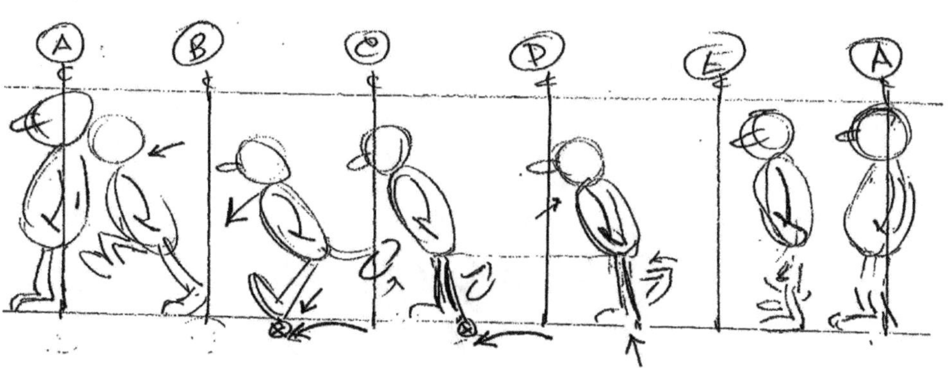

…but, just in time, the free leg, moving forward, strikes the ground and a new support base is formed.

The thrust of the new leading leg causes a counter force in the opposite direction

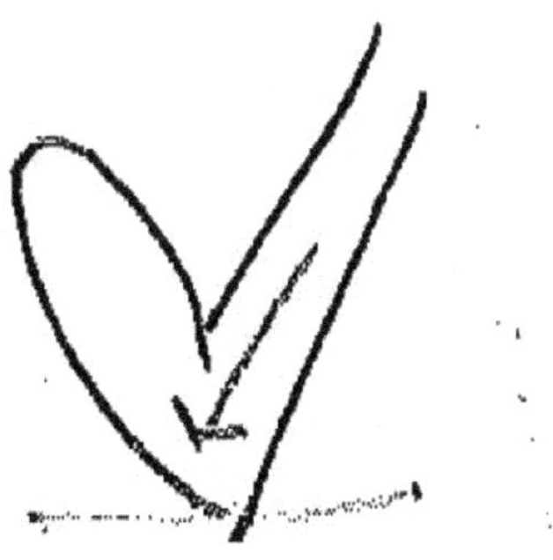

This counter pressure somewhat restrains the forward fall of the torso as the new support base is formed.

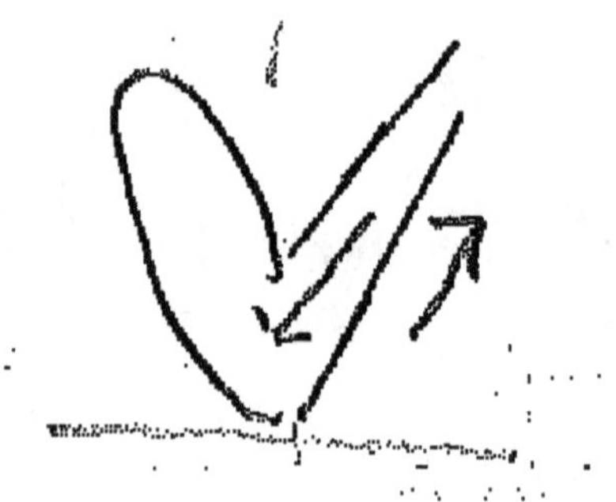

Note this diminishes as the leg assumes its vertical position – eventually to reverse itself and act as a pusher. Beside the momentum given to the torso by the thrust of the back leg, it is also affected constantly by the downward pull of gravity.

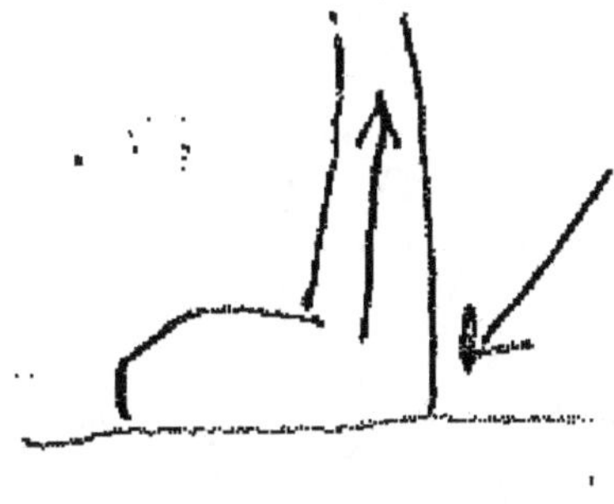

This force is opposed by the support leg.

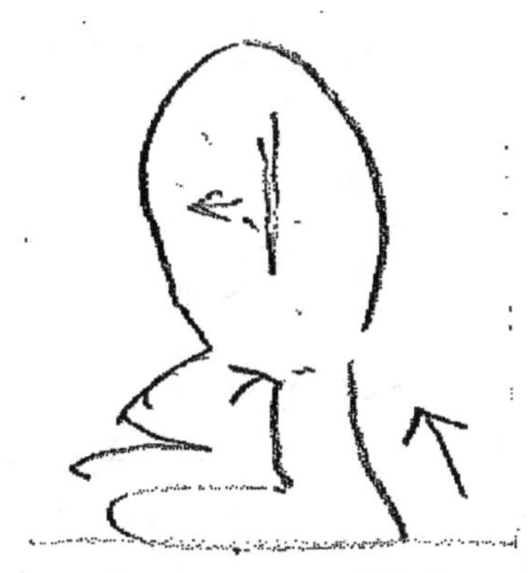

And during the phase of double support

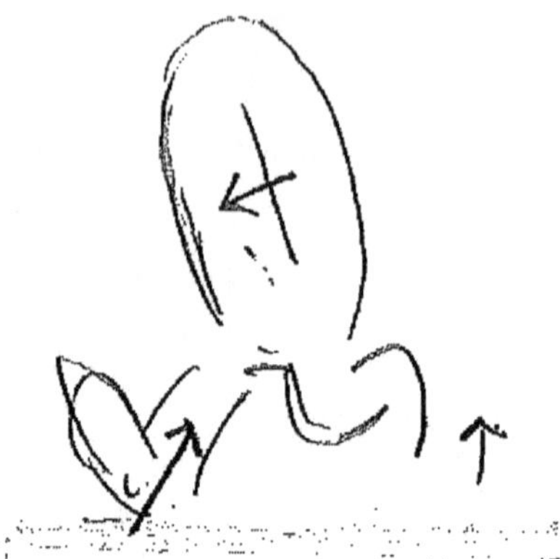

Each leg is applying vertical force. If you have exceptionally strong legs or are deeply in love with yourself, the vertical force may so exceed what is needed to counter gravity that a gait develops having an upward spring or an unusual amount of bounce.

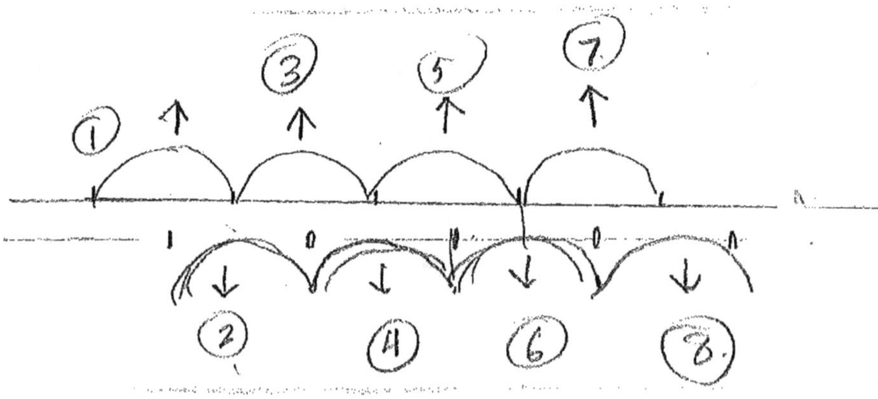

As I said a minute ago – applying such characteristics to animation without thought as to what they mean may be a way of adding "animation" to a character, but it also may destroy believability in that character.

I will be giving an assignment today, so I suggest you take notes. In animating a walk, the degree of inclination is very important as it will convey considerable information to the audience. If you recall in a previous talk I was calling this a "line of action or an action line" …

A=normal or mild resistance   B=a strong wind   C=no   resistance
        D=a hurricane

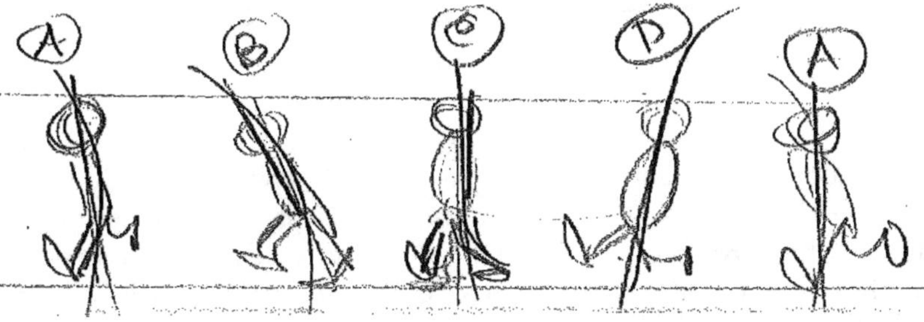

In the absence of noticeable wind or air resistance, these same inclinations tell us much about the emotional make-up of the person particularly when we realize that some of thee attitudes require tremendous muscular exertion.

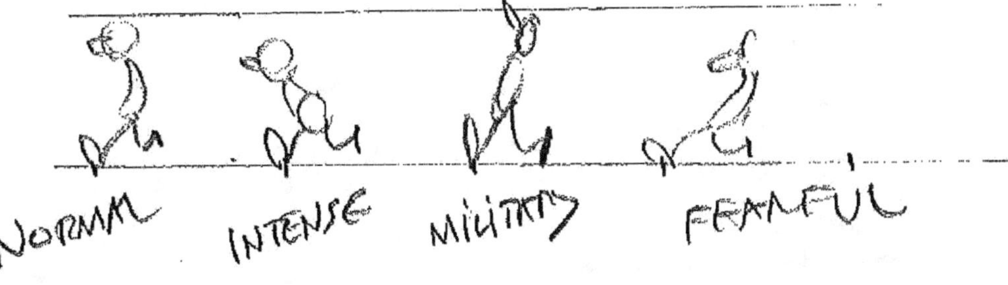

A=normal   B=intense   C=uptight—military   D=fearful?

The amount of pressure or thrust the foot can impart to the body – in the propulsion phase of the cycle relates to the counter pressure of the supporting surface.

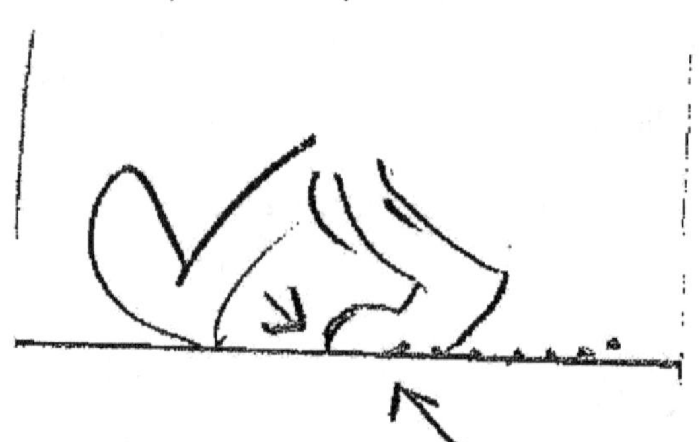

The surface on which you have your actor walk will affect the walk. If the
surface lacks solidity – as with snow-sand-mud – it will obviously not offer
enough resistance so that even greater exertion needs to be applied by the leg
to gain any forward motion. Friction is also an essential ingredient in the
recipe that constitutes walking. There must be sufficient friction to just
balance the horizontal force of the mass with the counter force of the leg.
Otherwise – as on ice – the force in the leg is not applied to the body – and
the foot slips.

I think this is a good place to illustrate walking as animators understand it, at least as this animator understands it. I will try to illustrate an entire cycle. Muybridge, in his famous book of photographs Animals in Motion, defines a step as lifting one of the supporting members from the ground – thrusting it toward the desired location – and placing it again on the ground where it resumes its function of supporting the body.

A stride is a cycle of steps. In a biped this stride is two uniformly executed steps.

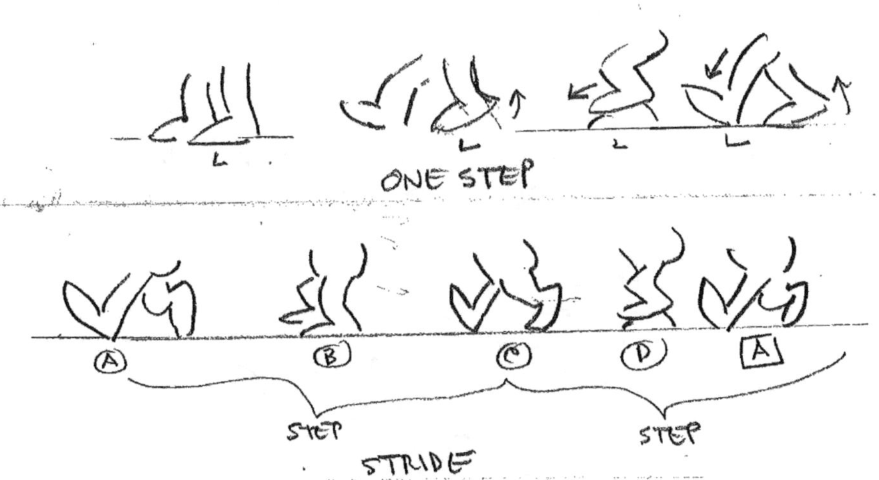

This cycle may be repeated endlessly – though now always in a new location.

The action of the arms plays only a small part in walking. You may have your arms behind your back – or your hands in your pockets-or folded – without appreciatively affecting the walk. Normally the arms swing opposite to the direction of the corresponding leg – when the left leg is moving forward the left arm is moving back....if the right leg is moving back...then the right arm is usually moving forward. This interplay is always slightly out of phase and overlapped. To explain why the right arm is back when the right leg is forward; think of a pendulum and the concept that for every force in one direction, there will be one in an opposite direction.

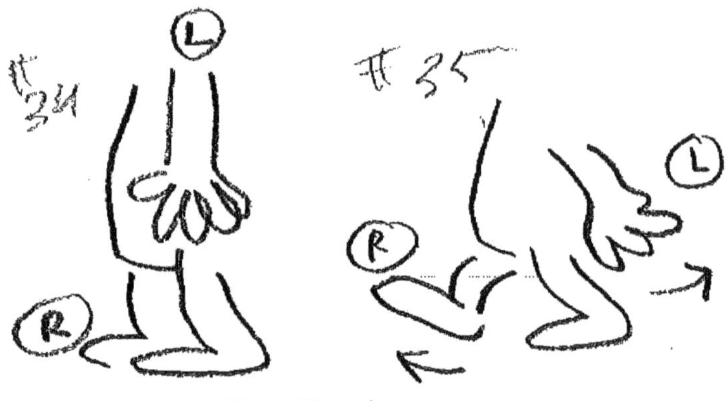

Unless you self-consciously do something with your arms they will ... if left hanging... always move in a direction opposite to the thrust of theppositeleg.

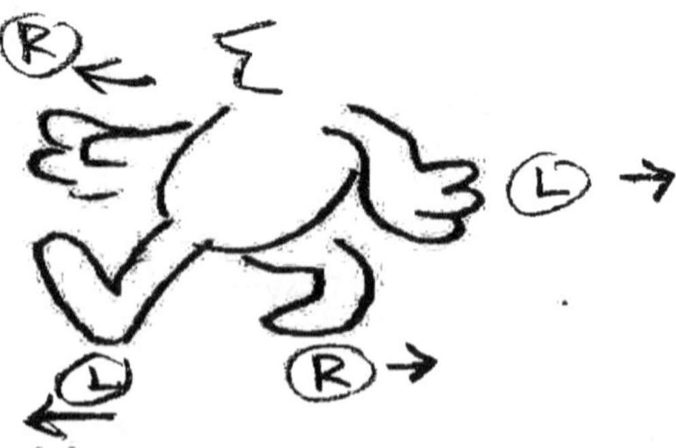

The first thing to decide when planning an animated walk is the speed of the walk – in the cartoon business we described the speed with a number. "I'd like to have him or her walk on x8s or how about a walk on x16s; no, that's too slow…let's settle for x12s."

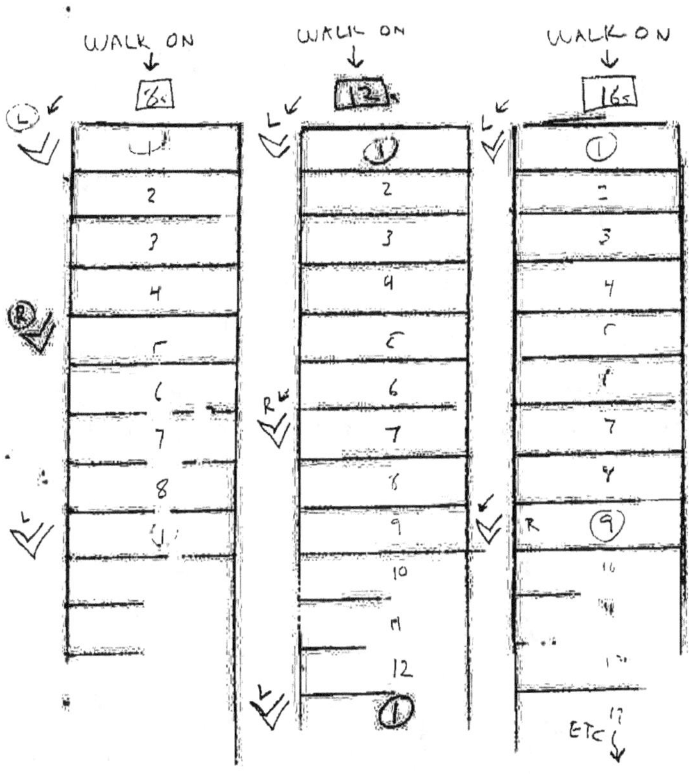

The numbers refer to frames of film per second (24 frames per second being the standard) and the number you choose – 8-10-12-14-16-etc., is the speed of the walk or the point in a step at which the heel strikes the ground – assuming this animation is exposed on two's.

Let's hear these walks or beats on a metronome – by counting the number of drawings between each step or beat, you also know how many in-betweens will be required for a particular walk. With regard to the number of in-betweens – I would like to give you a tip: it is always easier to have an odd number between each step than an even number – simply because it is easier to visually divide an odd number.

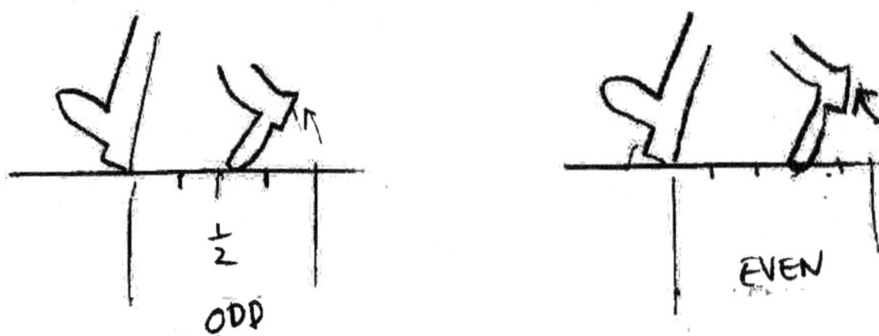

I know that most of you have a difficult time determining the path that the free leg should follow as it swings forward to get into position to become the support leg.

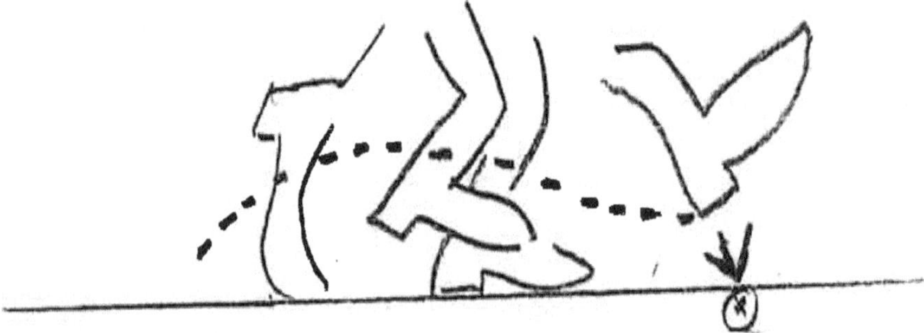

This path would vary in each walk – determined by weight, speed, mood, etc., in some walks the foot may drag or …

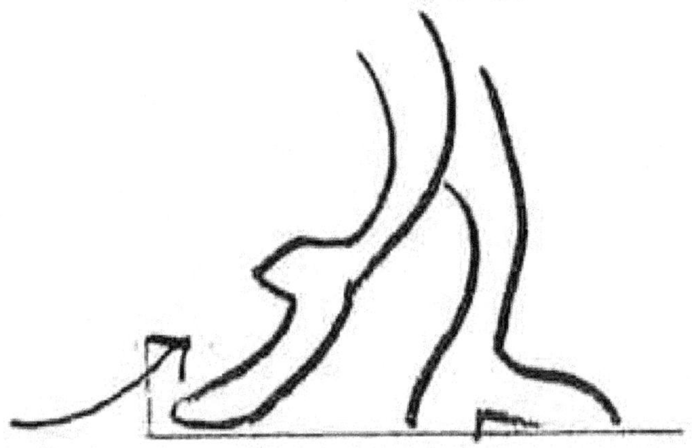

be brought forward late – almost reluctantly – it may wish to meet the ground with fear or great care as in the tip-toe

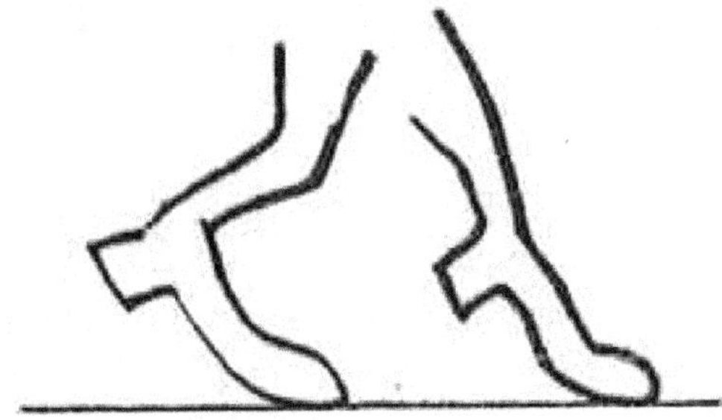

In other walks it may swing through the mid-point in a high step. And snap ... to meet the ground as in a strut or a goosestep. The variations are endless. There is a mean however – a normal path that the average foot does follow and I diagram it here.

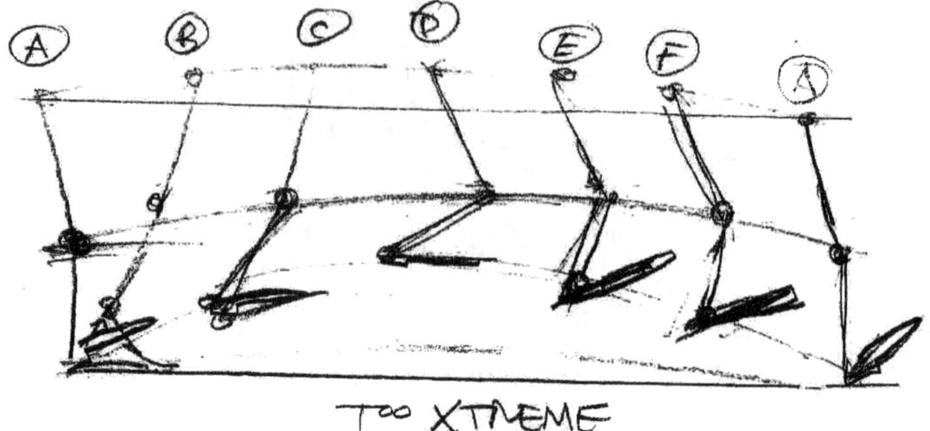

Another problem many of you have is a constant struggle with maintaining the correct lengths of the leg bones ... the upper half of the leg seems to

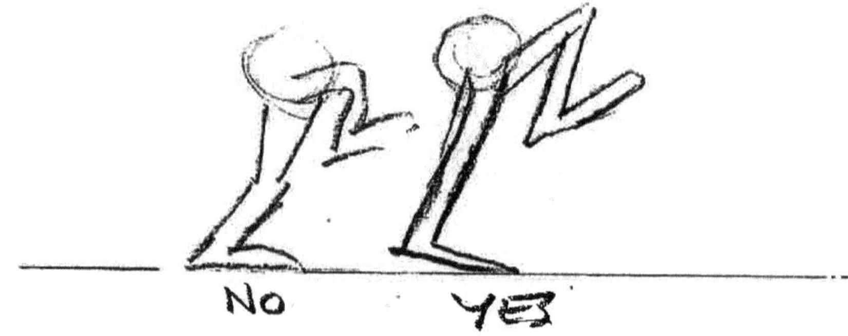

always grow longer or shorter to accommodate your placement of the foot.

If you can't fit the leg into the space you have left for it then your walk is
incorrect or impossible to perform.

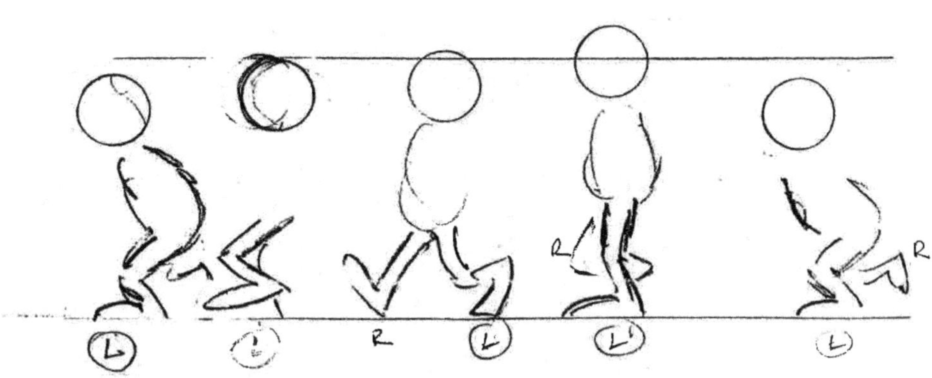

How much bounce or up and down movement should there be in a walk?
This is determined – at least physically, by the weight of the body – the
strength of the leg and the length of the stride. Imagine a mean head line
above the floor line.

To go above the mean line – means the support leg must push you there. A
buoyant personality or a dancer might do this...

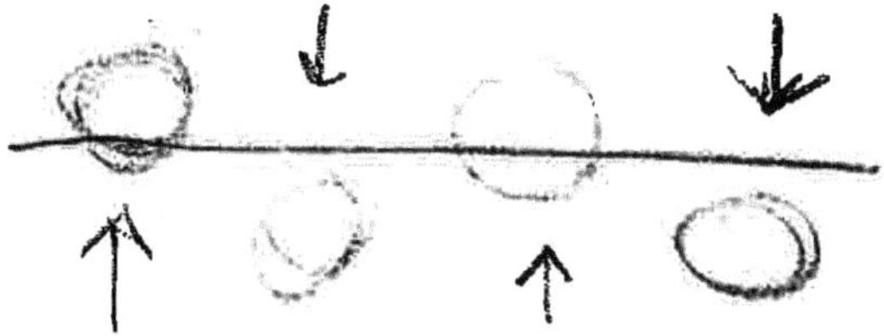

A fat man — with tremendous weight to lift would never do it — he may have a rise and fall in his walk, but it is apt to always be below the mean line and never above it.

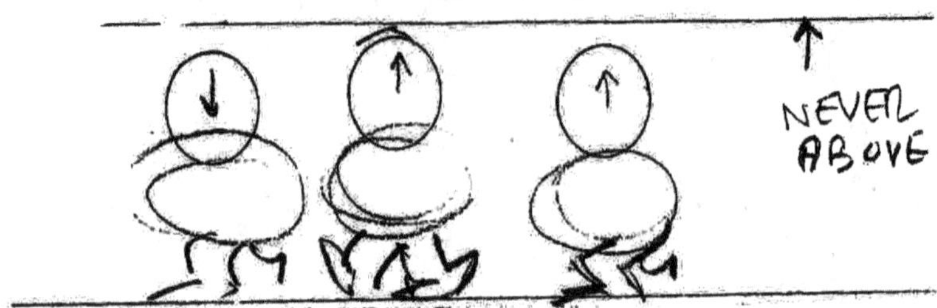

Why does the support leg bend when we walk? It is possible to walk without bending it and to a certain degree some personality types do — though, I do not think they remain personalities for very long. The leg bends simply to absorb the shock of your falling body — and in absorbing that energy it acts as a spring to lift the body and continue forward momentum.

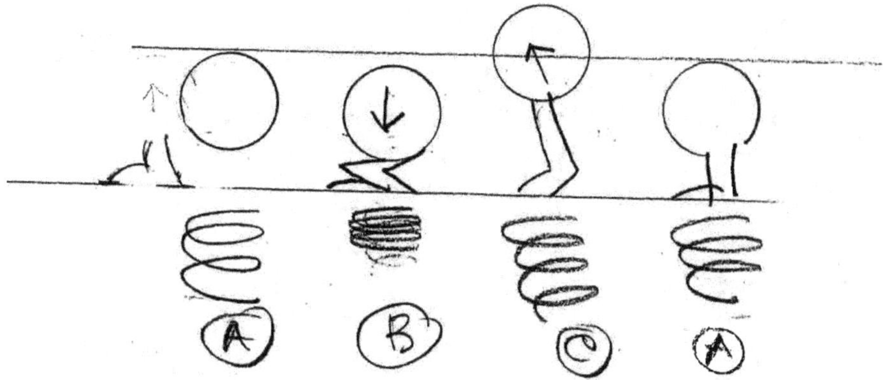

Think of the leg as constantly absorbing and releasing energy. If the legs did not do this, they would collapse from stress – literally break within a few years of learning to walk. It is not uncommon for people when their leg goes to sleep, to stand up – put their full weight on it and, the feedback mechanism failing, snap it.

I would like to give you an assignment – those of you who are not film graphics majors – or artists – can do it anyway if you choose-using stick figures. I would like each of you to decide on a character type – or physical type that you would like to animate. The character may be a man, a woman, tall, short, heavy, skinny, strong, weak, happy, sad – write the description of your character on a sheet of paper, and give it to Jules or myself with your name on it.

Then animate a walk – as your character would walk ... a simple walk across the screen – not a cycle.

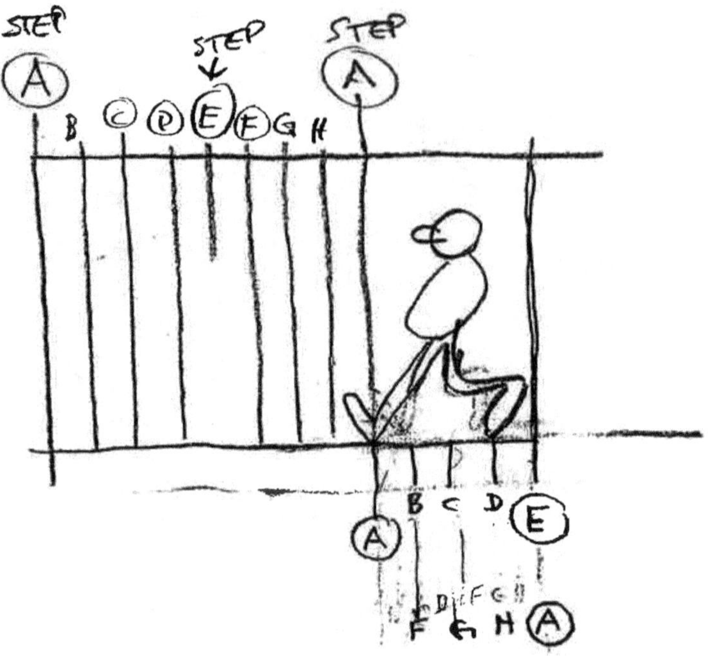

Keep the character design very simple – no hats – no eyes – no extraneous junk of any kind.

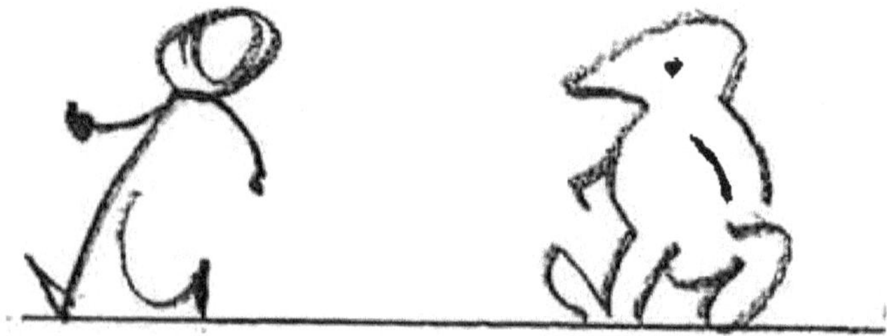

It may be as simple as this and no more complicated than this. Have this being walk across the paper – the stage – the screen – as only your character would. After shooting this walk, we can check it against your character description, analyzing not only the mechanics of the walk, but the character of the person you described. Not easy.

Later we will explore a hop and a skip and a run; in the case of a run I think it should be a cycle in place and we will pan the background... otherwise the character will run across the screen so fast we won't be able to analyze it. Animating a cycle for a walk or a run is relatively simple in principle. The character walks or runs in place and the background moves past this point at a speed corresponding to the forward motion of the character as if it was actually progressing.

In a cycle all these drawings are piled on top of each other

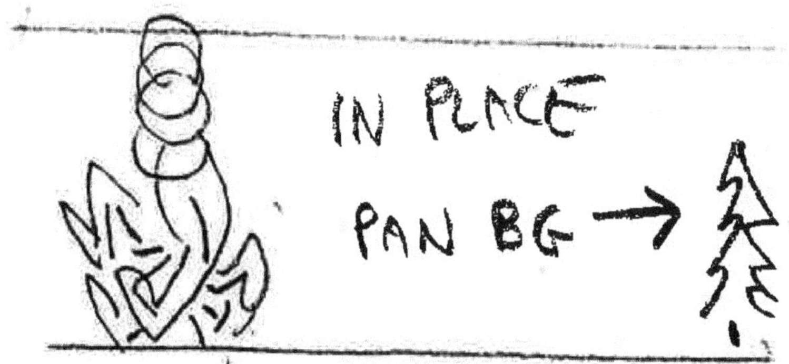

And a loop is made

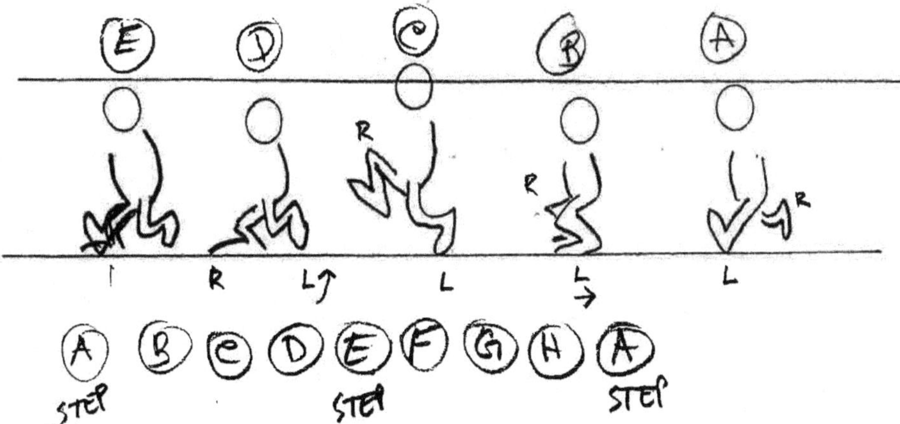

Assuming the background is on the same plane as the character – it moves past the character or across the screen at a speed equal to the distance that the feet slip back in the cycle. Now you have two assignments – one is a walk, the second is a run in place on a cycle. I would like all of the drawings to be planned so that they work on a 9-field center. I would prefer no figure be less than 3 inches tall or more than five. Each drawing will be shot on two's.

I will be available to help. Any questions? Thanks for listening. That's it for today.

Chapter 12

Behaving much like a Prussian General on an inspection tour, accompanied by a small entourage of petty officers, Disney director Wolfgang Reitherman (The Sword and the Stone) marched into my first lecture. Jules Engle introduced us. Wolfgang glowered and the look said, "Who the hell is this guy having the audacity to talk about animation at OUR school?!" It was a snob thing.

More than once I applied for membership in the Academy of Motion Picture Arts & Sciences and, more than once, I was rejected.
How come?

There was no problem in getting a friend and member to sign my application but that was as far as it ever got. The short subjects screening committee was turning me down. I had one screen credit as an animator on an Academy Award winner, but my other credits were all for TV production. The Academy saw TV as inferior to movies made for theatre - a snob thing.

After I was anointed VP of John Sutherland Productions I applied again. This time I was accepted even though my work was still not for movies. I figured someone on that committee might be looking for work someday and pressed my acceptance.

A few years later I was sitting on that same short subjects committee, an all male group of ten or twelve. One evening we were discussing whether or not to accept an applicant. Some on the committee were thumbs up and some were thumbs down: "This person has been in the business a long, long time." "Yes, but this person has no talent."

It was getting tedious when a silver haired elder sitting at the far end of a long table interrupted the discussion with, "Gentlemen. Gentlemen. Let us remember this is a private club." It sure is. A snob thing.

In 1972 I was having a very early Friday lunch with Duane Crowther at Boardners' Bar, a cartoonists hangout on Las Palmas Avenue in old run down Hollywood. Just a few doors down was the old Las Palmas theatre, also tired. (When I was in high school my brother Howard took me there more than once. There were a lot of wonderful character actors in Hollywood and the performances were always marvelous. I particularly remember Moliere's The Inspector General.)

"But Duane what am I gonna do?"

"Only one thing you can do. Quit."

We drank some more and mid-afternoon I went back to the studio. I picked up my briefcase and started toward the elevator and the parking garage. Harry Love, production manager and spy-pimp intercepted me.

"We gotta meeting. Where yuh goin?"

"Home."

"How come?"

"I just quit."

"You got a contract. You can't just quit."

"Just quit. Give my regards to Ralph Bakshi."

Robert Crumb, author of Fritz The Cat, hated what feature animation director Ralph Bakshi did to his creation. I agreed with Crumb, but I could not know, in 1972, that I would actually come to despise Bakshi. So, this is the story:

I had always wanted to direct an animated feature. Too much so, I guess. I was running the animation department at John Sutherland Productions and teaching animation theory and technique at Cal Arts when, just before Christmas, I got the call. Producer Steve Krantz had a feature and no director. Steve and Ralph Bakshi had had a falling out. Would I take over and direct the film?

My sister Dorothy spent most of her working life as an executive secretary for a Hollywood labor union. Labor union business agents seem to have inside info on everything that goes on in the movie business and they told her that the outfit putting up the money for this animated feature was not exactly legit. Oh well.

Listening to my dream and not my gut I had a Saturday morning breakfast with Steve and we discussed the deal. He was in a hurry. A contract would be ready Monday morning. I was uneasy. Something said NO but my dream won.

The picture was Heavy Traffic. I signed the contract, resigned from Sutherlands and Cal Arts, and walked into a mess. It would take weeks just to sort it out. There was no final script, no continuity boards, not much had been recorded and a staff of artists had nothing to do. I reported all this to Steve.

"Lay them off."

"But it's almost Christmas Eve. Can't it wait 'til after Christmas?"

"I don't give a shit about the Goy. Give them notice. NOW!"

The staff loved Bakshi. They hated me.

Late one afternoon Steve summoned me to his office for some

reason or other. When I entered he was on the phone and while continuing to talk, and listen, he managed to let me know he was chatting with a good friend, a Chief Justice of the Supreme Court of the United States. I was impressed and a little worried about the country.

Harry Love, the slimy production manager, told me with glee, that Ralph Bakshi was back as director of the picture. I was just a pawn in a contractual dispute. I had never met Bakshi. I had seen a couple of his vulgar movies. He swaggered into my office (his office) and sat down across from me - it was Friday.

"I'm gonna get you."

I confronted Steve. What about my contract?

"Don't worry we'll find something for you to do. You can make the trailer or the titles or something."

"Don't worry? I wasn't hired to make a trailer!"

"So make a trailer."

So I went to early lunch with Duane Crowther and then I went home and called my lawyer. He advised it was legally okay to quit, so not to worry. Not to worry? Everybody is telling me not to worry. Suddenly I have no job and I feel really stupid. How could I have been such a dumb fool? I told my wife if Steve Krantz calls tell him I'm on my horse and riding somewhere in the Big Tujunga Canyon. He called. He called again on Saturday. Same story, I'm still riding. I received a wire ordering me to return to work on Monday. Late on Sunday afternoon the phone rang. I picked up the receiver. Steve was friendly and understanding and gentle and when he started telling me what a lovely nice little family I had; I sensed his not so veiled and sickening threat.

"Listen Krantz, if you're implying what I think you are, if you even hint at harm, I'll kill you! Shoot you, and get away with it!" He hung up.

I have often wondered why Krantz was so insistent on my returning to the movie, to Give Ralph a little polish? Was he just a control freak? I'll never know. I immediately started looking for work and it would take a long, long time to recover from the damage I did to myself by not listening to my gut. Goodbye Shadow Hills, sell the ranchette, back to the house on Haines Canyon.

Truthfully, I never could have made Heavy Traffic. It was too autobiographical. It was Bakshi's story. Writing this now I can see it was Steve Krantz, who was the villain, yet I continue to deeply despise Ralph. Not because of the way he introduced himself, but what he did to Lord of the Rings is reason enough.

In 1974 AT&T made a decision to sponsor a high quality television series for school children. The Big Blue Marble ran in syndication for almost a decade and was indeed high quality. The cartoon elements for the show were produced by Ron Campbell Films Inc. Later, Ron would be the most important and productive storyboard artist on The Smurfs.

Despite very low budgets and never enough time, some very good animated films were made. I remember adapting the tale of Athene and Arachne. As the story goes Princess Arachne was so skilled in the art of weaving that even the Godess Athene was jealous. Athene caused the Princess Arachne to hang herself and then turned her into a spider. My adaptation of this myth and a few others turned out to be charming little movies. They are lost. They have disappeared into that great television vault in the sky.

I don't know about now but Wabac in 1975 animators and directors were members of an all-male club.

There was no way of telling who might show up at a gathering of the thirsty but for sure almost never a female. There was this belief that women could never be outstanding animators because they couldn't impart enough strength or power into their work. The concept of the female being the weaker sex was still prevalent. One would think Bette Davis would have shattered that myth but no, females never rose above being layout artists, background painters or assistants. Fifty years ago there were only two women animators in Hollywood: Laverne Harding and Ruth Kissane. Kissane did a lot of animation on my films and her work was very strong.

After 22 years of a sometimes wonderful and many times difficult marriage the light dimmed and our marriage died. I moved out of the house and nearly a year later Pat filed for divorce. It went amicably enough. Pat got alimony, child support and the house. I kept some cash and a half -acre lot on a hillside in Shadow Hills.

As the 1970s came to a close, I was an unmarried man living in an apartment and not liking it and spending more evenings in bars than was good for me. One Sunday afternoon, on an impulse, I went to the Los Angeles Home Show. A small geodesic dome was on display. I liked it and ordered one on the spot, the kit to be delivered to my half acre. This house would sit high on a hill with a spectacular view of the San Fernando Valley. It would certainly be the most interesting house I ever lived in. My son Michael and I were watching the yellow John Deere dozer cut a slice out of my half-acre when I got a call from a secretary at DePatie Freleng Productions. When could I meet with Friz and Seuss.

When tall and stately Doctor Seuss, aka Ted Geisel, and very short and unimpressive Friz Freleng interviewed me for the possibility of being director on the next Grinch television special, I was forewarned. In spite of its enormous success I knew that Seuss hated How The Grinch Stole Christmas. Chuck Jones had been the director and being the great draftsman that he was, he could not help but "improve" Seuss's drawings. Seuss, being the great Prima donna that he was, hated what Chuck had done to his work. That slick Warner Brothers' look was not for the good Doctor. The next Grinch special would not be directed by Chuck Jones.

"Tell me, my boy," said Seuss," how do you see yourself as a director of the Grinch?"

"Well Ted, I see my role as one of putting your drawings on the screen exactly as you draw them."

So I signed a contract to direct Halloween Is Grinch Night and the studio won an Emmy for a prime-time special.   Boris Karloff, the voice of the first Grinch, had died and we had to find another. Several actors tried out for the part, including that pompous singer with the deep, booming voice, "You're a mean one, Mister Grinch . . . " A friend of the doctor's, no doubt. The only actor that came close to Karloff was Hans Conreid, in my opinion better than Karloff, less of a ham and not quite so evil. Hans had a long and distinguished career on radio, the Broadway stage, movies and television and I knew him as Snidely Whiplash when I was directing and animating Dudley Do-right episodes.

Conrad and I were rehearsing his lines. They demanded a lot of energy and he was tired. He told me this was the first gig he'd done in over a year. No one in Hollywood would give him a part for no particular reason except that the new young hot shots thought he was old hat. In Hollywood being old is not good. He told me, sadly, he had to do road shows just to make ends meet and support his good wife. It is a cruel town.

I directed a second TV Special for Seuss, Pontoffel Pock Where Are You? It was not one of his better stories. I think he wrote it to fulfill a contractual obligation with ABC. As with the Halloween Grinch, this would be a David Depatie-Friz Freling production. The songs by Joe Raposo were particularly good.

One afternoon Friz dropped by the large room wherein I worked to take a look at the storyboard's progress. The storyboard, hundreds of drawings, was covering the walls. There was a sequence where a group was singing.

"Where's the orchestra?" said Fritz.

"The what?"

"You can't have people singing and not see an orchestra."

I thought to myself this guy is becoming senile. He's slipping back into those old black and white musical films of the thirties. They always had an orchestra.

"Put in an orchestra. You can't have songs without an orchestra." Friz left and went on a long cruise with Seuss. I did not add an orchestra and on his return he didn't seem to miss it, so I guess his mind returned to the present.

My deal with the studio was one third up front, one third on the completion of the storyboard, and one third when the picture was finished, by a certain date. When that date arrived the Special was far from complete, the reason being that Friz had taken my animation crew and assigned them to another show. On the due date I expected my final payment and assumed they would put me on a weekly salary until the film was done. "Oh no….you don't get paid until you finish….that's the deal!"

"That is NOT the deal! I want a weekly salary until it's finished plus my final payment upon completion." Dr. Seuss, oblivious in La Jolla, was not aware of this conflict. I called my attorney. Am I right? Yes, you are.

I cleaned off my desk and took all of my directorial material home. They could damn well get somebody else! A Thursday and a Friday and a week-end passed. Seuss called me at home.

"My boy, what's the problem?"   I explained.

Sans Seuss we had a meeting at the studio composed of the studio production manager, David DePatie, Friz Freling and myself. Friz, happily innocent, offered, "Well here we are, experts in communication, and we have this terrible misunderstanding."

BS!

Once or twice a week, while we were in production, Seuss would fly up from his home in La Jolla. I would pick him up in the morning at the Hollywood-Burbank airport and take him to the studio. We would work all day getting his signed approvals of storyboards, layouts, models, and color backgrounds without which we could not continue. The day was broken by a long and dull lunch with Friz always in attendance and always in command of the conversation, which always lacked any depth. Sometimes Friz and Seuss would talk about all the bores they had to dine with on their last cruise.

After a day of this tedium I would drive Seuss back to the airport, always early, so as not to miss the last flight to La Jolla. There was always time for a cocktail and a chat and I learned a lot about Doctor Seuss—his past, his politics and his Patricianism. I also learned, much to my surprise, that Ted didn't much care for children and had none of his own. The city of La Jolla always celebrated their most famous resident with news of his upcoming birthday and their most famous resident always made sure he was not at home when, carrying their favorite books, the little children came to call. Not all of his books are great, but there is no doubt in my mind that he was a man of genius. It was an honor to have worked with him. He died in 1991.

Besides Disney, the last place in the world I would ever think of looking for work was Hanna-Barbera, BUT there was one department at H&B where quality counted and was even exalted. This unit, independent of the rest of the plant, was run by a guy named Ross Sutherland. He had been the head salesman for John Sutherland Productions. He was also John's brother. Ross, from years of experience before joining H&B, knew all about pitching films to corporate sponsors, advertising agencies, school systems, federal agencies, the Army, the Navy, the Air Force and the Marines.

My first experience working at H&B was with Ross. Well, that's not exactly true. Many years before, when Hanna and Barbera were leasing space in the old Charlie Chaplain studio on La Brea Avenue, I had done some animation for them on a freelance basis. I worked on Quick Draw McGraw and Yogi Bear but I found it difficult to adapt to their restrictive formula and was soon gone. So in 1977 I went to work with Ross at Hanna-Barbera as a freelance idea man, writer and director. Ross taught me just about everything I ever knew about the business of pitching and producing animated films.

Even though we sometimes used the studio's famous characters, like Fred Flintstone or Yogi Bear, our films never got caught on the H&B assembly line. It was more like running a body-shop for customized cars. We made movies for oil companies, the Air Force, big banks, John Deere, the U.S. Chamber of Commerce (extolling the thinking of John Stewart Mill) and TV spots for Ocean Spray Cranberries and much more.

Soon I had a new role. Many of these companies frequently showed up with story concepts of their own, which were almost always seriously flawed and so it fell to me to be the story doctor. Much of the writing, from pitching a premise to writing the final script, was mine to do.

A Washington think tank decided it was time to explain the oil crisis and the need for conservation to the American people. They would do this via a prime time television special. The Center for Strategic and International Studies would provide all of the technical data and the research that would compose the content of the project. The King Feisal Foundation would provide the money. The form that this show would take was to be decided by a retired U.S. Navy Captain who was also a consultant to the Saudi Royal Family. The Saudis were also interested in conservation, wanting their oil revenues to last as long as possible. The Captain, whose name I cannot remember, was a Fred Flintstone fan and thought Fred would make the perfect spokesman to speak to the American people about oil and its relationship to our use of energy.

The Center for Strategic and International Studies provided me with a two-foot tall stack of very dry information concerning world oil reserves, current and future consumption, and price predictions. The key to understanding this mound of information was labeled M.B.O.D. -- which stands for Millions of Barrels of Oil per Day consumed. M.B.O.D. Great. I'll write a song about that. Hoyt Curtin, the studio's music director, put my lyrics to music.

Ross and I went to Washington and the Center helped me understand the numbers and what it all meant. We visited Jack Valenti and he promised, since this was a worthy project, to help us with public relations and distribution of the TV special which did not yet exist, just MBOD. Ross felt we needed more than Fred Flintstone. We needed a narrator who could deliver the straight talk while Fred provided the entertainment, a narrator with a great voice, but also a movie star that could attract a larger audience, someone beyond Fred's appeal. I began writing a script and developing a storyboard that would translate MBOD into entertainment.   As yet we had no contract and Ross was gambling the sale would finalize. Script and storyboard completed we now had to present it to the good Captain, who, very busy, was always off to somewhere. We could intercept him in Dallas at a tarmac hotel where we would have one evening to present the concept and the morning to talk about business.

After dinner the Captain took us up to a Top of the World lounge where a rock band was playing. We sat at the back so we could hear ourselves talk. The band kept rocking as I read the script, played all the parts and sang all the songs. The Captain nodded, "Yes, yes, yes I like it fine. Good job." He went to bed early and Ross and I had a couple more drinks. Whew.

At breakfast with the Captain, Ross pulled a budget figure out of the air, just like that. How much? I thought it was a staggering sum for a one half hour animated television special. The captain said, "Okay," just like that. Cash to be deposited into Hanna-Barbera's account designated for the production of ENERGY: THE NATIONAL ISSUE.

Concurrently Ross had sent the storyboard to Charlton Heston. He also liked the project and would do the narration, not more than an hour's work, for $10,000, the money to be donated to his favorite charity.

Alan Reed was the voice of Fred Flintstone and in the recording studio, as we went over my script, I began to offer input with respect to the inflection of certain words and the meaning behind some of the dialogue. He cut me off with a glare: "Listen, kid. I AM Fred Flintstone!"

I shut up.

Actually there were two Fred Flintstones. Alan Reed couldn't sing so, at a separate session, we called in Henry Corden. He always sang Fred and eventually when Reed died, Henry became Fred Flintstone. He was a super pro and held no delusions about who HE was.

On the morning Charlton Heston was to record his lines, there was noticeable excitement in the studio. Ross hired a still photographer. Moses was coming! The Hanna-Barbera cartoon factory was not a place where you expected to see a real genuine Super Star. Some of the ladies went a bit ga-ga.

Charlton Heston took his recording script and stepped up to the microphone. The engineer said. "This is Energy-take one." Heston then proceeded to read his many, many lines in one long and perfect take. I couldn't quite believe it. Later that afternoon his agent called me. "Chuck" wanted me to know that prior to that reading he had not even read the script. Great Actor! Big Ego!

During the week that president Carter delivered his TV address on the oil embargo, our energy picture was seen by 40 million Americans.

Chapter 13

By the mid seventies the cartoon business in which Tex Avery had flowered was gone. TV production, almost all of it reduced to formula, had no room or patience for a creative genius like Tex. Follow the script! No surprises! He tried doing commercials. Too restrictive. Very few appreciated his enormous contribution to the Art of Animation. Avery's brilliant graphic invention showed possibilities not perceived before. He was past his prime and in early senescence when Joe Barbera and Bill Hanna hired him as a gagman, his job to wander about the studio and look for stories that could use a gag or two. It was very nice of them. He didn't plug in many gags. Ours was only a nodding acquaintance.

One day I was recording a Fruity Pebbles commercial starring Fred Flintstone, Reed, and Barney Rubble, Mel Blanc. Mel would not give up. He was hooked up to some kind of a machine that fed him oxygen. He had no energy left in his being and surely there was none in his voice. It was decided he would finish recording his lines at his recording studio at home in Beverly Hills. This may well have been his last recording. Seated in the semi-dark control booth was a recording engineer, myself, and a couple of Ogilvy-Mather people—an account executive and a copywriter trying to squeeze her one-hour story into 28 seconds.

Somewhere into the second hour I became aware that someone else had slipped into the room and was standing behind me. It was Tex Avery.

"Okay let's have a ten minute break." Everyone left except Tex. He spoke softly, "Hey kid, just who are you, anyway?"

"Oh, hi Tex. Well, Howard Baldwin is my oldest brother and you used to go to the fights with Dot and George Cannata; she's my sister, and Cal Howard is my nephew's godfather and Rudy Zamora is my niece's godfather and I'm Gerard Baldwin the younger."

His hand barely touched my shoulder as he turned to leave, as if to reassure, to give me his imprimatur: "Well, then it's ok, kid."

A few days later Tex collapsed at the studio. An ambulance was called. Tex pleaded to someone "...please don't send me to a hospital - I'll never come back."

And he never did.

Although I usually worked at home there was many a day when it was necessary to be in the studio and then, at the darkening of the day, it became customary for Ross and I to wander into Bill Hanna's office and have a glass of wine or two or three from his well-stocked bar.

On one of these late afternoons, as the studios fourteen hundred cartoonists inched out of the parking lot, we dropped in on Bill to wish him a happy birthday.

Ross offered that now he could collect Social Security. Hanna expressed a genuine conflict about taking any S.S. money. He would feel guilty -- some people had so little and he had so much. Ross argued seriously, "Bill, what are you talking about? They've been taking a bite out of your checks all these many years! That's your money." Bill, equally serious, pulled on his ear. "I suppose your right and I guess it would help with the upkeep on the yacht."

I've been teaching a class in drawing at Kingwood College for the past eleven years and students frequently ask me, "How did you get to be a producer of animated cartoons?" What they are asking of course is how do I get to be a producer? There is no standard qualification, but most animation producers come from backgrounds with experience as animators, directors and writers. Once in a while someone is simply anointed but that is rare.

Bill Hanna and Joe Barbera were the directors of Tom & Jerry at MGM. Ross Sutherland's background was in sales. Convincing U.S. Steel they need a movie about the history of man's use of metal is no easy task.

Ross was in Detroit pitching an idea to General Motors and getting a great "deal" on his new Cadillac. It was a Friday. It was getting dark. Alone, I dropped by Hanna's office for a glass of Chardonnay. I had just wrapped up a film for Shell about how an oil refinery works and needed something to do.

"Not much going on around town. Ross says things are slow. Anything coming up?"

"How about producing?"

"I've never been a producer."

"Now you're a producer. On Monday morning there will be a meeting at ten and Gerard, please don't saunter in."

Production meetings were usually held on a Monday morning, in a thickly carpeted conference room at a very long highly polished ten thousand dollar table that could easily accommodate fifteen or more people. Bill Hanna sat at the head. His secretary, Ginger, sat beside but slightly back, as if she knew her place in this hierarchy of the largest animation studio in the world. This gathering was a mix of line producers, production managers and department heads. I thought it odd there were no directors. The talk was always about production schedules, deadlines, costs and pressure. There was pressure to produce more and more, faster and faster, for less and less. As the meeting droned on, some of us, those that could draw, would doodle or make sketches of each other. The problems were serious, but this was not West Point.

I was assigned two shows -- Herculoids for CBS and The Best of Superfriends, for ABC. The line producer had nothing to do with anything that was really creative. My main job was to see that the scripts were not too long. It was okay if a script was too short, you could always add an insert, but Hanna hated shooting footage and then throwing it away. Using a film meter, which is just a stop watch, and reading the script aloud, playing all the parts and using your own voice for music and sound effects, you could come pretty close to length, within a second or two. I might enact a scene three or four times and choose the average.

"Superman, look out!" Deeedeee da taa taaaaaaaaa BOOM ... BOOM...BOOM...Ka-RASH

"Whew! That was a close one, Superman." (9 seconds)

The producers did not do this. They just counted script pages. Somewhere between 40 and 47 pages would be just about right for a 25 -minute episode. This approach was almost never accurate.

After a script was storyboarded, it was the producer's job to go over it in detail with the network executive, always a female Vice President in charge of children's programming. They were picky and correctly so. It was their money. But they were also somewhat helpless as there was never enough time. I would attend to their concerns by changing the storyboard, covering it with little drawings, directorial notes, timing notes, inserting new scenes where needed and finally, with the Execs approval, I would send it into production. Many weeks later when the network V.P. next saw the episode, it was on film and good or bad, nothing could be done. Air time -- FINISHED!

My efforts at improving the quality of the company's product did not endear me to board sluggers, sheet timers, production managers, and other functionaries down the line. My input was crowding their space. I was interfering with their freedom to do as little as possible. My effort made their jobs more difficult. Many of them didn't give a damn about making good films. The pervasive attitude was "it's all shit anyway" and, of course, there was some truth in that. They were tired and cynical. They complained to Hanna about the changes I was making.

The network executives, on the other hand, were very pleased. They could see that someone was trying to make their shows better. They also spoke to Hanna.

At the peak of a production season there was so much work to be done in so little time that just about any 25-cent sub-contractor could pick up an episode. Some of their films were atrocious and standing at a Movieola, I found myself berating, "Hell. You guys are concerned about run-away production, but this stuff is not as good as what we get back from Taiwan and they're just learning."

Much of the work continued to be poor. Even after band- aids it would be embarrassing to screen an episode with a network VP. They would give a look and the look said, "How can you even show this to me?"

"I'll fix it…"

But you couldn't fix everything. The episodes had to air on time. The biggest sin of all was missing an air date. The next biggest sin, in my opinion, was the poor quality of the studio's product. The cause of these gigantic log jams and the inability to do good work could be traced back to the big three—ABC, CBS and NBC—who never made up their minds about what shows to buy or when to start production until much of the time needed to produce a decent product was already expended in indecision.

With little pride in what I was doing, I was coming to the decision that maybe it was time to leave Saturday morning and find something else.

I can't say I ever got to know Joe Barbera or Bill Hanna very well. I can't say I even remember their corporate titles but Joe was #1 and Bill was #2. Why? Perhaps when they first formed the corporation and offered shares the board of directors, one being big time director George Sydney, simply voted Joe top dog.

Joe's office was much bigger than Bill's and might be described as a suite. There was a large bathroom, a conference room and a large well-appointed waiting room. Glass cases displayed all of their Oscars, Emmys, Gold records and Honorariums. A loud fading red head was Joe's secretary and defensive guard.

Bill's office, although still quite large was more modest, but it too had a private bathroom. Ginger, Bill's secretary, was nothing like her name implied. She was rather motherly and soft spoken.

I guess I related more to Hanna than to Barbera. Bill's job was to keep the assembly line moving and not exceed budget while Joe, it seemed, was always off somewhere creating and pitching new shows and was rarely involved in the daily drudgery.

Did I really know these guys? No. Our conversations were almost always about animation, Network concerns and production problems. They were older than me and had family and friends that went way back to MGM and Tom & Jerry. I think Joe saw himself as the creative force behind the studio and I sensed Bill Hanna resented this assumption.

Bill frequently ate lunch at the old Smokehouse restaurant across the street from Warner Bros. The Smokehouse was, and still is, I presume, a very good typically American establishment serving prime rib, good steaks, fish and chips, a large menu with no surprises. Starting at the cocktail hour, a piano offered favorites into the night. Lunch with Bill was always about production schedules, delivery dates, flow charts and budgets.

At the peak of a production season and over a weekend Bill would invite all of the line producers, board sluggers, sheet timers and assorted helpers aboard his yacht for a big party. This was an all male event. Of course the guests brought along animation work to be done—work first— then party. Bill did the cooking. I was never invited, nor would I have gone. I think Bill knew that I, as a former President of the Screen Cartoonists Guild, saw these "parties" as a form of labor exploitation. We never talked politics.

He had a reputation of being a real tough Ogre. Fax machines were new and when they first came out, very expensive.

"Bill, we need a Fax machine."

"How much?"

"Five thousand."

"No."

"You're flying drawings to Taiwan every day. That's time. That's money."

The Fax machine finally won.

One late afternoon when I was in the office with Bill, Ginger announced great animator Irv Spence (Jerry dancing with Gene Kelly) would like to see him. Sure, send him in.

"Bill, I need a raise."

"No you don't"

"I don't?"

"No."

"Oh."

Moral: Never ask for a raise unless you are prepared to quit if the answer is no.

Returning to my office from a long lunch, I would frequently shut the door, lay down on the floor, and hypnotize myself to sleep. During one nap I recall hearing the door open just a bit, and half-opened one eye to see Bill Hanna. I started to jump up as he crossed the room.

"Don't get up. Don't get up." He leaned down over my prone body and proffered a page of a storyboard over my face.

"Do you mean scene 372A to be inserted before or after scene 372? Not clear."

"...Oh. Yeah. Before."

"OK."

He walked back to the door and as he closed the door, glanced back at my still prone body.

"Feels good doesn't it?" Some Ogre.

But he could also be extremely forceful. After listening to Bill deliver a long list of "must happen," I replied, "Well Bill, I'll do my best."

"NO! That's not good enough!"

For many years the Hanna-Barbera studios had a near monopoly on the production of animated films made for television. The three networks, ABC, CBS and NBC, had a near monopoly on all television entertainment produced for children. TV had a huge appetite. There was little time for creativity and even less for quality.

Design and manufacture a television set and an assembly line can produce one million sets that, at the end of the line, will all work and be of acceptable quality. Design and produce a television show for kids and the assembly line can never guarantee or even anticipate what will come out at the end. There are too many variables. Joe Barbera saw himself as the studio's creative genius while Bill Hanna figured out, as best anybody could, how to run a cartoon factory.

The screen cartoonists union had a minimum pay scale for directors. The key to any film is the director, but there were no directors, as such, at H&B. Once a network approved a script, it was turned over to a producer (me) who turned it over to a storyboard artist who turned his work over to a board timer who turned it over... SO, nobody was a director and the producer had the final cut. None of these people had the credit "directed by" but rather some ignominious title like "sheet timer" or, and this one I really love, "board slugger." By splitting the director's role into its component parts and avoiding the word "director," the studio saved money. For a creative and talented artist to refer to himself as a "board slugger" must have been humiliating. They got used to it. Usually creative people with robotic jobs are not too happy and the paradox of doing more and more with less and less created an invisible anxiety that infected the studio. This method of turning out miles and miles of animated film was Bill Hanna's idea and it worked. All television animation studios were soon using the same system. The only trouble was that, sometimes, what came on the screen was enough to make a sensitive animator throw up.

In 1998 Warner Bros published a big over-priced hard cover book titled "Hanna-Barbera Cartoons.[2] This book tells the reader very little about Bill and Joe. Its sole purpose is to coin money. It is a catalogue of animation cells, none of them original and, therefore, all of them fake. Not a one of these cells was ever under a camera! The book offers no insight into these once famous, now fading, personalities. On page nine Barbera offers: "People sometimes ask me how Bill Hanna and I managed to work together for more than fifty years without fighting. My answer is always the same. "We did fight…the first week…and we haven't spoken since."

Joe was not invited to attend Bill's funeral service.

Quite often Joe Barbara ate lunch at an elegant Italian restaurant in old Hollywood. Unlike the Smokehouse, this place had a quiet elegance enhanced by a sparkling fountain. The Maitre d' always greeted Mr. Barbera as if he were a Prince of the Medici, a role Joe accepted with grace. After a couple of glasses of quality Chianti, lunch with Joe was always about ideas, concepts and imagination.

After one long lunch, Joe was driving us back to the studio when, somehow, the subject of an heir apparent came up. Joe turned ashen. Death? Retire? They never did. Even after the bean counters took over "their" studio, they went to work every day. Neither one of them seemed to have a life beyond cartoons. In a Jungian sense they were the thing they did. From my observation they were not much more than that. But I may misjudge.

In 1964 Joe Barbera said: "The days of showing little elves playing around a mushroom are gone forever."

In 1980, out of the blue, came The Smurfs.

Chapter 14

Saturday morning children's programming on the NBC television network was not doing well. For whatever reason, kids were not watching NBC. The Neilson ratings were so low the network was considering making a big, big change, dropping children's programming altogether and replacing it with news. That was the rumor. Someone else was also making a big change. Fred Silverman, NBC CEO, was resigning. I heard he was bored. I don't know how anyone could run a television network and be bored. Maybe he just needed a change. Legend has it his daughter returned from a trip to Europe and presented daddy with a couple of little blue figurines. Silverman was soon looking at Smurf hard-cover comic books. They were selling well in Europe but unknown in the United States. He thought the books could be the basis for a great show. Before leaving NBC he made a deal with the creator of The Smurfs, pen name Peyo. He also made a deal with Hanna-Barbera. Done.

Margaret Loesch was Hanna Barbera's Executive Vice President for network affairs. Prominent in her home was a large and imposing portrait of her father, who, at one time, had been the youngest General in the United States Air Force. Margaret had inherited all of those qualities one needs to be a General and she was a good one. She managed people, including me, very well. I don't know why she chose me to be the guardian of The Smurfs, perhaps I got good grades from the networks, or perhaps I let it be known I wasn't too happy working on hopelessly idiotic films that were empty of any meaningful content. I recall her introducing me to someone: "Gerard comes to us from Bullwinkle." To me, that was odd. Why not, "He comes to us from Dr. Seuss."

Many years would pass before I realized that "everything Bullwinkle" had become a cult with a large U.S. following numbering in the hundreds of thousands. As the children of the early 1980s mature, now in their thirties, so too will the Smurfs take on a cult-like status; only these happy memories, worldwide, will number in the millions.

I always felt, during my first season producing The Smurfs, that Margaret Loesch was my protector and guide. She seemed all business and motherly at the same time. If I had to go to the airport and welcome Peyo or go out to dinner with someone in product licensing, she would always advise, "Don't drive, Gerard. Feel free to take a limo anytime. That's what they're

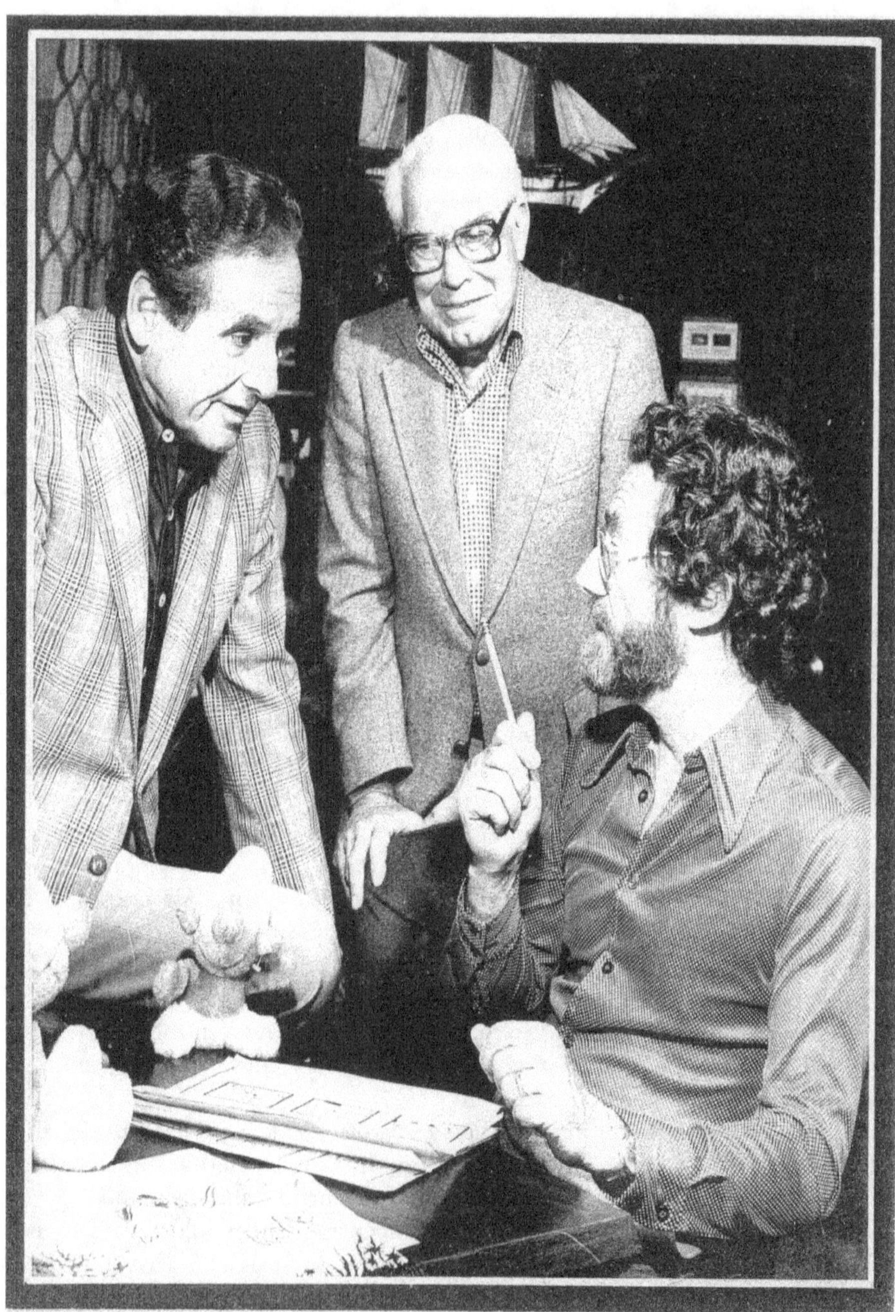

for." Bill Hanna would never have said that.

The people at children's programming in New York were not happy with Silverman's decision to air Smurfs. They were not the least bit enthused about the Smurfs. They were too soft, too wordy, too old fashioned: "I mean come ON! The Middle Ages?"

Mickey Dwyer, a woman in her fifties was the NBC Vice President of children's programming. H&B sent a delegation to N.Y. to meet with her and discuss the show and, of course, for her to meet and become acquainted with its producer.

Since the concept was something "new," she would need to see a pilot film and test it. I liked Mickey and thought she was an okay gal even if she did have grave doubts about the appeal of the Smurfs. All I was certain of was that the Smurfs were charming and unlike any of the Slam Bam stuff, like Superfriends, that was being fed to America's children. The folks at NBC were totally convinced the Smurfs had no appeal.

Back in Los Angeles I made a pilot film about six minutes long. I felt the same way about Peyo's Smurfs as I did about the good doctor's Grinch. In the translation from book to screen, nothing must change or become distorted. Peyo had complete creative control and this little film looked as if Peyo had drawn it himself. It was charming. On the assumption that to children, classical music would sound very old and thus help them enter the Middle Ages and believe that the stories were about a time long, long ago, I chose music by Beethoven and Vivaldi. At the first screening an NBC exec turned to me and asked: "Who did the music?"

"Vivaldi."

"Nice. Can we get him?"

Len Janson was the story editor on a Hanna-Barbera TV series, Space Ghost. He needed a secretary. An attractive young woman, by the name of Frances Novier accepted the job on the condition she could submit stories. Okay. She had ambition to be a writer. Len made her re-write her first one page premise five times. He made her re-write her five page outline five times and re-write the twelve page script for an eleven minute story five times. She finally sold her first Space Ghost story, but this guy was also doing his best to discourage her. He probably felt she had no talent. This very talented guy was also destined to be one of the two story editors for The Smurfs.

Peyo did not speak English. His writer, Yvan Delporte, spoke English very well. There would be many production meetings involving many people. Delporte spoke for Peyo, but did we REALLY know what

Peyo said? Delporte, in his own self-interest, might slant a translation and we would not know. We needed our own interpreter.

The odds of a young woman being born in Fort Worth, Texas and French being her first language are very slim. The odds of a young woman speaking perfect French and perfect English and being an aspiring writer who just happens to be working at the studio are even slimmer.

Tex Avery teased this attractive young woman with the long blond hair for being a clothes horse, and she was.

Frances Novier was now the "official" interpreter for the Smurf show and, in 1982, became Frances Novier Baldwin. Some folks thought, that at 53, I was a bit too old to begin a new family. Someone at NBC said I was trying to live twice. Alison was born in 1983. John was born in 1987. I love my four children and they love me -- most of the time.

As always, NBC tested the pilot on a focus group in New York and, much to their surprise, the pilot tested off their charts. If a pilot tests well and is still a flop the exec can always say, "Well, it tested ok." Children's programming gave a reluctant nod. The studio could proceed with production without any more input from the brains at NBC. BUT, I got a phone call from Mickey Dwyer. She grudgingly allowed that the pilot tested rather well, but there would be one change, the classical music would have to go!

"But why? That music reinforces the concept that the Smurfs live in the Middle Ages."

"NO. Got to go."

"I don't understand."

"Kids don't like classical music. They like Rock 'n Roll."

"But isn't it absurd to see a knight in armor on horseback and hear Rock 'n Roll?"

"Gerard, if you put ANY classical music on that show I'll break your arm!'

And she meant it. The Network is the ultimate boss. I was despondent until suddenly Mickey Dwyer, Vice President for children's programming, got fired! I don't know why. Perhaps the top Network brass saw her as responsible for their low Saturday morning ratings. As NBC searched for a new boss for children's programming, there was a short period of time when the kid department had nobody in charge. The studio already had an okay to proceed with production, so we recorded the entire musical library for the as yet unwritten episodes and pretty much spent the entire budget allowed for music, all classical.

From early storyboards we already knew that, more than once, we would see a line of happy Smurfs marching along as if on parade. Hoyt Curtin, the studio's music director, was having difficulty finding an old piece of classical music, just the right musical phrase and tempo that would express the "spirit" of the Smurfs. We were talking about it when, suddenly, I had a Eureka moment and offered how about...

LA LA♪
    LA LA LA LAAAAA♫
        ♪LA LA LA LA LA LAAAAA ♫   That was it! Too bad I don't own it.

Later, when ratings soared everybody was singing the LA LA LA song and the sale of little blue figurines topped hundreds of millions of dollars. The Smurfs was the most watched show on Saturday morning holding a 44 Nielson share, which means that 44 out of every 100 TV sets on Saturday morning were tuned to NBC. When Smurfs went from a half-hour show to a one-hour show to a one and a half hour show and kids stayed glued to their TV sets—when that happened—all of the NBC executives stood up and basked in their collective wisdom.

Joe Barbera said he thought the show was a hit because the Smurfs were blue. Odd. The Smurfs were a hit because the concept was great and the stories were good.

Although hundreds and hundreds of people are involved in the production of an animated television series only a few are key.

The creator of the Smurfs, Pierre Culliford (Peyo), and his writer, Yvan Delporte were a Yin and a Yang team, Delporte being the dark side. Peyo, looking out from under his large horn rimmed glasses, seemed open and happy, a family man. There was a time which his wife, Nine, referred to as the "old days" when the creation of comic strips was, indeed, a family project. His son did the inking. His wife did the coloring. I cannot recall the daughter's role but she had one. Peyo collected toy soldiers and the collection was elegant. The family lived in a lovely but unpretentious house in Brussels. The neighborhood was a mixture of private homes and apartment buildings that reminded me of the better parts of NYC in the 1930s. Someone told me Peyo was the second richest man in Belgium. I don't know if that was true, but in Switzerland his private elevator opened onto a most luxurious apartment. A movie art director could not have done a better job of conveying wealth. Although Peyo and his wife were very generous to Frances and my two little children, he also had a frugal side. I remember his first visit to Hollywood where he was to meet our two story editors that had been assigned to the series, Len Janson and Chuck Menville. Peyo asked me to take him to a liquor store where he carefully selected one bottle of moderately priced wine and then proceeded to offer it as a gift to the both of them. I don't think he was cheap, just innocent. He may well have been the most famous man in Belgium. The Belgian post office issued a stamp with a Smurf on it.

Yvan Delporte, Peyo's writer and interpreter was short, skinny, balding and brooding. He was an eccentric fellow and a bit rebellious for a man his age. At one Emmy banquet he wore some kind of a denim overall, black bow tie and white sneakers. I was told he'd had a son who committed suicide, which might explain his sometimes-dour disposition.

On Peyo's many trips to Los Angeles, he always brought his wife. When Delporte came to L.A., he always brought a secretary and always a different one. Delporte saw himself as the co-creator of the Smurfs and Peyo saw him as an employee…his writer. This was never resolved.

In 1984 Margaret Loesch left Hanna-Barbera to head up Marvel Productions and, without her shield, I was open to the snipers.

By the time NBC found a new VP to oversee children's programming, the Smurf show was well into production. Phyllis Tucker Vincent was a tall striking African American, new to her job and, at first, a bit unsure of herself. She got my admiration when she took me aside and asked me to help her play her part. Smart lady. Phyllis supervised not only The Smurfs but all other children's programming for the network; however, The Smurfs, being the most demanding, was also the most challenging. NBC had gone from the Saturday morning basement through the skylight. It was now number one and NBC wanted to keep it that way. Phyllis had to read and make input on every story premise, outline, script, storyboard, voice recording and finally, with a critical eye, view every foot of film. A difficult job. She was good at it and always listened. A 90-minute show might have three one-half hour stories and six ten-minute stories and each one had a beginning, a middle and an end. This was not soap opera writing and at the peak, staff and freelance, I am sure we had 14 writers working.

A student asked me recently how Lucille Bliss got to be Smurfette. I had never met Lucille. I only knew her from talking on the telephone as an aging actress looking for work. Sometimes her agent would call. I never had any work for her. Way back in 1949 Lucille was the voice of Crusader Rabbit, Jay Ward's first production and the first animated series made for television as well as the first show to use what later came to be called "limited animation," which means containing as little movement as humanly possible and as few drawings as possible.

The year 1949 seemed a hundred years in the past. I was still in art school and I'm not sure if I ever saw a Crusader Rabbit episode. Anyway, in 1981 I attended a large NBC Christmas party where I finally met Lucille. She was a petite old lady and her frilly white Alice-In-Wonderland dress was a bit girlish. I liked her.

"Anything coming up, Gerard?"

"As a matter of fact, yes. I'm going to do a show called The Smurfs. There are 100 Smurfs and only one is a girl, a young girl. Her name is Smurfette. Weird, eh? Your odds are terrible, but have your agent call me and I'll see you're there for the casting."

A good deed for Christmas, I thought.

On the day we were casting Smurfette, NBC executive types were crowded into the recording studio control booth. They were projecting their deep concern. The only thing more insecure than network brass is a doctor performing brain surgery for the first time.

The part was not an easy one. Smurfette, created by the evil wizard, Gargamel, enters the Smurf world as a bedraggled vamp.

"Do you like what you see?" she says.

And then, using HIS magic, Papa Smurf changes her into a sweet little blond. This sweet little blonde must survive in an all-male world. The Smurfs are male, but none of them had any Testosterone, so I guess Smurfette was quite safe.

We spent a good part of a day listening to female voice talent trying out for this one part. I don't know how actors can stand the constant rejection, but one after another actresses walked up to the microphone, glanced at a drawing of Smurfette and read the few lines we had prepared. Very late in the day in comes tiny Lucille Bliss in her dainty white dress, a lady of 60 trying to look 16. She reads the lines. We all gape and look at each other, eyes wide. It's HER! Lucille Bliss IS Smurfette. Think of it. She will soon be recording two or three episodes every week for five or more years with residuals in perpetuity and that is how Lucille Bliss, struggling actress, was, hopefully, very comfortable in her old age.

What Phyllis, the African American Vice President in charge of children's programming really wanted was a black Smurf.

My wife Frances, pen name Frances Novier, came up with a story that sort of satisfied the Vice President's desire.

Smurfette has never seen a blue rose nor has any other Smurf. Wouldn't a blue rose be the most beautiful flower in the world? Alas, there is no such thing nor can there be. A blue rose is impossible. Smurfette becomes obsessed with her desire to gaze upon a blue rose, even just once. Papa Smurf admonishes, "If Mother Nature had intended for roses to be blue she would have made one long ago. It's not a good idea to set your heart on something you cannot have."

Persistent Smurfette visits Mother Nature (June Foray) and the good lady succumbs to Smurfette's tearful plea and grants her wish. It is night and the moon is full when, standing before a beautiful white rose, Smurfette intones the Magic words:

"Oh Mother Nature, always right

I stand before this rose so white.

I've made my promise, my heart is true.

Delight my eyes with one rose -- Blue."

As the white rose turns blue, blue Smurfette, turns white. The Smurfs are shocked by her transformation. Shocked. Shocked. Shocked. She hates being white. Hates it. Hates it. Hates it.

Mother Nature breaks the rules again. Smurfette may have one more wish.

"Oh blue rose, blue rose, pity me.

Oh Mother Nature, hear my plea.

Like Sun, and moon, and evening star,

We each of us are what we are.

Please, Mother Nature, set me free.

Free of the promise I made to thee."

The blue rose dies and Smufette's white skin returns to blue. In a most roundabout way Phyllis got her wish.

Pre-production work on the Smurfs television series probably started in 1980 although the precise dates, to this historian, are not too important. What is important is that in the 23 years prior to the television premier of the show, Peyo had written, illustrated and published many hard-cover comic books and the Smurfs were only the latest in a rather long series and the most successful. These Smurf books numbered fifteen. At the studio our two story editors used up a near quarter century of Peyo's creativity in three weeks. Now it fell to our writing staff to come up with new Smurf stories at a prodigious rate. By 1982 it was a 90-minute show! This huge success brought much attention to anyone connected to its production and, as we entered the second season, our two story editors quit for opportunity elsewhere.

There was not one writer immersed enough in Smurfland to replace them except, of course, me. With the blessing of Margaret Loesch, I anointed myself Supervising Story Editor and with her further blessing found myself an associate producer and advanced to Supervising Producer. Heady stuff. We quickly broke in a new story editing team, but I remained supervising story editor until I walked away.

Frances, my wife, had submitted premise after premise after premise to the first two editors. Their response was always no, no, no. I thought her stories were pretty good but did not interfere for fear of being seen as nepotistic. It was a happy day for Frances when those two left. I submitted her story premises to NBC and most all were accepted—her stories were very good. "...Just what NBC was looking for." Ultimately she became a story editor. Busy times.

Animation being so labor intensive there was always a search for artists outside of Hollywood where wages were much lower. Bill Hanna found them in Taiwan. The Chinese learned very quickly and soon Cuckoo's Nest studio was doing most of the Smurf production, animation through camera. This was a company Hanna had nursed from a seedling to a first class production house and, in appreciation, at the studio in Taiwan, you were greeted in the lobby with a bronze bust of Bill.

James Wang, president of Cuckoo's Nest, wanted me to visit his studio and see how it functioned and thus solve some serious communication problems, which were considerable. Our man in Taipei, Peter Aries, was doing an excellent job and he too thought I should visit and see how the place worked.

Hanna, being the short-sighted cheapy he could be, did not want me to go on the grounds that I was needed at the studio. But actually he didn't want to spend the money. Finally James Wang paid for my visit. It was First Class all the way.

Soon after General Chiang Kai-shek and his army fled the mainland to escape the Communist juggernaut and settled on the island of Formosa, Madame Chiang Kai-shek ordered the design and construction of The Rice House On The Mountain. This hotel is a huge grand palace located outside of the city and stands atop a high hill surrounded by a lovely park. It overlooks the city of Taipei, which was not only the capital of Taiwan but the magnet for all cultural and business activity on the island. The hotels original purpose was to welcome and impress visiting businessmen and dignitaries, but these days it was not very busy because most of the travelers preferred the downtown Hiltons.   The hotel's lobby was awe inspiring and made me feel like I was an actor in a DeMille film about a Chinese version of ancient Rome.

After the long flight and that first day of familiarizing myself with the workings of the Cuckoo's Nest, I was very tired. As the sun was going down a taxi dropped me off at the Rice House On The Mountain.   I remember clearly standing on my balcony having a last gin and tonic and gazing out over the city. Far away and below I could see men fishing in the river, a black river. The phone rang. It was Frances. My sister, Dolores, had died. Oh. She is 9000 miles and twenty-one hours away and I just got here. There is no way I can make that service. Oh well, there are sure to be many more deaths and many more services to come. I'll make the next one.

Peter Aries had married a Chinese woman. His mother-in-law was involved, in some way, with a Buddhist Nunnery. Their monastery was perched high up on the side of a steep crag. I was invited, as an honored guest, to join the nuns for Sunday supper. The monastery could not be reached by car so, leaving it far below, Peter and I scrambled up the rocky escarpment and, a bit breathless, were greeted by the Head Mother. As the nuns performed their Sunday service, I was allowed to sit, Lotus position, at the door of the Temple and contemplate a prayer wheel. Its hypnotic effect was reinforced by the tintinnabulation of melancholy bells and I thought a lot about my sister and of the service I had not attended.

In the second, third and fourth Smurf seasons we needed at least six stories for a 90 minute show plus the scripting of 5 prime-time specials. Linearly, that's a feature a week. The procedure for creating a story worked like this: Every story premise was translated into French and faxed to Peyo and Yvan Delporte. Their input, in French, was faxed to Hollywood and translated into English. This premise would then be sent to NBC. With the network's okay the premise would be expanded into an outline of perhaps ten pages -- translated into French -- faxed to Brussels -- comments returned in French -- translated into English and then forwarded to NBC. With their nod the outline would morph into a script of 40 or more pages which would then be translated into French and sent to Peyo -- his comments returned in French -- translated into English -- and then sent to the network for an okay to proceed with recording. More often than not there would be a second and third draft. This plan did not always work as it was supposed to.

Sergeant-Major John Novier, retired, and his charming wife, Madeleine, took on the near overwhelming job of not only translating, but interpreting all of these many, many stories. They lived in Texas. Literal translations have no poetry. A joke in English may be totally flat in French and vice-versa. Nuance is everything. Wherever their origination, all words moved through a triangle: Hollywood—Texas—Brussels—or Brussels—Texas –Hollywood and when Taiwan, a sub-contractor, became involved this pathway evolved into a quadrangle. John was a Frenchman and got this role not because he was my wife's father, although it didn't hurt, but because at the close of World War II he had been an interpreter for the advancing American army and a translator of some highly technical books coming out of the Albert Einstein College of Medicine in New York

Imagine an assembly line with over a thousand people all being paid, but they have nothing to do because they are waiting for a story. Very expensive. The show must go on air, on time, no matter what. More than once a script would be put on the conveyor belt before Peyo ever saw the final. This would really anger him and he'd throw a tantrum resulting in the arrival of a long, sometimes angry, diatribe concerning our failings with respect to holding onto the Smurfy concept -- Smurf characters out of character -- story ideas he didn't like -- a long, long list of faults and cautions -- thirty or forty points to be addressed NOW!

Poor Peyo, far away in Brussels, could only be reactive to the onslaught of stories. Although he had complete creative control, he understood television's gaping maw and was usually cooperative and helpful. Only rarely did he angrily stiffen in defense of his concept. Nothing could be injected into the show that was not Smurfy. Nothing, at least not for the first three years.

I don't remember what betrayal of Smurfiness caused Peyo to demand an immediate audience, but you cannot say no to the King of the Smurfs. Since, contractually, Peyo had total control, his intense concerns had to be placated. Thus, at great expense of money and time, five people schlepped to Switzerland.

June 13, 1985   Lusanne, Switzerland

Meeting with Peyo. Present at the meeting…..

Peyo - His Majesty

Bill Hanna - An ambassador from far away

Alvin Furleger - The studio's agent

Jean Macurdy - Deeply concerned for NBC

Frances Novier - My wife and trusted interpreter

And Yours Truly - Supervising Producer, Story Editor and Director.

We met for a full day in some hotel conference room that the King had rented for this event. Everyone took notes and there was no end to nodding and smiling and agreeing and paying obeisance to the King. I thought it interesting that Delporte wasn't present.

The next day we left.

What I learned about the Swiss: On the return trip, at the airport, I was looking out through a glass wall and watching a large sweeper cleaning the tarmac. Suddenly it stopped. The driver glanced back. Oh No! One cigarette butt had escaped! The driver backed up about 50 feet to pick it up. Whew! A close call.

Frances and I flew home with Bill Hanna. Everybody, it seemed, knew those two words—Hanna-Barbera—stood for animated cartoons and that animated cartoons stood for America and apple pie. When we arrived in New York the customs agent said, "Hello, Mr. Hanna, welcome home." And he waved us by without even a glance at our luggage.

Chapter 15

The hallway that led to Joe Barbera's office was long, wide, richly carpeted and lined with mediocre paintings that no one ever looked at. At the far end of this hall, resting on an ornate stand was one of those big old leather-bound Webster's that no one ever looked at.

As a story editor I would be looking to find and define the absolutely perfect word to scribble on some young writer's first draft of a Smurf script. It was on one of these walks down the long hallway that Joe Barbera came round the bend dressed in his usual Hollywood version of sartorial splendor. Elegant loafers met cowboy boots. Although there were just the two of us he spoke quietly as if not to be overheard, "Gerard, be careful. You know that Jerry Fallwell has declared the Smurfs to be the work of Satan and a bad influence on children."

"Yeah, I heard that too. As Papa Smurf would say, 'Amazing!'"

"Lunch tomorrow?"

"Great."

The need for more and more scripts was so demanding that sometimes Frances and I would write a 22-minute story over a weekend. It was on one of these working weekends in 1984 that we would write The Moor's Baby.

It was against Hanna-Barbera policy to use the word GOD on children's programming. We didn't know.

'Twas the Middle Ages when the Moor, with his entourage of camels, guards, wife and little baby decided to set up his tents not far from the Smurf village. He doesn't know about the Smurfs. While the Arab is teaching algebra to Omnibus, two bad guys kidnap his baby. All the Smurfs are soon involved in the search and rescue. When the Arab Prince finally has his baby back, he hugs it close and says, with great feeling, "Oh thank you God!" as just about anyone would in a similar situation.

NBC had given the script its okay as had their department of program standards and practices.

I arrived at the recording session for this story quite late, just as the actors were doing the last few pick-up lines. Perusing the recording script I noticed "Oh thank you, God!" had been crossed out.

"How come?" I asked, and the reply was, "We don't say God on children's TV."

"How come?"

"Company Policy."

"That's pretty stupid."

"Company policy. Joe Barbera's policy."

"Look. I'm the producer and it's my script, so just record it anyway. I'll be responsible."

A quick check with Jayne, the studio production manager, who just happened to be Joe's daughter. She was not motherly.

"We don't' say God on children's programming. That's Joe's policy."

"That's ridiculous."

"No God. That's it!"

I called NBC. Did the VP have a problem? No. Did standard and practices have a problem? No.

Back to Jayne.

"It's okay with the network. In fact they think the line is most appropriate and just fine.

"No God."

"Well, I guess my next step is to call Jerry Fallwell and all hell will fall upon this company."

The line stayed in. I'm sure Joe Barbera heard about this trivial incident, but he never said a word. An interesting thing about this story is that it is a fine example of television's far reach. The following letter was forwarded to me that same year. It was from the American-Arab Anti-Discrimination Committee, Washington D.C.

Ms. Betty Hoffman, Vice President NBC
30 Rockefeller Plaza
New York, NY 10020

Dear Ms. Hoffman

We have received several calls about a recent cartoon featuring an Arab Prince on the Smurfs (April 21, 1984). On behalf of the staff and membership of the American-Anti-Discrimination Committee, I want to congratulate NBC for introducing a positive Arab character on Saturday morning cartoons.

Remarks we received from our members indicate that the introduction of the character was done tastefully and in a sophisticated manner. Callers especially appreciated the fact that the character was regarded as kind and loving toward a family member and willing to help in a crises. In addition, in an apparent attempt to free a fairy, he used an algebraic formula. This is, of course, a gesture indicating one of the most important contributions of the Arab world to culture and science.

It sounds very good and I thought that you would appreciate hearing from us. My best wishes to all involved in the production of this fine cartoon. Keep up the good work.

Sincerely
James Zogby
Executive Director.

At one point there were 1400 people working on the show and another number in Taiwan. For me, it was a relentless, usually seven days a week grind. As for Bill Hanna and Joe Barbera, it was their studio, but they stayed out of Smurf's way. Bill gave me access to the computer read outs and I could track every nickel including his.

I first heard the expression "He's a character" from my brother Howard and his friend, New Yorker cartoonist, Sam Cobean. They both used this descriptive frequently as did a lot of people from Hollywood, a place overflowing with "character" actors, though I doubt that this is the origin of the expression. "He (or she) is a character!" was applied freely and often to anyone who was somehow unique or eccentric or cast from a mold with a crack in it.

I can only think of one person involved in The Smurfs to which this descriptive was apt: Freddy Monnickendam was a character! He was a Belgian businessman, the head of Sepp, a branch of Dupuis and responsible for merchandising everything Smurfy. Merchandising is where the big BIG money is. It was Freddy who negotiated the contract between Dupuis, Peyo, NBC, and Hanna-Barbera and he had a screen credit as Executive Producer along with Joe and Bill.

Freddy was tall, graying and imposing in his $3000 suits and was never without a white limousine standing by. When it came to spending money he was extravagant. The artists at the studio referred to him as "Freddy Moneygodamn."

I don't remember what we had to talk about, but always pressed for time, Freddy could only give me 45 minutes for a speedy lunch. Reuben's restaurant was one block down the street from the studio and, naturally, we took the ever-waiting white limo. As we ordered a couple of burgers with onion rings, Freddy told the waitress he'd give her a big tip if she could hurry them along. She did, and after he paid the bill and we rose to leave, Freddy

Moneygodamn dropped a $100 bill on the table.

A serious conflict arose between Peyo and Freddy Monnickendam about the division of rights and the distribution of money. Freddy had access to lots of it. Annoyed with the legal haggling over The Smurfs he decided to create a TV series of his own. The first thing he had to do was introduce himself to CBS, NBC and ABC so he threw himself a big birthday party and invited a few hundred TV folks. If you needed a ride he'd send a limo. Freddy gave a speech and toasted his wonderfulness. A small choir sang the happy birthday song as Freddy cut his cake…and ate it too.

Since NBC had the highest Saturday morning Nielson rating, it was the logical place for Freddy to pedal his Snorks and soon NBC was seriously considering commissioning the series. The deal was pretty close and would be even closer if I would agree to be the producer. Being responsible for one and a half hours a week was a huge work-load and adding The Snorks would increase it to two hours.

My ego won out over common sense and I agreed. At first it was like being a test pilot about to break the Smurf barrier. I have often wondered if Freddy's lavish expenditures and access to Swiss bank accounts helped the sale.

The Snorks were little creatures just like the Smurfs, but they were multi-colored, lived on the floor of the ocean and survived there because they had snorkels growing out of the tops of their heads. How or why these snorkels worked was never explained. Other than their location and weird anatomy, the Snork show was just another family situation - action — adventure - comedy for children, although I didn't think it was very comedic.

One day Freddy had to see me "right away!" to show me the new Snork figurines that would soon be distributed to every potential market in the country and, Freddy hoped, the world. Frances and I must meet him for dinner. He sent a white limo to pick us up. His white limo was already there when we arrived at L'Orangerie. Freddy spread a line of Snorks across our table and we spent a couple of hours in serious conversation about Snorks. The wine was great but I dawdled over my duck breast, which was much too rare for a Yankee.

I anointed a young protégé, Larry Latham, to become Associate Producer on the Snork show and he carried a lot of the load. The under water effects would be accomplished by panning a "ripple" glass or "distortion" glass between the camera lens and the animation giving the scenes a kind of waviness. This was time consuming and therefore expensive, so the studio dropped the under-water effects after the first season. I wasn't very happy about that. This kind of cost cutting was going to destroy any chance the Snorks had of surviving. I declined producing the second season and sure enough, the ratings dropped and The Snorks were soon gone.

At a Smurf recording session there was always a cast of wonderfully talented actors that sometimes would number fifteen. Other than having an occasional chat, and that being almost always about performance, I don't think that in a career spanning sixty years I was ever close friends with an actor. Animation artists? Yes. Directors? Yes. Producers? Yes. Composers? Yes. But actors? No. The one exception being June Foray (Rocky-Natasha-Jokey Smurf), an extremely gifted actress, a good friend and a great person.

Gordon Hunt, father of Helen Hunt, was the recording director. He was terrific. Paul Winchell was Gargamel and his characterization was superb, but he was also a pill. If I asked him to do a pick-up line for an episode he had already recorded, he felt as if he was being exploited. At one session he threw a tantrum and just walked out. Perhaps he was just tired. His agent called me to apologize for his client's unprofessionalism. No big deal. We just went back to work.

I talked so much all day and to so many, my voice began to dry up and sound like a tire on gravel. A voice therapist helped me to learn that it was not necessary to project so intensely. I had a recurring dream that during the morning coffee break, when the Taco truck was host to a crowd, all would look up on hearing the loud chatter of a large military helicopter as it descended onto the parking lot. Joe and Bill would be agape as some U.S. Army Colonel types, in full dress uniform, would disembark and hurry up to me, "Mr. Baldwin, the country needs you." Feeling no guilt I would clamber aboard and just wave good-bye and fly away.

Sometime at the beginning of the fourth season Phyllis Tucker Vincent, VP of Children's Programming at NBC needed an assistant to help her with what was becoming an overwhelming work-load. She hired a young woman who had taken a course in film at NYU or Columbia or some such place and this young lady was given a lot of freedom and power. She began to interfere with the Smurfs in a way I saw as extremely negative. My job was demanding enough, perhaps almost crushing, without this girl insisting on new camera angles, putting her mark on our stories and having much to say about everything Smurfy. Margaret Loesch would have defended me from this meddler, but she was no longer there and had not been replaced by anyone brave. It was not proper protocol for me to protest directly about anyone on the NBC staff. I complained to Bill Hanna and Joe Barbera, but, always fearful of alienating a Network, they did nothing. I heard that this dame was also offering her critiques to a Disney television production but the Disney people, unafraid of the big three, backed up their producer and her "creative" input was thwarted. The interference from this brat, nameless for all eternity, was only one of the many reasons I ultimately walked out on the Smurfs.

As with all long-running television series, stories were getting increasingly difficult to come by and there was growing concern that this goldmine not play out. All were searching for a new vein. I thought our writers had only to reach down into their guts for new material, but most of our writers were not very gutsy. There were many long meetings with story editors, writers, NBC execs, marketing folks, comic-book publishers, even agents - all trying to come up with the magic injection that would energize The Smurfs and lengthen their TV lives. Joe Barbera, of course, suggested we add a dog (he loved dogs). Someone suggested a time-machine - Clockwork Smurf would invent a time machine and then the Smurfs could go to New York (the agent's idea - he loved New York), or somehow the Smurfs would visit another world, or another world would visit them and on and on and on.

At first Peyo and Yvan remained resistant, but there was increasing pressure to add new concepts. Peyo was making an awful lot of money and, fearful this money might someday cease to flow, he was beginning to weaken.

First to arrive and be accepted was the dog. Barbera was happy. Or was it the baby? Once in a blue moon a baby comes along, a Peyo story. I wondered how it was conceived or who nursed it. Perhaps there was an immaculate conception? Tribes of ugly little creatures began to find their way into the Smurf village and new villains with names like Hogatha were giving Gargamel a rest.

Greed was causing the rivets to pop out of Peyo's armor. At one hotel breakfast, just before a big meeting that would forever change the original concept of The Smurfs, Frances begged, on bended knee, for Peyo to hold on, to not give in, but he was afraid that NBC would cancel the show. He was afraid he would make less money. He could not be persuaded and greed won. A few hours later the total deterioration of his sweet and simple concept began. Everyone was happy except me. . . and Frances.

I have been told that, in 1950, Papa Smurf was 542 years old. This cannot be true since it brings him into being in 1408 - way too late. If he is, indeed, of the middle ages and I use 1250 AD as a reasonable although arbitrary starting point for the beginning of his existence then Papa, in 1950, was 700 years old.

I was always totally convinced that the Smurfs were an asexual lot but here come Smurflings and then another female, Sassette and finally a Grandpa Smurf, voiced by Jonathan Winters. The year is 1250 and if Papa Smurf is 700 years old then Papa came into being in 550 AD and if HE had a father, then the great grandpa possibly met someone that knew one of the Apostles.

Just before my sudden and impulsive departure from the Smurf show, I had lunch with a mysterious stranger at a restaurant where nobody in Hollywood would ever want to be seen. Another company was offering me thousands of dollars to cover legal fees if I would break my contract with Hanna-Barbera and join them, the presumption being the Smurfs would follow. Any lawyer, including Hanna-Barbera's own, could see this was a dumb idea. Even the company tempting me was not thinking clearly. Yes, I was important to the show but not THAT important. Word of this little morsel got out and when I drove out of the parking lot and headed home, all assumed that I was leaving the studio and going to try and take the Smurfs with me.

INCORRECT.

I didn't want to have anything to do with the Smurfs ever again. The wonderful concept had been destroyed and was now empty of meaning. It was now just another same-as show. I stayed home for weeks. Not wanting to break their end of the bargain the studio continued to send me my paychecks and I continued to cash them. Some thought this was a terrific deal, but it was a very depressing period in my life. Finally my attorney pronounced that if I did not return to work I would be blackballed from the industry.

"Can they do that?"

"Yes. There is precedent."

"But that's illegal."

"Yes, but the industry is powerful and you are nothing."

I returned to the studio with a letter from my doctor of many years who reviewed my history of stress related symptoms and strongly implied that a return to the Smurfs might be injurious to my health, or worse. No more Smurfs.

No more lunches with Joe. No more wine with Bill. Never heard from Peyo or Delporte again. I was persona non grata. The studio assigned me the task of producing the Fred Flintstone 25th Anniversary Special. The uninspired script was written by Tom Ruegger, also a Smurf writer.

Four years hence Tom Ruegger would be the producer of Stephen Spielberg's Tiny Toon Adventures starring Bugs Bunny and all of the Warner Brothers cartoon characters as little children. Working for Tom would not be pleasant. Finally, after a few weeks of not doing much of anything, Hanna-Barbera released me from my contract.

It was 1986 and I immediately went to work as a producer and VP of nothing for the newly opened Hollywood branch of Tokyo Movie Shinsha, soon to be referred to as TMS. The President and Samurai chief of this company, Mr. Fujioka, was very formal. The whole studio was very formal. Japan is very formal.

Back in his homeland Mr. Fujioka was producing an animated feature based on Winsor McKay's wonderfully imaginative Sunday color comic strip, LITTLE NEMO. The strip first appeared in 1905. Fujioka would pay homage to McKay and rightly so, since he regarded McKay as the father of animation, a view I agreed with. What this Samurai intended to do was to top Walt Disney and thus bestow great honor and prestige upon the land of the rising sun. The original comic strip was a series of short plot-less episodes and not the stuff of a feature film. My read of the so-called script he was working from told me more likely he would insult the memory of Winsor McKay and embarrass Japan.

More than one script had been written and all of them, including a treatment by Ray Bradberry, had been rejected. To date no script had satisfied or projected Mr. Fujioka's vision of what Little Nemo was to be. I was reminded of my failed effort years back when I had a vision for an animation sequence in Rhapsody Of Steel. My inner vision was so wonderful I could not explain it, but I could "see" it. I could "feel" it and they let me do it and when we saw it – IT – my vision, up on the screen was a meaningless mess. I feared for Fujioka.

In Tokyo TMS was an animation production and distribution company, supplying mainly the Japanese market. Their venture into the American TV market, as I understood it, was mainly to increase revenue so that some of the new money would help with financing Little Nemo.

I hired and sent off to Tokyo my mentor #5, Bill Hurtz, his roll to tend to the culture gap that was always there and always a problem. Every so often some Japanese animator would think it funny to have one of our cartoon characters give our audience the finger. It wasn't. Hurtz was soon involved in giving Fujioka advice about the production of Little Nemo and, eventually, working with two Japanese directors, saw the film to its completion. Three directors cannot be good.

Japanese animation is very good and was, at that time, superior to what the U.S studios were turning out for television. The reason was simple. Traditionally in America animators were paid by the 35mm foot. A foot of 35mm film runs 24 frames per second, potentially offering 24 drawings per second as in a Disney feature. Other cost savings aside, an American animator had an incentive to make as few drawings per foot as possible. A Japanese animator on the other hand was paid by the drawing, so he had an incentive to make as many drawings as possible per film foot. Therefore Japanese TV animation was more fluid, richer, and had much more movement than a Hanna-Barbera product. When the networks, ABC, CBS and NBC realized they could get more animation for their money, they began to see TMS as a possible supplier.

CBS was interested in a concept for a series created by Chris Columbus who someday would be the director of Harry Potter and the Sorcerers' Stone. Judy Price, CBS VP for children's television would conclude a deal with TMS but only if the producer was an American and preferably, Gerard Baldwin. She ordered 13 half hours of Galaxy High School -- a season.

Scripts, recording, storyboards, key layouts, model sheets, direction and mixing would be done in Hollywood. TMS would only do the animation. The Japanese resented the intrusion of all these wide eyes. Although they never said so, you could sense it.

After signing my one-year contract TMS revealed there would be a co-producer. SO! Japan had not told me this up front. My co-producers name was Barry Glasser and he, apparently, had been oozing around Fujioka for quite a while. Barry, in my view, was a giggling twit but no matter, he would be the head writer and story editor and direct all of the recording. My job was simply to shovel the rest.

About a year or more later, Bill Hanna suggested we have dinner. NBC was not happy with my successors and ratings were beginning to slip. Would I come back? It was a good offer but, "No thanks, Bill, I think I'll stay with the Japanese."

When John Patrick Baldwin was born on April 8th 1987, Mr. Fujioka summoned me into his office. We sat on the floor, Japanese style, while his secretary brought in a big gleaming black lacquered box and set it down before us. This Asian beauty was also his lover and she joined us. I had never seen anything like this stunning box. It did not touch the floor but floated on six legs, two indented from the corners front and back and one leg centered on each side. It reminded me of a floating oil rig. It was decorated in gold and had an elegant sash draped around it. As Fujioka lifted the lid and began to remove the contents he told me, quietly and sincerely, that now that I had a job forever, my son, when he came of age, would be Samurai. Fujioka proceeded to assemble a Samurai ceremonial helmet, brilliant gold. The colors were violet, blue and red with gold wings. A leaping dragon adorned the top. John Patrick was never much interested in becoming Samurai. I still have the stunning box. It sits, like a little shrine, on top of an armoire, waiting for a Samurai that cares.

TMS was well qualified to produce animation of high quality, but they did not sense the cultural gap that separated East and West, at least in so far as it applied to animated cartoons.

Galaxy High School was a wonderful concept. Chris Columbus wrote the pilot. The episodes were beautifully executed yet the ratings were not good. I don't know why. Probably the stories were too complex and lost the young children who were far from high school age. TMS thought the problem was with the opening title, which I had designed. They made a new one. It was totally Japanese and loaded with action and super special effects. It didn't help. Galaxy High School was a flop, but even now, 25 years later, it does have a small following of animation aficionados.

The next project for TMS was a really big one. The Music Corporation of America, known as MCA, had an interest in a toy company. Who could not notice the hundreds of millions of dollars little Smurf figurines had generated, thanks to all that free Smurf show advertising. MCA would develop a line of toys and an animated TV show to plug them.

I never quite understood where the idea for the Bionic Six came from. Perhaps from some writer that worked for MCA? The series would be distributed in the syndicated market. Sixty-five half-hour episodes were to be completed in one year, at which time the figurines would be ready for distribution.

The MCA Vice President in charge of this huge project wanted no part of Barry Glasser. I, alone, would be in charge and I was happy. Again, American artists would dominate with TMS only providing the animation. All design, background color keys, storyboards, music, recording and final mix would be done in Hollywood. As it turned out, of necessity, Barry Glasser would continue directing the recordings. And he did well.

A former Smurf writer, Gordon Bressack, would be the story editor and he was able to pull together enough writers to supply us with 65 one half hour episodes in twelve months. That is the equivalent, linearly, of twenty features in a year. My wife, Frances, wrote the opening episode and Gordon wrote one of the most original and clever scripts I ever had the fun of producing, "That's All Folks!" You can find reviews on Wikipedia.

MCA immediately began selling the concept to independent stations. One of their colorful brochures began the pitch with… "The super animated series that's got the thrills, the adventure, the Bionic power that'll keep the kids turned on without turning their parents off!"

Whoever wrote this tired copy must have written, "Coming Attractions" in the 1940's. Ugh.

I read in Daily Variety, "Producer-Gerard Baldwin. TMS has brought on a veteran producer to head up THE BIONIC SIX. Gerard Baldwin has a long and distinguished career in animation..." When Variety starts referring to you as a veteran, you know you're not a hot-shot kid anymore but a tough older guy with a few scars.

So what does this "veteran" animation producer actually do? Think of building 65 ships. As a class the ships are all the same basic design and they are all the same length and have the same function. Each ship is to arrive at the same port but each on a different day. It is okay to be early but you'll walk the plank if late. Some crews are reliable. Some drink too much rum. If something breaks aboard one of these rigs, parts are rarely interchangeable.

And then there is the problem of command and loyalty. MCA put up all the money, but TMS paid my salary.

Not all voyages begin on calm water and I wrote the following memo addressed to Mr. Fujioka and key staff as storm clouds loomed on the horizon. It is typical of many.

MEMORANDUM

TO   : MR. FUJIOKA   cc: SACHIKO
FROM: GERARD BALDWIN   SANDER
DATE : NOVEMBER 10, 1988   IKEUCHI-SAN
                                       IRENE

SUBJECT: PRODUCTION SCHEDULE AND BUDGET

TMS requested a preproduction cost sheet to cover special categories of work to be done on the *Bionic Six*. On October 15, 1986 a cost sheet was submitted. In some areas it was quite detailed…in other areas it was, of necessity, less so.

Comparing the amount of work to be done with the time allotted for this work as specified on the production schedule indicates clearly how many roles had to be filled and by what date.

On Oct. 17th the show was picked up. As of November 7th (three weeks later) there was still no authorization to hire <u>all</u> of these people.

I have used Oct. 20, 1986 as the earliest date we could begin preproduction as any earlier start would have been speculation.

At one point we were told that as many as nine storyboards would be done in Tokyo. Later we were told as many as 50% would be done in Tokyo. This no longer seems to be the case. This budget, therefore, presumes that <u>all</u> preproduction work will be done in Los Angeles. How many Japanese artists can be dovetailed into this schedule is unknown to me but they are welcome and needed. I leave it to a production manager as to how this can best be accomplished.

Using Oct. 20, 1986 as a start date I am projecting preproduction work of one kind or another through the second week of May, 1987…28 weeks.

On November 17th five scripts will be ready to go to storyboard. Five scripts of 3 acts each will require 10 storyboard artists on <u>that</u> day with a hoped for delivery of 2 1/2 weeks. On Nov. 18th another script is due…on Nov. 19th another script is due…thus on November 19th, 14 storyboard artists should be working. We anticipate that at some point 3 storyboard artists per show will be required to meet the TMS schedule. I detail this to demonstrate the magnitude of this production. Five scripts per week also impacts on every other category.

Obviously we do not have enough space for all of these people nor are they waiting

182

in the street for TMS to engage them. The best are almost always busy. We may have to entice some of these artists with more money. Certainly we will have to guarantee many of them an "x" number of weeks' employment. Will they accrue vacation time or expect medical coverage? What might happen if 25 of these SCG members decide to call for an NLRS election? Not likely, but possible.

This is not the place to go into the ramifications of such a sudden expansion. I have not included myself in this budget since it is not clear to me if I am part of overhead or on the line. If on the line add to the total the appropriate amount.

I suggest that head key artist, model artist, prop artist be in one room, keep their own files and be a direct link to the six other artists.

Spoke with David Hilberman. He would find it interesting to review and fix storyboard for us. I would find him welcome. From David the particular board would go to a producer / director to be slugged. I recommend this—either at a per board price or a salary for "x" number of weeks. Add to budget. -GB

The Bionic Six family was composed of a Caucasian dad, a Caucasian mom and Eric and Meg, their teenage children. Then there was J.D, who was black and Bunji, who was Japanese. I guess they were adopted. Naturally this family had to own a very special super aircraft to zip around in whenever they morphed into being the Bionic Six.

TMS sent me two designers from Tokyo. They were very hip guys and very talented. Their job was to design the jet. They spoke no English. I said, "Design a plane something like a Convair." They went off somewhere to work on the design of this plane and two weeks later presented me with a Convair, perfect in every detail inside and out. There may have been fifty detailed drawings.

"Hmm. Well, you know that's not quite right. It looks like... a Convair." Now, an American designer would have said SHIT and, grumbled back to the drawing board. Not these two guys. They threw a tantrum, packed their bags and flew back to Tokyo. Somehow, inadvertently, I had insulted or humiliated them beyond repair, or Fujioka would not have allowed them to leave. It is possible that "...something like..." does not translate into Japanese very well.

Being a loud mouth extravert who usually said what I thought about almost everything made the Japanese very nervous. They cautioned me, more than once, with one of their favorite proverbs:
"A nail that sticks out is soon hammered down." The entire Japanese staff

was extraordinarily sensitive to how others might feel so that no one ever lost face except when they were drunk, which was quite often. It might be in a restaurant or a bar when, after a few drinks, a group's mental barricades would be shoved aside and then all those rusty old nails would pop up and the loud recriminations would begin.   I was always astounded to see these oh so cool and controlled people just explode and scream at each other and then, on the following morning, back on the job, their mental coffins were all nailed shut again as if the night before had never happened.

On a short trip to Tokyo I was very impressed. The Ginza beats Broadway by a mile and I was impressed when a Japanese executive stomped his foot to tell me one square foot of Ginza sidewalk was worth a million dollars. I was impressed when dinner for six cost eight thousand dollars and impressed with some footage for Little Nemo that was truly impressive. I was not impressed when a young Japanese director got dressed down for making a mistake and shaved his head in atonement.

I was coerced into allowing a Japanese animation director to do a storyboard for The Bionic Six. It worked okay but was excruciatingly slowly paced, very Japanese. I could not reject it for fear of humiliating him. I showed it to the V.P. at MCA. He understood my problem and not giving a damn about Japanese feelings rejected the board and made it clear he never wanted to see another. The Bionic Six was an okay show. The toys were crappy. They did not sell well. The Bionic Six family morphed into oblivion.

The Lionel Train Corporation came to TMS looking for someway to revitalize their company. Lionel was looking for an idea, looking for something really new and exciting. Of course, it had to include a train. A TMS writer, some no talent gal hired by Barry Glasser for reasons of his own, came up with a terrible idea about a family of super heroes who travelled about on a train. GREAT! Super Heroes travel by Super Train! We flew to Detroit to make the presentation. Lionel headquarters, just outside of Detroit, was dark, gray and gloomy. This was a mausoleum filled with toy trains from years back, a museum that no one ever visited. The intended audience for this show – children – had probably never been on a train or even seen one except in old cowboy movies. Lionel gave an okay to a short pilot film. We made one.

Super Heroes travelling about by train is just dumb. Where could they go? Nothing came of it and nothing new came into TMS. Although TMS continued to sub contract work from Hollywood studios, there was nothing that I could work on, so I tried writing my own treatment of Little Nemo, but no one ever read it or cared.

Fujioka increased my status by promoting me from Vice President to Senior Vice President, a compensation for promoting me into a smaller office. I could see it coming. One of Fujioka's underlings was designated to fire me from my lifetime job. I could tell it gave him pain. Hollywood's staff of Japanese artists were very uncomfortable and almost tearful since they assumed, that for me, this was a great disgrace. It wasn't.

John Patrick was one year old and Alison Margaret three when it became obvious the little geodesic dome was soon going to be too small. Brilliant Waquadi Falicoff designed us a spectacular and beautiful addition that more than doubled the size of our house. It also more than doubled our mortgage. The construction was ongoing when TMS fired me. Shall we stop? No.

I always thought that since I was so very talented and had a wide breadth of experience, I would always be secure and that nobody could ever catch up. I was wrong.

It was quite clear to me that my role in the animation industry was in decline. Leaving the Smurfs as I did, studios may have perceived me as unreliable. There were a lot of talented young animation directors happy to do my job for half my salary. There is no doubt money can trump talent and experience. I needed work to support my new family and began bouncing about taking any work that was available. I found myself being a sequence director, a sheet director and finally, just another board slugger. I recalled Sir James Frazer's marvelous book The Golden Bough wherein he discusses a common tribal rite: The King Must Die.

Chapter 16

It was about 1988 when I did some direction on Garfield's Thanksgiving television special. My filmography credits me at this time with Rude Dog and Dweebs, Jim Henson's Muppet Babies, The Fantastic Four, Iron Man and others. Most of this work is just a blur in my mind and it's just as well. I decided to retire. It was okay with Frances. The California real estate bubble was big, so it was easy to sell the house. Costa Rica would be nice. No. Texas would be better because that's where Grandpa and Grandma lived and a bunch of her brothers and sisters. We were not a super hero family, so it made sense to travel by train. We Amtracked to Houston. Frances would look for a house. I would return to LA and work a bit longer to wrap up a few large credit card bills.

I was encouraged when I got a call from Paul Strickland, who had been a production manager on the Smurf show. Warner Bros. and Steven Spielberg were into production on a new series. Tiny Toon Adventures would feature all the old Warner Bros. characters as little children. Tom Ruegger, who had been a Smurf writer, was the producer. They needed another unit director. In some Looney way they were trying to recreate the old Warner studio, which was impossible. From my first day absolutely nothing I could do would please Tom Ruegger. Perhaps I had been hard on his writing. Was it pay-back time? After a few weeks he gave me notice on a Friday. On Monday morning I was waving goodbye to my older son, Michael, and a big long white land yacht was headed East and in October of 1989 I joined Frances and the kids in Houston, Texas.

We've been living in Houston now for over 23 years. At first we experienced a serious cultural shock, especially Frances, who missed our life in Los Angeles very much.

When we first moved here, thanks to some old cartoonists back in L.A., mostly guys whose careers in animation, I had a hand in promoting, I began receiving directorial work of one kind or another. Some of the shows I worked on I saw as vile and ugly. Duckman comes to mind. Many of the shows were just the same old stupid crap. I flew back to L.A. a few times to direct Fred Flintstone in his role as pitchman for Cocoa & Fruity Pebbles cereal. Long distance meant less work but also gave me more time to paint and write and I enjoyed a burst of pent up creativity, which is still blooming.

I first met Alan Zazlove in art school and his growth as an animation artist paralleled my own. He was the key director on the Smurf show when the Disney studio offered him a producer's role and stole him away. Alan produced Aladdin, the TV series, and he kept me busy as a director for a year or so. After Alan retired, no more Disney, but I did receive an Emmy nomination for "outstanding contribution to animation" for Disney's Aladdin. I found it puzzling. The only reason I can think of for receiving this nice nomination is that the Disney Company has such a huge block of Academy members nothing can stop them. I didn't win that Emmy.

A young Houston entrepreneur type had an idea for an animated television series. It had some merit. His concept was clear enough but he knew absolutely nothing about animation. To this young man it seemed almost miraculous that the producer of a very successful TV series was living in Houston. Now if he could just get George Foreman, who also lived in Houston, to be the hero of his show, he figured he had a good chance of a sale.

Presenting Frances and me to a local Investment house he was able to raise seed money and for 50K Frances and I developed an impressive presentation. George Foreman was optioned and this made it possible to raise even more money, mostly from athletes. It was not easy to get close to Foreman. He was always accompanied by relatives and hangers-on and one silent constant I presumed to be a bodyguard. It was at his beautiful ranch that I finally got to speak with him privately – well, not quite – the entrepreneur was taking pictures as I outlined to Foreman the role we had created for him as a molecule-sized Black Super Hero. He liked the idea. We were greatly encouraged but the young president of this newly formed production company got a bit cocky and so sure of himself he began to waste much of the capital and when it came time to renew Foreman's option there was no cash left and, without Foreman, the project died. Too bad. I liked George and it would have been great fun.

Everyone dreams about all kinds of fantastic, crazy and bizarre stuff and experiences an occasional nightmare. Of all the energy I have burned in my too short life I cannot help but wonder what percentage of that energy was expended on dreaming about animated characters like Mr. Magoo or Papa Smurf. I bet Peyo dreamt about his Smurfs, but since he didn't say we will never know and I doubt if Hanna or Barbera did. Most likely they dreamt about Yogi Bear or Fred Flintstone, but when they left so did their dreams and now, to me, they are only shadows.

I don't know if Peyo had a favorite Smurf but mine was Papa. There was great personal satisfaction in giving Papa things to say that were positive and good for children to hear. Sometime after Peyo died I was at a TV fair in some convention center in Las Vegas. Every producer that had a show to sell or a pitch to make had set up booths, hundreds of them. I was there to help pitch the show starring George Foreman. There was a large banner hanging over one of the booths that proclaimed, "Yvan Delporte - creator of the Smurfs!" The attractive young receptionist told me he was off somewhere and would not be back that day. I never saw or spoke with him again. Delporte died in 2007.

Once upon a time the two words, "Hanna-Barbera" pronounced as one, were synonymous with animated cartoons and conjured up Fred Flintstone, Yogi Bear, Quick Draw McGraw, Superfriends and more, much more. These two words, "Hanna-Barbera" are already fading from our collective unconscious, soon to be familiar only to animation buffs.

I still remain close to a handful of artists of exceptional ability and warmth, but most of the cartoonists I worked with closely for so many years are fading. Work was the chain that bound us and when the chain was broken we all, like the stars in our ever-expanding universe, drifted further and further apart.

If you Google Smurfs you will find all kinds of bizarre and crazy assertions. There are quite long and serious dissertations about the Smurf stories trying to indoctrinate our young children with doses of Communism, creepy. Another creep writes, "...when I worked on the Smurfs as a designer for a while... the cruel blandness of the Smurfs and Gerard Baldwin and his team of moronic evil writers..." Funny!, or as Papa Smurf would say, "Amazing!"

There is also, and often, some sexual innuendo directed toward Smurfette. The most frequently asked question in my drawing classes, usually delivered with a knowing smirk is: "Why is there only one Smurfette?" Peyo would laugh and reply, "Because one is enough." But that is not a satisfying answer to a sincere question.

There are 100 Smurfs, or at least there were at the beginning of time. With the exception of Papa Smurf they are all one-dimensional characters. Handy is certainly handy and that's all that he is. Brainy is certainly brainy and that's all that he is. Vanity is vain and that's all there is to him. Etcetera.

There is not much more to any of them than their one trait. Papa Smurf, however, is a fully realized character. He is not at all one dimensional but a Smurf of depth and complexity; a very wise and benevolent little dictator with a fully realized persona. Smurfette is also a fully realized character and that is why one Smurfette is quite enough.

Recently, a young woman in one of my classes told me that, as a child, she was not allowed to watch the Smurfs because her mother said they were the work of the Devil. I wonder what Peyo would think of all this garbage. He was a good and kindly man, now in Heaven. I cannot help but wonder where the good reverend Fallwell wound up.

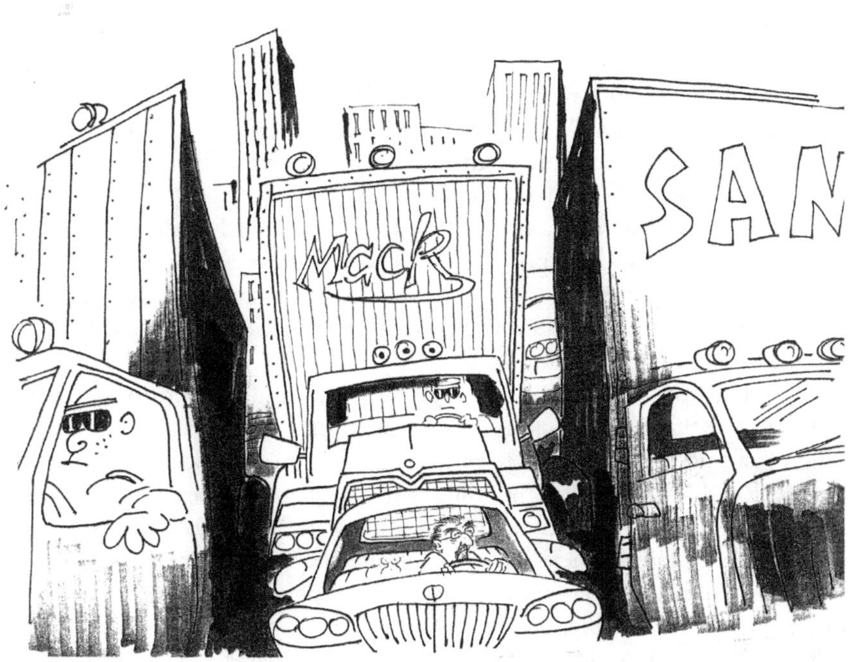

Chapter 17

It's 2012! I am approaching 84 years of age and can write that I have been blessed by being part of a big project, especially one that, in a positive way, has engaged and entertained young children across much of the world.

I just had a sudden realization that I might be a metaphor for an old car, one with about 300,000 miles on it. It is still running pretty good, not all original parts, so it doesn't even qualify for being a genuine antique. A full restoration is probably not possible but, even if it were, which it isn't, it would cost more than this old car is worth.

I've got a couple of good mechanics that go over the works twice a year. They check out pumps, hoses, gaskets and insist on all kinds of additives.

These guys, from long experience, can anticipate a breakdown. They can advise that, yes, it's in good shape but don't test it. Don't push it. Yes, it's running good NOW, but don't take it across the Great Divide on a hot day. They don't recommend any high-octane fuel, but I never pay attention to any of that "it's bad for you" advice. I've considered a new paint job, but without a complete body overhaul, removing every dent, that paint job wouldn't be more than a shiny cover up.

I can't trade me in and even if I could, which I can't, life without me wouldn't be the same. Nope. I'm stuck with the car.

Catharsis, July 21, 2012: The last cartoon studio in the whole world opened and closed in one short night, last night, close to dawn. I was there and the reality is still with me --

The space that houses these many hundreds of screen cartoonists is divided into three interlocking and overlapping structures at the center of which is a huge rotunda that reminds me of St. Peters Basilica. Section #1 is a typical eight-story office building with its parking garage, the kind they grow in Burbank California. This building is, somehow, encased within Section #2, a huge Disney-like castle, or maybe it's a fortress, constructed of Paper-Mache bricks that rise up to brightly painted parapets covered with cute Gargoyles. Finally, section #3 is a vast off-white Bedouin tent that hides the sky and could cover all of Arabia if it had to. This tent filters the intense California sunshine so that, within the rotunda, the air is cool and the light is soft. From my uncertain position in the rotunda I feel central yet adrift. I gaze about me trying to comprehend all that is going on even though

I know exactly what is going on since, as a full bird colonel, it is my job to know exactly what is going on.

Yet, all around me like spokes on a wheel, there are many dark recesses and what is going on within these dark shadows is not always mine to see or understand! What I can see high above me on cantilevered balconies are long lines of artists, male and female, all dressed in blue denim vests. Some are happy and some are sad, but all are creating thousands and thousands of drawings, which are swiftly carried by wheeled carts to a one hundred foot tall animation camera where a crew of seven uniformed operators, wearing white cotton gloves, feed its gaping maw. I cannot recall the melody, but they were, all seven, whistling a happy tune. To that I can swear.

Well apart, there are two large grottos. They can only be taken in one at a time. Within each grotto hangs a very large and ornate gold frame and each frame houses a portrait painted by John Singer Sargent. This is, of course, impossible yet there they are. These are nice flattering portraits without a hint of Dorian Gray. I know that every portrait has some Dorian in there somewhere but, great artists like Sargent bury it deep beneath an impasto veneer.

The first painting I gaze upon is a standing full figure portrait of Joe Barbera as a five star general. His hair is much too black for a man his age. Although his studio represents a triumph of quantity over quality, you would never guess it from his royal countenance. Joe's velvet cloak is trimmed with fur. His delicate left hand rests lightly on the be-jeweled hilt of a ceremonial sword. His stance is that of Prince of the Medici and his expression is that of a man who has just delivered a successful and major speech about new shows and his search for the next Scooby Doo. The painting of General Joe recedes as the second portrait, Bill Hanna as a four star general, comes into focus. His gleaming white hair glistens like smooth snow in the sun. He is deep in thought and I know what he is thinking. General Hanna is thinking about the cost of Blackwing pencils. Maybe if the animators had to supply their own Blackwing pencils they wouldn't use them up so fast. No. The union would never stand for that. Perhaps the electric pencil sharpeners could be modified so they wouldn't chew up cedar so fast. Old-fashioned hand-crankers are the least wasteful but also slower, so that what you gain in longer pencil life you lose in productivity. Some think General Bill will be remembered for discovering the principle known as MLF = P. This is the law that proves "Doing more for less and doing less faster = profit." But he was more than that. As can only happen in a dream, my mind's eye zooms in on the painting and I fly over Bill's right shoulder, his four stars far below me now and race toward a distant mountain. This is Mount Rushmore of Toon whereon are carved, as major figures in the Pantheon of animation, Tom and Jerry.

A short and simple movie cross-dissolve returns me to my place within the rotunda. There are other Colonels, but I rarely see them. I figure each has his own rotunda and his own battalion and, I am certain, each answers to a different Hanna and a different Barbera than the two I serve.

From Studio A I can hear ten actors, at the top of their lungs, singing my great LA LA song. LA LA♪LA LA LA LAAAAA is reverberating throughout the basilica and it warms me. Now I can almost taste the cool Chardonnay, so it must be near the lunch hour. Well, lunch hour for them. Rank has its privilege. I am reminded of Rome again and that Colonels are to a General what Cardinals are to a Pope.

The singing stops and some cartoonists, trying to look casual about it so as not to be noticed, leave ten minutes early. These are the brave. Some leave two minutes after the clock says twelve. These are the timid.

On this very special Noon I'll be damned if the whole battalion, although now singing the LA LA song, started marching out onto Ventura Boulevard parading west toward the sea and lunch with Steven Spielberg. I was wondering if Jay Ward might be free for lunch when brilliant morning sunlight sliced through my closed bedroom blinds and, in a cartoon flash, took away the last animation studio I would ever be a part of.

FIN

Epilogue

Who is Evolution?

In an endless universe our solar system is just another Mom & Pop Stop & Shop convenience store, a place to refuel on your trip to eternity. I feel as if time is passing me by but it is not. Rather, I am a passenger on a train christened Time. I have no memory of climbing aboard or any idea of where this Zephyr is going as it accelerates toward its unknown destination. I have always been aboard, or so it feels. I can't remember where or when this journey began or remember a beginning of self. For some inexplicable reason I'm in no hurry to reach the end of the line and return to that state we call Stardust. No. We cling to life.

The seeds of life were not planted on this planet by the pilot of some passing space ship who, in a billion years or so, intended to return, someday, and reap his crop. More likely the first living things were created right here on Earth by events and forces we can only imagine.

To make a really great stew you need all of the just right ingredients in exactly the just right amounts: a big pot, a master chef and a bolt of lightning. Dr. Frankenstein was definitely onto something.

What was life like when it first appeared thousands of millions of years ago? It may be described as that which moves of its own volition, or life is that which can replicate itself -- must replicate itself. We say life behaves in such and such a manner in order to survive. Survive for what purpose? The survival of the species? Why? Who cares? Can an amoeba care about the survival of amoebas? Does an amoeba even know that it is an amoeba?

In our search for the why of things we, man, created the idea of a force that acts upon molecules in such a way as to make simple life increasingly complex. Science calls it Evolution. Apparently this process was at work millions and millions of years before primates existed. The big question for me, right now, is not what is Evolution but WHO is evolution, and asking who, does not imply anything more than the freedom to question the what, where, when and why of the Cosmos. I just want to see a framed portrait of this Evolution, something I can relate to. If the first life was an accident, well that's okay with me but who is this buttinski that seems to be meddling? Was evolution waiting for life to occur so it could act upon it, or did evolution occur so that the possibilities for life could expand? Something weird occurred way back then, that's for sure. That's the trouble with Mr. Peabody's Wabac machine. No writer of animated cartoons ever turned that clock back to zero, either because they were fearful, or knew they were incapable of writing the greatest story ever told.

Our five senses set limits on our perception of the universe and our beliefs set limits on our understanding of the universe. A belief in God the Creator limits perception, but so does our easy acceptance of the Big Bang as Creator.

It is much easier to understand a continuum than a beginning and an end. That the universe has always been and always will be seems to ring true. I can't conceive of anything so vast and plentiful of matter being compressed into something the size of a golf ball or a pea or a period.

Why not go all the way with that idea and say that, finally, all the matter in the Universe compressed into a point of non -existence. Then there would be no explosion.

About 60 million years ago this Earth, our Earth, was teeming with life. This was the age of the dinosaurs. If evolution was at work and there is no reason to think it wasn't, evolution had created a grand environment for life. We do not know why creatures evolved from the simple to the complex--from the tiny to the huge--but all living things were having the time of their lives consuming each other, one way or another. The fire of life needs to be constantly fed. Each furnace, unaware of its fate, lives in a state of eternal bliss. To steal from Shakespeare "All the world's a stage, And all the creatures merely players: They have their exits and their entrances; And one man in his time plays many parts [. . .] ending in "oblivion, Sans teeth, sans eyes, sans taste, sans everything."

At the time of the dinosaurs Evolution, like some potter sitting at his wheel, was still molding molecules into new and ever more complex combinations. I wonder if, given enough time, the hands of evolution would have ultimately produced a man. No, not in that chapter, Fred Flintstone would be no match for a REX.

If the function of evolution is movement in the direction of making life more secure and enduring, it's not doing a very good job. The age of the dinosaurs was destroyed by a meteor 60 million years ago. Evolution, not to be discouraged, and ever diligent, went back to work and so, here we are--the chosen ones.

The myth of Adam and Eve tells the story of man's ascension very well. At first the happy couple was, like all of the other animals, living in a state of eternal bliss. The five senses were more than adequate for short-term survival. There was no sin. There was no guilt. They had many children and society was not too different from that of the elephant or the chimpanzee.

The line of descent was matrilineal and so it was Eve who plucked the Apple and in doing so became sentient. The good part of becoming self-aware was man's sudden shift from being a social animal, like all the others, into that of being a cultural animal, but the price of culture is the realization that we are unique and alone. The negative of being "man" was, and still is, the foreknowledge of death. Much of our creative energy, be it magic, religion or science, is spent in avoiding, denying or delaying oblivion.

Just as I step on ants, evolution sends entire life forms, plant or animal, into the blackness of extinction.

If a species is on the edge of obliteration, does its last living member shed a tear? Probably not. How sad.

Richard Feynman once said to me, "Gerard, your questions are beyond the realm of science and if you keep asking questions like this you will surely go mad." Well, that was many years ago and I am still sane—and, still asking questions.

I am not like the other life forms I see all about me. A tree is clearly alive. It moves in its own way and reproduces in its own way and means me no harm but I cut it down. I step on ants, cut flowers, rob bees, tear living meat from bones and enjoy, now and then, a trip to the moon on gossamer wings.

Like an automobile transmission my life is so complex it cannot hold itself together for very long and so it breaks down and returns to that junkyard in the sky or, carried by a solar wind, again flows across the dunes of time--and I will run out of time if I don't get back to the train of my thoughts. "Run out of time?" Time, it seems to me, is not going anywhere. Obviously there never was "a time when" and surely time is more than what the clock reads.

Since I cannot experience my beginning and I cannot experience my ending, perhaps that sense I have of moving "along", sometimes passing through space and sometimes space passing me by -- perhaps this very moment, may be all of the time I will ever have.

If molecule A and molecule B are always in motion, then the distance between A and B is never fixed or repeatable. Thus the time it would take to travel from A to B or vice versa is not repeatable or reliable.

Does this mean time cannot be measured or even exist with any certainty -- that a train "on time" is only an approximation of reality?

If life reacts to its environment or adapts to its environment in order to survive, then what is the motivation behind the adaptation? Why does life desire to continue? Let's return to my original question: Who is Evolution?

In man's search for the why and how of things he became aware of a force that acts upon life in such a way as to make the simple increasingly complex. Apparently this force was at work many millions of years before we existed. We call it evolution and we are the result of its desire. We know quite a bit about how it works, but the why of it remains a great mystery. There is always myth.

In our culture Mother Nature is usually depicted as a very happy old dame who, without pain, is always giving birth to life. You cannot think about good old Father Time for very long before he morphs into the Grim Reaper. Mother Nature keeps offering life and he keeps killing it. What a marriage! These two clearly begat everything including the expanding universe, the possibility of a contracting universe, the concept of life and death, beginning and ending, black and white, Yin and Yang -- well, the list goes on and on. They are very busy. They can also be excruciatingly slow with their work yet, at other times, they can create an event with the touch of a finger as beautifully shown by Michelangelo. We do not know if they are a very old couple or eternally young. Do they have a script?

I first became really acquainted with Mother Nature and Father Time when they appeared on the television series, The Smurfs. She was a jolly old grandmother type and he a benign very old man with a dry soft voice. They lived in an enchanted cottage that always smelled of warm waffles drenched in melted butter and maple syrup. No Smurf ever noticed Father Times scythe or questioned its function.

Well, having enticed you to travel with me this far on my search for the answer to an off-the-wall question, I am well aware that unanswered questions are difficult to live with and unacceptable to the human psyche.

A Jesuit teacher once said "give me one year with a good student and that person will be a Catholic forever." Well, forever didn't happen, but there is no doubt that many early years of Catholic schooling have wired my brain in such a way that I think like a Catholic and so, in trying to find the answer to my question "who is Evolution?," I keep coming up with the need for a formula that can unify and make whole my disparate notions about the answer, much as Christianity did with its creation of the Divine Trinity.

The Divine Trinity of God the Father, God the Son and God the

Holy Ghost clearly always had something missing. A female? How could those wise old ones leave her out? Easy. The ancients did not hold females in high regard so they didn't even notice she was missing. I find it hard to believe but after 1500 years of Trinitarian doctrine Mary, Mother of God, was only officially assumed into heaven in 1950.

Please forgive this arrogance and allow me to offer this not quite so Divine Quaternity:

God the Father IS Father Time

God the Mother IS Mother Nature

God the Son and God the Daughter … that's us: Man!

We are the creators of magic, religion and science and all the Gods are in our image. We are the eyes that perceive and speculate on the nature of being and pose unanswerable questions.

Every time I look up at the Big Dipper, the one that hangs in Mother Nature's vast kitchen, I fantasize about what she's cooking. Perhaps she and Father Time are reminiscing about the old days as she slowly stirs the big steaming pot -- round and round and round -- while Father Time, staring off into space lovingly sharpens his scythe.

"So, Mother. what's cooking?"

"Your favorite, dear. Cosmic stew."

"Easy on the Gravity."

"You know it's funny. I don't know why but for some reason just now I've been thinking about the people."

"That bunch. They're asking for extinction if you ask me."

"Oh Father, try and be kind. You must admit I got the convex lens just right. At least they don't see their world upside down anymore."

"Upside down or right side up they're making a mess."

"I wonder if they might be better off with two heads?"

"Now where in the universe did you get that idea? They'd bump heads."

"I could widen the shoulders."

"Top heavy."

"Shorten the legs ?"

"Legs—pegs! Leave, 'em alone. Besides, I think I smell a Meteor."

"Oh dear."

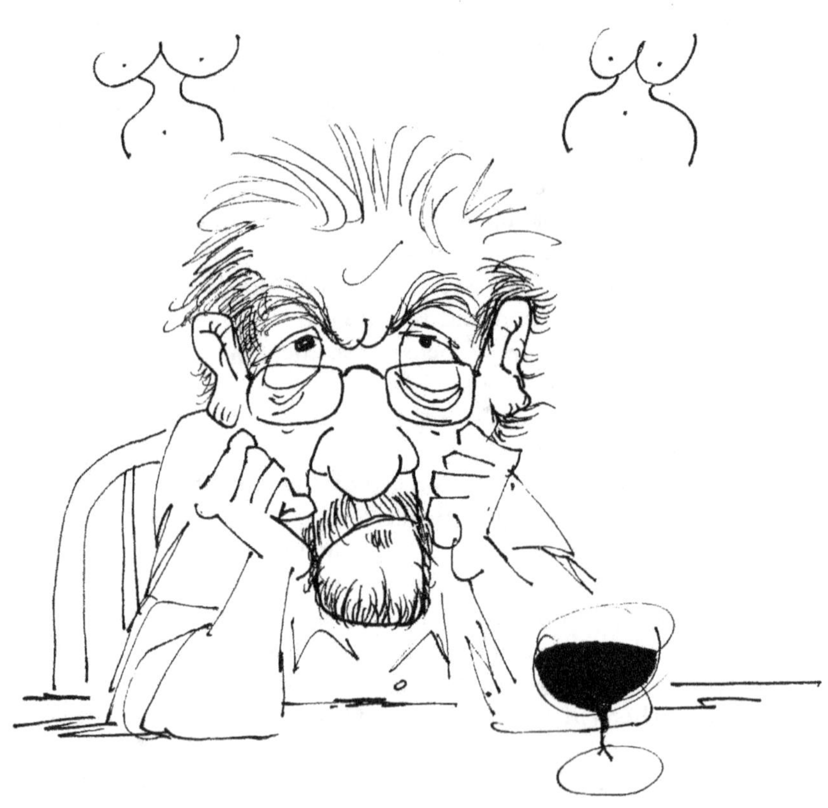